The Garden Lover's Guide to the Northeast

PRINCETON ARCHITECTURAL PRESS   NEW YORK

PAUL BENNETT

The Garden Lover's Guide
to the Northeast

Princeton Architectural Press
37 East 7th Street
New York, NY 10003
212.995.9620

For a free catalog of other books published by Princeton Architectural Press,
call toll free 1.800.722.6657 or visit our web site at www.papress.com

LIBRARY OF CONGRESS CATALOGING-IN-PUBLICATION DATA
Bennett, Paul, 1970 –
    Garden lover's guide to the Northeast / Paul Bennett. — 1st ed.
      p.   cm.
    Includes bibliographical references (p.   ) and index.
    ISBN 1-56898-163-5 (alk. paper)
    1. Gardens—Northeastern States—Guidebooks. 2. Northeastern
States—Guidebooks. I. Title.
    SB466.U65N7525   1999
    712'.5'0974—dc21   98-53015
                                              CIP

EDITING: Jan Cigliano
DESIGN: Sara E. Stemen
MAP DESIGN: Jane Garvie
Special thanks to Eugenia Bell, Caroline Green, Clare Jacobson, Therese
Kelly, Mark Lamster, and Annie Nitschke of Princeton Architectural Press
                                  —Kevin C. Lippert, publisher

PRINTED IN HONG KONG

03 02 01 00 99   5 4 3 2 1
FIRST EDITION

Contents

How to use this book

Refreshments in vicinity 🍽️

Formal garden ⬥

Landscape garden ▨

House major feature 🏛️

Historic garden 🏛️

Kitchen garden 🏛️

Botanic interest/rare plants 🌿

Topiary 🦆

Borders 🗻

Water features ⛲

Architectural features 🏺

Regional maps show
locations of gardens.

Each regional map includes a
numbered key to make finding
garden entries easy.

This guide is intended for travelers who wish to visit the most historic and beautiful gardens in the northeastern United States, from the pleasure gardens of Acadia, Maine, to the colonial gardens of Mount Vernon, Virginia.

The book is divided into five chapters covering the major states. Each chapter comprises an introductory section with a regional map and a list of the gardens, followed by entries on each garden. The numbers found on the regional maps can be used to locate the numbered entries within the chapters. These entries are accompanied by detailed at-a-glance information telling the reader about the garden's defining characteristics and nearby sights of interest. The guide also includes seven feature gardens, beautifully illustrated by three-dimensional plans.

Entries begin with at-a-glance
information on opening times,
directions, nearby sights of
interest, and how to receive
further information.

Major gardens include watercolor
plans that note special features.

Foreword

Besides those included here, there are hundreds of gardens throughout the northeastern United States—private gardens of resplendent beauty, meadow and woodland gardens with an educational purpose, and plenty of excellent arboreta. In choosing the gardens included here, however, I focused on one central question: Did the landscape exhibit noteworthy garden features? But one might also ask: What are garden features, in the first place?

In the case of the major gardens, such as Longwood, Winterthur, and Dumbarton Oaks, the answer to both of these questions seems self-evident. But there are many other unusual garden spaces in America, many of which certain gardeners, garden writers, or garden enthusiasts wouldn't even consider gardens at all. Some are quite small and, to the untrained eye, seemingly inconsequential; others, lacking a good collection of spring bulbs, might be classified as parks or woodlands. Yet in many cases such landscapes are excellent gardens as well. In the case of the arboreta, for example, my assessment revolved around several ancillary questions: Were there significant floral features? Was there an artful arrangement of plant material? Did the architecture—pathways and terraces—create a heightened experience of the landscape? Did I simply feel like I was standing in the woods when I visited the site, or was there something here that transcended the quotidian experience of nature? More than anything else, this last question became the litmus text for deciding which gardens made their way into this book, and which did not.

The garden is a powerful expression of human spirit, executed most often in the context of the natural world (although not always). The following gardens, to greater and lesser degrees, all attempt this ultimate feat: to show us something new, about ourselves and our relationship to the world.

An ancient Chinese proverb guided the spirit of Harvey Ladew at his estate in Maryland.

Introduction

Architecturally speaking gardens are protean places. Impelled by the powerful hand of time, gardens are naturally transformed and the arrangement and intention of their original planting scheme gradually evolve into something different—sometimes something radically different. In most cases this is due to the vicissitudes of history: some gardens bear the mark of many hands, the impress of which, measured over time, can be read as a narrative of aesthetic history. In turn these histories can often reflect trends in the culture at large. For instance, many of the gardens in this book—in fact, a significant majority—fell into disrepair and neglect sometime between 1960 and 1985. At Winterthur, for example, du Pont's masterpiece suffered the ravages of mismanagement for over a decade, only now reemerging—ten years into a vigorous restoration—as a major American garden.

Outside the garden, these decades were marred by social upheaval, a series of tremendous recessions that included a period of outrageous inflation. Garden preservation, never a priority in times of strife, necessarily suffered. But in the recent decade this has changed, dramatically. A renewed interest in gardening has brought people out to public gardens, and in no time since perhaps the heady days of the Colonial Revival movement (roughly 1870-1900 and again 1920-1930), have we seen such a sustained effort at rescuing significant American landscapes. An excellent example of this (and no doubt a fairly controversial one) are the Colonial Revival gardens at Gunston Hall in Lorton, Virginia, which were designed in the 1950s by Alden Hopkins, one of the landscape architects responsible for Colonial Williamsburg. Although a beautiful creation in themselves, the gardens are currently being excavated using magnetic resonance imaging and other new technologies to determine the composition of the original garden planted by George Mason in the eighteenth century. Although postmodernists might quarrel with the idea, the latent hope here is to provide a single, final narrative for these gardens.

At the same time that gardens are inherently protean due to their inextricable connection with that most protean of forces, nature, they can also be solidly consistent expressions: Like architecture or art, each garden has its own unique structure, character, and aesthetic—a Japanese Zen garden is as different from a modernist American garden as a Palladian dome is from Frank Gehry's Guggenheim Museum in Bilbao. Although a wild diversity is perhaps the most salient feature of gardens in the Northeast, there are a few, distinct garden traditions that have indelibly shaped the region. The first are Colonial gardens and Federal-era gardens, dating back to the eighteenth century and earlier. Although few of these actually

OPPOSITE: *Sleeping Ariadne is just one of many works of art that grace Kykuit, the Rockefeller estate in Tarrytown, New York.*

ix

still exist, museums like Old Sturbridge Village in Massachusetts (*page 47*) and Strawberry Banke in New Hampshire
(*pages 13–15*) and small historic houses like the John Whipple
House in Ipswich, Massachusetts (*page 40*), have mounted significant re-creations based upon scholarly research. These gardens addressed themselves to the entire household, providing
not only vegetables for food but plants that were used as dyes,
soaps, air fresheners, and medicines. Surprisingly, as garden
historian Ann Leighton points out in her seminal history on the
subject, many colonial gardens were also beautiful, incorporat-
ing roses and other flowers to create a bright, sunny extension
of their typically dark and dank houses. Although several contemporary restorations are under way on these gardens, the
vast majority were restored and preserved in the late-nineteenth and early-twentieth centuries when a patriotic love of the
past gripped the country, and reflect, in their Victorian flourishes, the aesthetics of Colonial Revival.

In the mid-nineteenth century, a significant new direction
emerged as American gardens were transformed by the writings of Andrew Jackson Downing, whose influential *Treatise on
Landscape Gardening and Rural Architecture* interpreted English
ideas of landscape aesthetics into a form particularly suited to
the American geography—specifically to Jackson's home in the
Hudson River Valley of New York. The great gardens of this era
are what we call estates, but which are in reality carefully
designed landscapes reflecting Jackson's demarcation between
the *beautiful* (pristine lawns, intimate copses and groves, or soft
areas) and the *picturesque* (grand vistas and rocky crags that
evoke nature's terrible majesty). Frederick Law Olmsted transferred these ideas onto a vast public stage with his designs for
Central Park (with Calvert Vaux, an associate of Downing's),
Boston's Emerald Necklace, and several estates in New England
and New York. Blithewold at Bristol, Rhode Island (*page 56*),
was designed in this fashion by a protégé of Olmsted.
Lyndhurst at Tarrytown, New York (*page 91*), is a sublime example of this style; while Montgomery Place in Annandale-on-
Hudson (*pages 101–2*) bears the mark of Downing himself.

The last significant historical trend took place at the tail
end of the nineteenth century and the beginning decades of
the twentieth as wealthy Americans turned to the pleasure gardens of Europe for inspiration. Whereas in Europe gardens
developed as the leisure activity of an idle aristocracy, here they
became the passion of a class of ambitious businessmen. At
Pierre du Pont's Longwood estate (*pages 131–3*), Alfred du Pont's
Nemours (*pages 142–3*), and the Blisses' Dumbarton Oaks (*pages
165–7*), the panoply of European garden history—from Italian
gardens of the Renaissance to the Sun King's Versailles—was
imported and reformed into ebullient displays, of which the
water symphony at Longwood remains the last word.

Painting with broad strokes is always risky, and several other crucial developments influenced gardens into the twentieth century, including the American renaissance in botany, fueled in large part by Charles Sprague Sargent at Harvard University's Arnold Arboretum, whose hand is evident in many landscape gardens in New England. A natural extension of this development was the establishment of the great botanical gardens and conservatories built by the great architecture firm of Lord and Burnham, as well as the recent advent of eco-sensitive and sustainable gardens that explore the newest ideas in environmentalism—some of all of these types of gardens are included here. Modernist gardens, such as Fletcher Steele's Naumkeag (*pages 49–51*) also dot this history, although many of his great works are private and thus not included here. And of course, no seemingly seamless linear narrative would be complete without some outstanding anomalies, such as the prescient Henry Francis du Pont's Winterthur (*pages 147–9*), which has influenced contemporary garden design perhaps more than any other garden in the country.

I can think of few tasks as enjoyable as traveling through the northeastern United States on a tour of gardens. My fellow travelers will witness a world of tremendous diversity, which reflects as much of what I call the protean nature of gardens as it does the protean nature of America as a whole. Although traditionally the purview of a very few, over its brief but rich history American gardening has imbibed (however sparingly) at the fountain of democracy. That these gardens are open to the public without prejudice is but one reflection of that fact. How the democratic process has been expressed in the beauty and intellectual grandeur of our public gardens, I'll leave to my readers to decide. Happy travels.

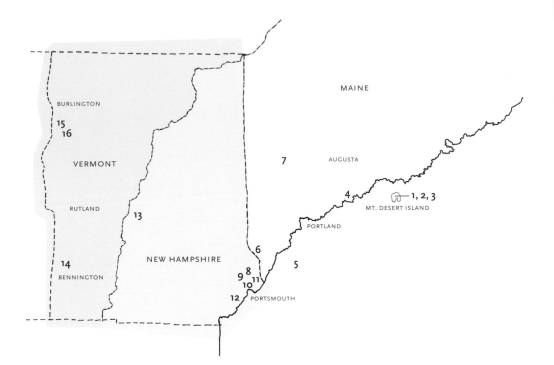

MAINE

BURLINGTON

15
16

VERMONT

RUTLAND

AUGUSTA

4

🏛 1, 2, 3
MT. DESERT ISLAND

7

13

PORTLAND

NEW HAMPSHIRE

6

5

14
BENNINGTON

9 8
10 11

12 PORTSMOUTH

NORTHERN NEW ENGLAND:

Maine, Vermont, and New Hampshire

The single most determinate factor in a northern New England garden is the climate. Cold, long winters and early frosts have traditionally limited the plant palette, while plenty of rain has given the landscape a lush character. In some areas anomalies exist; along the Maine coast certain southern species have been deposited by glacial action, and the ocean has a tempering effect on the weather. It is perhaps not surprising that Maine is also the site of some of the greatest pleasure gardens in the region, most of which center around Mount Desert Island, where several wealthy families (the Rockefellers among them) maintained summerhouses. Beatrix Farrand lived here, and her influence continues to be felt in the collections of the Asticou Azalea Gardens (*page 3*) and Thuya Gardens (*page 4*), both of which were created from the breakup of her estate. Celia Thaxter's small garden on Isle of Shoals (*page 7*) was also a product of these climatic variations, while Bernard McLaughlin braved the harsher zones inland in his very private, very eclectic garden, which was thankfully rescued after his death and opened to the public (*page 8*).

In New Hampshire, Portsmouth's zenith predates Mount Desert Island by a century, at least. A vibrant trading port at the mouth of the Piscataway River, Portsmouth's garden history dates back to the colonial era. Wealthy merchants such as John Langdon (*page 9*) and John Ladd (*page 10*) constructed large town houses adorned with gardens of roses, fruit trees, and grape arbors, modeled on British traditions but with peculiar American twists— such as the helical rose trellis, which can be seen in

OPPOSITE: *A Maine mist settles over the Japanese azalea garden at Asticou.*

I

Old fashioned peonies frame magnificent views at Hildene in Manchester, Vermont.

several Portsmouth gardens. North of here, the mountains of Vermont and New Hampshire have traditionally provided refuge for artists, such as the sculptor Augustus Saint-Gaudens who emigrated from New York City to a quiet spot along the Connecticut River to complete some of his greatest work (*page 16*).

Of course all of these gardens have their roots in colonial traditions, not to mention the soil, of this region. Gardens were central to the lives of European settlers. Even in townships like Portsmouth, where a division of labor and active trading gave people access to a wider variety of goods, most families subsisted in large part from the yield of their own gardens. Literate and plucky, these colonists relied not only on the wisdom of their neighbors to guide their gardens but benefited from European garden books that were imported to the colonies, including Dioscorides' guide to medicinal herbs (*De Materia Medica,* published 1 AD). These texts were widely disseminated throughout the colonies, producing a vibrant, diverse, and highly interesting garden tradition. Strawberry Banke in Portsmouth (*pages 13–15*) presents a vivid and scholarly re-creation of a typical colonial garden, combining vernacular aesthetics, learned traditions, and utilitarian need. Here we see not only the re-creation of colonial gardens but the preservation of styles and traditions that have emerged throughout the intervening 400 years.

Northeast Harbor:
Asticou Azalea Gardens

LOCATION: SEAL HARBOR AND PEABODY DRIVE, MOUNT DESERT ISLAND

GARDEN OPEN: dawn–dusk, daily, June–October.

ADMISSION: free

FURTHER INFORMATION FROM: Box 59, Mount Desert Island 04660

NEARBY SIGHTS OF INTEREST: Acadia National Park, Bass Harbor Lighthouse, Thuya Gardens

Garden historians still cringe to think of Beatrix Farrand's great test gardens on Mount Desert Island being dismantled in the 1950s. At Reef Point, as her ancestral home was called, Farrand cultivated a famous garden in which she experimented and tested her ideas, but one that, alas, was impossible to maintain in perpetuity. Lucky for gardeners everywhere, Maine resident Charles Savage recognized the value of Farrand's work and with the help of summertime neighbor John D. Rockefeller Jr. removed many of the fine specimens to the newly created Asticou Azalea Gardens nearby. Although azaleas, rhododendrons, and mountain laurel grow here to great effect (lining neatly designed paths around a glistening pond), the gardens have evolved over the years under the tutelage of many different designers. Perhaps drawing on the Asiatic roots of the azalea, several Oriental gardens now make their home at Asticou, including a *kare sansui* garden, or dry landscape, composed of raked sands and gravel and artfully placed rocks that describe greater landscapes in miniature. Stepping stones, trickling water, and stone lanterns are direct overtures to Oriental traditions, while the plant selection infuses Americanism into the mix. Korean firs and Japanese maples stand beside Canadian hemlocks and the shrubbery of ubiquitous blueberry to achieve a fusion that complements the natural scene. Of course the garden is best in June, when the azaleas explode; however, good design can be enjoyed at any time and fall in this area is ritually spectacular.

ABOVE: *Proportion and form meld in the Japanese garden.*

3

GARDEN OPEN: 7am–7pm
daily, July–September.
10am– 4:30pm daily,
September– June.
ADMISSION: $2.

FURTHER INFORMATION FROM:
Box 1120, Northeast Harbor
04662. (207) 276-5130

NEARBY SIGHTS OF INTEREST:
Acadia National Park, Bass
Harbor Lighthouse, Asticou
Azalea Gardens

2 Northeast Harbor: Thuya Gardens

LOCATION: PEABODY DRIVE, ELIOT MOUNTAIN, MOUNT DESERT ISLAND

In the early part of this century, when Boston landscape architect Joseph Henry Curtis vacationed in Bar Harbor, Maine, he couldn't leave his work behind. At his summerhouse, Thuya Lodge (named for the stands of cedar, *Thuya occidentalis,* that grow there), he set about constructing a landscape of terraces, picturesque paths, and framed vistas, much in the romantic vein. In the 1930s Charles Savage, progenitor of nearby Asticou Azalea Gardens and caretaker of the trust that Curtis established for the land before his death, converted the lodge into a horticultural library and transformed the nearby orchard into a formal flower garden. Much of the original plant material at Thuya was acquired from Beatrix Farrand's private garden in neighboring Reef Point, and in design the garden mimics Farrand's interpretation and reworking of Gertrude Jekyll's English cottage garden style within the peculiar climatic and geographical context of coastal Maine. A tall cedar fence, penetrated by cob gates, surrounds the garden. The two major beds, lying at cross axes, have seen several different designers come and go since Curtis's original design: sometimes with the intent of restoring the garden to a more Farrand-like presentation, with masses of phlox and astilbe moving through each other in impressionistic waves; at other times, with the intent of moving toward a native, rustic feel; while still at other times, rigidity and formalism have held sway. Lately the resident gardener has made it a priority to push the growing season out to three full months, no small feat in this climate. A wishing well and a pond in the far reaches of the garden give the space a residual country feeling and ambiance that avoids being "cutesy." Outside the garden, Curtis's original path system winds through 200 acres of forest up the side of Eliot Mountain.

Acadia: Wild Gardens of Acadia

LOCATION: OFF PARK LOOP ROAD, ACADIA NATIONAL PARK,

MOUNT DESERT ISLAND

Due to a "glacial accident" that deposited many southern species of flora onto the surprisingly mild Maine coast, the natural landscape in this area can be quite lush in the summertime. All too often this character is achieved through the importation of exotics—daisies, rugosa roses, and clover, to name but a few. But at the Wild Gardens of Acadia, these intruders have been stiffly turned away, and instead the focus is on native species. The gardens were first begun in 1909 by George Dorr, one of the boosters of Acadia National Park, as a way of preserving naturally occurring plant communities. An inventory of native species conducted in 1928 continues to serve as the guiding light. Several different habitats comprise the gardens, beginning with an attractive woodland area that contains a swamp and dry brook. A canopy of sugar maple and beech are underplanted with many different ferns and wildflowers. The most florid display takes place in the wildflower meadow, which blooms throughout the summer in a continual rotation of blossom. Annual mowing has served to reinvigorate the flowers while keeping the forest at bay. A rocky crag nearby with well-drained soils serves as an alpine plant observatory. The gardens are meticulously cared for, and in many instances show the guiding hand of man in the pursuance of the purely natural—such as in the Seaside, a streambank that has been maintained as a salty environment through the introduction of seaweed and beach gravel. Although the nearby creek contains freshwater, the plants here, which include the rare sedum roseroot, are typical of the shore. There has always been a heritage of ecological gardening at Wild Gardens (and Acadia in general), which illustrates that contemporary eco-sensitivity has deeper historical roots.

GARDEN OPEN: dawn–dusk daily, May–October.

ADMISSION: free.

FURTHER INFORMATION FROM:
Sieur de Monts Spring
Acadia 04609

NEARBY SIGHTS OF INTEREST:
Abbe Museum, Acadia
National Park

ABOVE: *The Wild Gardens exude a sensitivity for the natural environment.*

GARDEN OPEN: dawn–dusk
daily. **ADMISSION:** free

FURTHER INFORMATION FROM:
P.O. Box 244, Wiscasset
04578. (207) 633-4333

NEARBY SIGHTS OF INTEREST:
Pemaquid Point Lighthouse,
Monhegan Island

4 Boothbay Harbor: Coastal Maine Botanical Gardens

LOCATION: BARTER'S ISLAND ROAD OFF ROUTE 27, TWENTY MILES EAST OF BRUNSWICK

A botanical garden in its infant stage, such as the Coastal Maine Botanical Gardens, offers little of interest beyond its natural |setting. But that is precisely what is intriguing about this garden, set along a large swath of Sheepscot River waterfront. Eventually these woodlands will include theme gardens, flower collections, a children's garden, and conservatories. Presently two small garden areas exist along the trail that winds through the beautiful woods of the property. The Fern Walk contains indigenous species of shade-loving ferns, scattered carpetlike through the cool forest. The second garden, the Shore Walk, passes along a 3,600-foot parcel of shoreline planted with desiccation-tolerant herbaceous plants and grasses. The windy coastline, littered with the detritus of the tidal river provides a wild setting—far from what the word *garden* conjures in the mind. But the arrangement of the experience and the highlighting of architecturally unusual plants make this nascent garden wonderfully pregnant with possibilities. Entering the woodland again, wildflowers such as the coy pink lady's slipper—a wild orchid native to the area—color the understory in informal fashion. A devoted organization of gardeners and fund-raisers ensure that the garden will eventually take off. Until then, the main attractions are the seascape views and deep woodland ambiance that seems to brim with possibilities.

The Sheepscot River provides a dramatic backdrop for a tidal garden.

5 Isle of Shoals: Celia Thaxter Garden

LOCATION: NINE MILES OFF THE COAST OF KITTERY

On a typical summer morning in the Gulf of Maine, Isle of Shoals appears in the haze like a miraculous vision. The island must have presented itself in just this way when Celia Thaxter arrived one April morning in 1893 on a steamer bedecked with seedlings, ferns, and the fronds of houseplants. Thaxter, a popular poet, cultivated a small flower garden on Isle of Shoals, near where her family ran an inn. An attractive spot presided over by an engaging individual, the garden set the stage for the growth of a small salon, which included Robert Lowell, Sarah Orne Jewett, and the painter Childe Hassam, whose greatest works depict the flowers in Thaxter's garden. The inn was destroyed by fire in 1914, and the garden eventually reverted back to nature. But in the 1970s a group of dedicated gardeners replanted Thaxter's island paradise according to the writer's journals. The poet was an enthusiastic gardener who wrote as eloquently about battling slugs as she did about the beauty of an iris. Her garden reflects these sensibilities in its relaxed, sensual appearance. Although quite small (50 feet by 15 feet), almost sixty different plants are included within its confines, such as a proliferation of asters, sweetpeas, and poppies in pinks, yellows, and reds. "I love to pore over every blossom that unfolds in the garden, to study it and learn it by heart as far as a poor mortal may," wrote Thaxter in her gardening journal. As her legacy attests, such a student needs only a small plot and a big soul.

GARDEN OPEN: Cornell University runs a tour of the garden every Wednesday. The ferry leaves at 8:30am.

ADMISSION: $10

FURTHER INFORMATION FROM: Shoals Marine Lab, G14 Stimson Hall, Cornell University, Ithaca, NY 14853. (607) 255-3717

NEARBY SIGHTS OF INTEREST: Gulf of Maine

6 South Berwick: Hamilton House

LOCATION: FOLLOW SIGNS FROM BRATTLE STREET, OFF ROUTE 91, FIFTEEN MILES NORTH OF KITTERY

This Georgian-era house sits high above the Salmon Falls River, giving excellent views of the wild countryside of Maine. In marked contrast, some of the best formal gardens in the region have converted the proximate grounds into a highly civilized state. Although the house dates back to the beginning of the nineteenth century, the gardens were created in the early twentieth, when the estate was purchased by Emily Tyson and her daughter Elise, who lovingly restored the grounds and mansion with the help of their neighbor, the writer Sarah Orne Jewett. The style, in keeping with the spirit of the time, is Colonial Revival and shows Ms. Jewett's knowledge of

GARDEN OPEN: dawn to dusk Wednesday–Sunday, June 1– October 15. House tours on the hour, 11am–4pm.

ADMISSION: $4.

FURTHER INFORMATION FROM: 40 Vaughn's Lane South Berwick 03908. (603) 436-3205 www.spnea.org

NEARBY SIGHTS OF INTEREST: Sarah Orne Jewett House

European traditions gleaned from her many travels there. The main gardens are partially enclosed by a long pergola, lines of hedges, and several outbuildings. The flowerbeds, arranged along strong axial lines, are planted and maintained in a full, abundant manner, with vegetation flowing over borders and onto paths. Ms. Jewett had a penchant for old-fashioned materials such as phlox, tiger lilies, and golden hollyhocks, which repeat throughout the landscape to great effect. There is also a cottage on the property, which is enclosed by a vaguely English-cottage-style garden. Currently, a restoration effort has commenced at Hamilton House. The magnificent elms that once overhung the house and were lost over the years to Dutch elm disease are being replaced with newly developed, disease-resistant varieties.

A tasteful elegance presides over Hamilton House.

GARDEN OPEN: dawn–dusk daily, through "the growing season." **ADMISSION:** free.

FURTHER INFORMATION FROM: P.O. Box 16, South Paris 04281. (207) 743-820 www.dma.net/garden

NEARBY SIGHTS OF INTEREST: Jones Museum of Glass and Ceramics, Snow Falls Gorge

McLaughlin transformed a common garden through care and character.

7   # South Paris: McLaughlin Foundation

LOCATION: MAIN STREET (ROUTE 26), JUST BEFORE THE RAILROAD TRACKS, TWENTY MILES NORTHWEST OF LEWISTON

Bernard McLaughlin's father was a potato farmer in Aroostook County, deep in the northern wilderness of Maine—a cold, snowy land that imbued him and his progeny with dogged determination. But perhaps as a countermand to his heritage, McLaughlin spent his summers in Florida, where he developed a deep love for flowers. In 1936 he settled down in South Paris with his young, wealthy wife and began planting an epic garden that for many years was the best-kept secret in Maine. After his death a few years ago, a group of garden lovers banded together to save the plot from the bulldozer, and today much of McLaughlin's vision remains. Beginning with a simple patch of phlox, the garden grew into large borders of daylilies, sedum, and irises—an intriguingly architectural combination of contrasting forms. But the garden is less a statement of design finesse than a showcase for one man's abundant love of nature. Wildflowers make a major statement, as do some 200 lilacs of 98 different varieties. McLaughlin was primarily interested in plant variety, and although he possessed a certain horticultural élan, the garden is decidedly vernacular in aspect, reflecting the inner meditations of a mind untrained in the traditions of garden design. Few gardens of this type have been recognized for their value. But, lucky for garden lovers everywhere, this one has been preserved—due to the advocacy of a few avid Down-Easters, and much to the chagrin of the Ford dealership across the street.

8 Portsmouth: Governor Langdon House

LOCATION: PLEASANT STREET, NEAR THE INTERSECTION WITH STATE STREET

John Langdon rose to prominence in New Hampshire politics after the Revolutionary War, serving as governor of the state for two terms. He was also a figure on the national stage, as a signer of the U.S. Constitution and host to George Washington who dined at his house in 1789. After successive owners, Langdon's descendants repurchased the property in the late nineteenth century. The two-acre landscape, situated in the middle of busy Portsmouth, bears the signature of that time. The Victorian accents of the Colonial Revival design are evident in the geometric axis of the formal garden, which contains two twelve-foot-deep, perfectly balanced perennial borders. Together with the 150-foot flanking arbor covered with grape vines and climbing roses, these ostentatious elements create a lovely setting that Langdon surely wouldn't have experienced in the eighteenth century, but which are beautiful nonetheless. The rear wing of the house, containing the dining room, opens into the gardens and is a twentieth-century addition, built by McKim, Mead, and White in 1905. The informal landscape flows through an Adirondack glade composed of spruce, tamarack, and other evergreen species unusual to Portsmouth. Additional specimen trees on-site include a copper beech and several smoke trees.

GARDEN OPEN: dawn–dusk Wednesday–Sunday, June 1– October 15. House tours on the hour, 11am–4pm.
ADMISSION: $5.00 adults, $4.50 seniors, $2.50 children.

FURTHER INFORMATION FROM: 143 Pleasant Street Portsmouth 03801. (603) 436-3205 www.spnea.org

NEARBY SIGHTS OF INTEREST: Jackson House, Wentworth Coolidge Mansion

A profusion of climbers luxuriate in the summer sun.

9 Portsmouth: Moffatt-Ladd House

LOCATION: MARKET STREET, JUST NORTH OF TOWN CENTER

GARDEN OPEN: 11am–5pm Monday–Saturday; 1pm–5pm Sunday, June 15–October 15. **ADMISSION:** $1 for the garden; $5 for the house tour.

FURTHER INFORMATION FROM: 154 Market Street, Portsmouth 03801. (603) 436-8221

NEARBY SIGHTS OF INTEREST: Fort Constitution

This handsome old house was built by John Ladd in 1763, a merchant who ran a lively import-export business from the docks that once stood immediately across Market Street. The present gardens, which enclose the house on two sides like a custom-knitted glove, were designed by Ladd's descendant, Alexander Hamilton Ladd, in the nineteenth century, although several of the original Federal-era features still exist. These include a conglomeration of bee houses (no longer in use), a damask rose planted 1768 by Mrs. Samuel Moffatt (a married relation), and the enormous horse chestnut tree planted by General William Whipple (Moffatt's son-in-law) in 1776 after his return from Philadelphia, where he signed the Declaration of Independence. Beyond these, the garden is an approximation of Alexander Hamilton Ladd's design, based upon his garden journal, in which he meticulously recorded his plant selections. Quince trees, lilacs, and old roses twined to a helical trellis— an unusual design distinctive to Portsmouth—are just a few of the nineteenth-century features that still exist. Several beds include annuals and perennials arranged in a rustic manner, where color and form flow into one another. Taken as a whole, although situated on less than one acre of land, the garden provides hours of interest, due mainly to its intimate scale and winding brick paths that carry visitors to a separate terrace where an orchard once stood but which now mainly offers views of the rest of the garden. The house contains one of the best collections of period furnishings in northern New England. Antique books are for sale in the old barn behind the house, and the gift shop madam is good for lengthy conversations.

Jumbled and eccentric combinations in this historic garden.

10 Portsmouth: Rundlet-May House

LOCATION: MIDDLE STREET, THREE BLOCKS FROM MAPLEWOOD AVENUE

James Rundlet made his fortune in the textile industry that flourished in Portsmouth in the late eighteenth century and proclaimed his wealth by situating his Federal-style mansion on a terrace high above the street. The gardens behind the house are faithful to Rundlet's time owing to the conjunction of a good historic record (including an 1880 photograph) and a continuity of ownership. Within the house, his ostentation extended to imported English wallpaper, whereas outside his tastes ran to European formalism without the grandeur. The gardens are laid out along a regular—but not severe—grid that overlays a series of terraces. Old-time plants predominate, including peonies, lilacs, tiger lilies, and the climbers: roses and grapes. The romance of the scene is inspired, as it is throughout Portsmouth, by a distinctive helical rose trellis that occupies one corner of the lot (and provides a strong visual anchor to the garden). Fruit trees dot the perimeter of the garden and culminate in an old orchard of pear and apple in the rear, which gives way to a small forest of intrusive Norway maple. Several original outbuildings exist on-site, including two privies surrounded by annuals. One of Rundlet's descendants was a founder of the New Hampshire Society for the Prevention of Cruelty to Animals (SPCA), and there is also a small pet cemetery on the grounds.

GARDEN OPEN: dawn–to dusk Wednesday–Sunday, June 1– October 15. House tours on the hour, 11am–4pm.
ADMISSION: $5.00 adults, $4.50 seniors, $2.50 children.

FURTHER INFORMATION FROM:
364 Middle Street
Portsmouth 03801.
(603) 436-3205
www.spnea.org

NEARBY SIGHTS OF INTEREST:
Jackson House, Wentworth Coolidge Mansion

ABOVE: *A small urban garden transports visitors to the eighteenth century.*

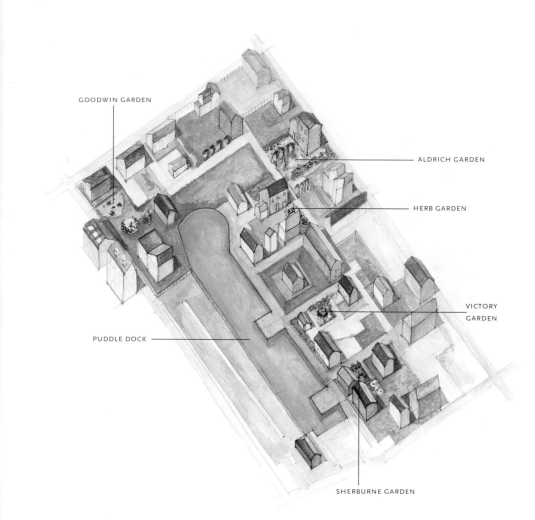

GOODWIN GARDEN

ALDRICH GARDEN

HERB GARDEN

VICTORY GARDEN

PUDDLE DOCK

SHERBURNE GARDEN

II Portsmouth: Strawberry Banke Gardens

LOCATION: MARCY STREET, ACROSS FROM PRESCOTT PARK

When Captain John Smith sailed past the mouth of the Piscataway River on his way to Maine in the early seventeenth century, what caught his eye wasn't the excellent deep-water port or the sheltered anchoring ground, but a profusion of strawberries lining the banks. Soon afterward a small settlement was established here, calling itself Strawberry Banke. Today the museum at Strawberry Banke, south of the main shopping area in Portsmouth, is devoted to preserving not only this very early colonial history but also the history of the intervening four hundred years up to the mid-twentieth century, when the property was converted into a museum. There are four significant gardens at Strawberry Banke, each of which speaks to a different era in the settlement's history. The Sherburne Garden (c. 1720) is the oldest. Located just inside the entrance to the museum, this garden provided a single family with most of its food, as well as sundry other important items. Although not beautiful in the modern sense, the current appearance is one of the best re-creations of colonial gardens in the region, based upon extensive archaeological exploration of the site and the existence of deed records for the property. The gardens are planted in raised beds built with wood and contain many herbs, such as peppermint and hyssop, and vegetables, such as beans, squash, orange calendula, and apples.

GARDEN OPEN: 10–5 daily, mid April–October.
ADMISSION: $12 adult; $8 children; $28 families. Garden tours by appointment.

FURTHER INFORMATION FROM: P.O. Box 300, Portsmouth 03802. (603) 433-1100

NEARBY SIGHTS OF INTEREST: Portsmouth Maritime Museum, Prescott Park Arts Festival

ABOVE: *Strawberry Banke features architecture, gardens, and the cultural artifacts of local history.*

OPPOSITE: *The 19th-century Goodwin Garden presents a typical formalism.*

Colonial gardens were utilitarian to an extent that we can't even imagine today, and yielded a profusion of seeds, fruits, and flowers that served a variety of nonculinary purposes. According to garden historian Ann Leighton, Puritan settlers were well acquainted with the classical botanical writings of such Roman and Greek authors as Galen and Dioscorides, and many colonial gardens contained medicinal herbs derived from those sources, such as lovage—one of the herbs in the Sherburne garden—which was a well-known cure for digestive ailments. Industrial purposes also dictated the colonial garden. Many plants were used as preservatives, dyes, and paints. Even the rose had a use. Littering the floor with its petals ensured that a fresh smell would be released with each footstep, to liven up the rather dank, dark surroundings. But lest we think the colonial mind some brutish, dim chasm, Ann Duncan, director of landscape at Strawberry Banke, reminds us that roses were also probably included in the garden for their own sake, to create a pleasing display throughout the summer.

Sarah Parker Goodwin and her husband, Ichabod, who served as Governor of New Hampshire from 1860 to 1861, lived in a little white house on Islington Street. However, facing possible demolition, the structure was moved onto the Strawberry Banke property in 1963. Mrs. Goodwin's garden has been re-created according to her meticulous journals and knowledge of typical nineteenth-century gardens. She was particularly enamored of her naturalistic grove of deciduous and evergreen trees, which she called "tanglewood"—only partially planted here. A curious arch between two hemlock trees signifies where this feature would have been located. Within the formal garden proper, several beds of annuals and perennials, including a liberal dose of orange poppy, form two central beds; a summer house hides beneath a population of climbing vines; and roses climb over cedar fence posts—all touches of gardening glamour and inventiveness indicative of the period, and of which Mrs. Goodwin partook. The third garden at Strawberry Banke is the Aldrich Garden, designed in 1913 to commemorate the obscure poet Thomas Bailey Aldrich using plants mentioned in his work. Mainly this garden documents the Colonial Revival period, so crucial to gardens in the East, when historical preservation groups began restoring homes and gardens from colonial times. More than colonial aesthetics, however, gardens from this period showcase early-twentieth-century tastes, such as symmetrical geometries and naturalistic groves and nooks, all accentuated by English-cottage-style borders of what were thought to be "period" herbs and flowers.

The Victory Garden, located just off Mast Lane, was a common feature in the mid-twentieth-century landscape. During World War II, the Department of Agriculture urged Americans to conserve food products by tilling gardens. It was also thought that gardening might provide a method of fostering

TOP: *The Sherburne Garden displays colonial herbs and flowers*

BOTTOM: *Savoy cabbage and other staples fill Mrs. Pecunies garden.*

patriotic pride and bolstering home-front morale; certain color schemes and "American" vegetables were propagated to this effect. This particular victory garden was the handiwork of Emma Pecunies, whose home once stood only a few feet away. The garden is re-created from the memory of Pecunies' descendants and an archaeological investigation. One striking feature is the intermingling of vegetables with bright flowers, which garden boosters also stressed were good for morale. Amidst the broccoli and onions you will see many exquisite dahlias—to strange, interesting effect. A homely wire fence encloses the garden, redolent of the "use-what-you-can" philosophy of victory gardens, and supports climbing roses. Only one plant is original: a resilient yucca that has clawed its way through several feet of rubble and fill.

Besides these four gardens, there is much to see in the way of cultural landscape at Strawberry Banke. Of particular note is a small plot next to the Shapiro house, in which an immigrant family lived during the early part of the century. Oral histories have revealed that Mrs. Shapiro was famous for her carefully tended garden. Although not restored per se, the thin strip of land next to her house does contain red Russian kale, a variety brought to this country by Eastern European immigrants, as well as poppies and lilacs. Elsewhere in the museum there is an orchard, and many of the lanes that transect the property are lined with period flowers and herbs. A small herb garden near the Victory Garden attracts many visitors; however, it is neither historic nor artistically noteworthy. The large greensward in the middle of Strawberry Banke was once an inlet called Puddle Dock. Two of the many wharves that lined the waterway are marked near the entrance by wooden structures, although interpretive signs are lacking. A cultural landscape report of a few years back noted the need to create a vigorous interpretation program. Once done, it will complement the already informative gardens nicely.

TOP: *Victory gardens were common during World War II.*

BOTTOM: *Castor bean surrounded by ageratum makes a strong 19th-century impression.*

12   North Hampton: Fuller Gardens

LOCATION: WILLOW AVENUE, JUST PAST THE INTERSECTION OF ROUTES 1 AND 1A, TEN MILES SOUTH OF PORTSMOUTH

GARDEN OPEN: 10am–6pm daily, mid May–mid October. **ADMISSION:** $4.00 adults, $3.50 children.

FURTHER INFORMATION FROM: 10 willow Avenue, North Hampton 03862. (603) 964-5414

NEARBY SIGHTS OF INTEREST: Hampton Beach

A sense of American antiquity pervades the Fuller Garden.

New Hampshire Governor Alvan T. Fuller (served 1924–1928) hired landscape architect Arthur Shurcliff to surround his mansion with beautiful rose gardens. One might say that Shurcliff's design is typically Colonial Revival in style. This is true. But the gardens also exemplify his facility within that mode to create engaging and spirited places. Each rose garden was oriented toward the house in a specific manner; however, the mansion was torn down in 1961, so one must use the imagination. Shurcliff's showpiece is the Front Garden, a sunken rose garden with beds set into an alternating diamond pattern that widens along its length to create a false perspective from the entry steps. Many different rose varieties are featured, including modern hybrid teas and classic floribundas. Crab-apple trees at the far end anchor the space, while a perennial border travels the length, seeming to open it up further. Hid-den behind this ostentatious display is a small Japanese garden oriented around a koi pond and small bridge. A local nursery was hired in 1930 to design the Side Garden, a radial rose garden in which an array of hybrid teas animate a selection of small statues and fountains. A hedge and cedar wall of espaliered fruit trees enclose the garden on one side, while a wood screen stands along another. A narrow path leads to the Back Garden, the most private of all. Here a selection of floribundas sit in a small but open garden presided over by old-time climbers—a quiet, romantic spot that would have appropriately adjoined the inner sanctum of the house.

13   Cornish: Saint-Gaudens National Historic Site

LOCATION: ROUTE 12A, TWENTY MILES SOUTH OF LEBANON

GARDEN AND HOUSE OPEN: 9am–4:30pm daily, late May–October. **ADMISSION:** $4 adults, children under 17 free (includes house tours).

FURTHER INFORMATION FROM: Box 73, Cornish 03745. (603) 675-2175 www.sgnhs.org

NEARBY SIGHTS OF INTEREST: Dartmouth College, Queechee Gorge

Augustus Saint-Gaudens first came to Cornish in 1885 on the advice of a lawyer friend who suggested that in New England, he might find many tall, hearty Yankees on which to model the statue of Lincoln he was preparing for the city of Chicago. Although the journey was long and he was little impressed with the former tavern that his friend rented for him, something about the fog-laden hills and the romantic Connecticut River got into his bones. He kept returning annually, finally purchasing the house, which he named Aspet, in 1891, and moving in permanently in 1900 when he was diagnosed with cancer.

Turtles and Victory in the atrium garden.

Saint-Gaudens did some of his most important work in Cornish and attracted a small colony of artists and writers to the area, including Kenyon Cox. When he wasn't transforming American sculpture with his monumental bronzes, Saint-Gaudens dabbled in landscape architecture at Aspet. Local pines were planted as hedges to create a series of rooms around the house, but over the years gardeners have substituted hemlock, which is somewhat better suited to the task. A bowling green, a formal ellipse, a cutting garden, and a rectangular, terraced perennial garden are all arranged around the central house. According to photographs, Saint-Gaudens completely planted this last area with an effusion of flowers. In the 1940s garden designer Ellen Biddle Shipman was commissioned to re-create the neglected garden, which she did as perennial borders separated by an intelligently proportioned lawn and adorned with a few of Saint-Gaudens' burnished putti. Several replicas of the sculptor's work, made from the original casts, are displayed throughout the garden, including the renowned Shaw Memorial, a bas-relief of the famous Boston brigade of black soldiers that fought during the Civil War. Nearby, set into a quiet copse of hedge, is a replica of Saint-Gaudens' memorial statue commissioned by the essayist Henry Adams, in memory of his wife, Clover. Entitled "Grief," the dark brooding face seems to reflect Adams's own sober sensibilities, and prompted him to write when it was complete: "Saint-Gaudens held up the mirror and no more, he meant to ask a question, not to give an answer." A small, open-air museum contains displays of other work, including a cast of the Farragut Memorial, Saint-Gaudens' first commission, sitting atop its original bluestone base, designed by the architect Stanford White, a frequent collaborator. The area is designed as an intimate, Roman style atrium, with a columned portico and pool of water lilies fed from each side by burnished bronze turtles that spit a steady stream of water. There is also much onsite not associated with Saint-Gaudens per se but also notable, such as a stunning birch walk that runs along the edge of the bowling green and several miles of nature trails.

GARDEN OPEN: 9:30am–5pm
daily, mid May–October.
ADMISSION: $7 adults,
$3 children.

FURTHER INFORMATION FROM:
Rt. 7A, Manchester 05254.
(802) 362-1788

NEARBY SIGHTS OF INTEREST:
Bennington Battlefield,
Appalachian Trail,
Sky Line Drive

LOCATION: ROUTE 7A, THIRTY MILES NORTH OF BENNINGTON

Robert Todd Lincoln, one of Abraham Lincoln's four sons, first came to Manchester as a boy in the summer of 1863 in retreat with his mother from Washington and the Civil War. Almost forty years later, in 1902, as the successful millionaire president of a railroad company, Lincoln returned to Manchester to purchase a small hill on the outskirts of town, on which he proceeded to build an impressive Georgian Revival mansion. Lincoln's daughter, Jessie, designed the gardens behind the house to resemble a Gothic stained-glass window, probably observed during one of the family's sojourns abroad when Lincoln served as ambassador to Britain. Four squares topped by an arc are delineated by a privet hedge, which acts as the lead, while the stained glass is re-created in a mélange of colorful flowers. It takes less imagination than one might suppose to see the "window," as the color scheme consists of large, bold blocks of pink, white, yellow, and blue. When the local nonprofit group that now administers the site first came on board in 1979 the gardens were in pretty rough shape, with privet running roughshod over everything and colors bleeding into one another. Over the last twenty years, however, a handful of indefatigable gardeners have beautifully restored the place. Each year they get a little better at the feat of maintaining consistent color throughout the season. In particular, the garden is regionally renowned for its peonies, which fill out the white and pink sections in June.

ABOVE: *An imitation of a stained-glass window is best viewed from the second floor.*

Elsewhere on the estate, the gardeners are undertaking a restoration of the kitchen garden. Archaeological digging, archival records, and some creative guesswork and experimentation have coalesced to make for an auspicious beginning. But like all new gardens, it will take a few years before things are truly established and looking their best. For now the garden contains many period vegetables, such as brandywine tomatoes. Nearby are the beds where the master peony growers ply their trade. Although they don't sell any of these wonderful plants, the staff freely gives helpful growing advice. There are several miles of walking trails at the estate, which turn into cross-country skiing trails in the winter. Lincoln hired Frederick Todd, a protégé of Frederick Law Olmsted, to site the mansion and lay out the grounds, with the result that there are many excellent views of the Green Mountains and the valley into which this little hilltop is tucked like a bean in a pod. The best views of the garden are achieved from the second story of the house.

15 Shelburne: Shelburne House

LOCATION: HARBOR ROAD, ON THE GROUNDS OF SHELBURNE FARMS

William Webb fell in love with Vermont about the time that he fell in love with Lila Vanderbilt. It wasn't long after their marriage, in the first decade of the twentieth century, that the millionaire couple purchased four-thousand acres along Lake Champlain and hired Frederick Law Olmsted and conservationist Gifford Pinchot to design this magnificent 1,400-acre working farm and gentleman's estate. Olmsted left the project about halfway through after arguing with Webb about fundamental aspects of the landscape design; he immediately took on another Vanderbilt commission, the Biltmore estate in North Carolina. For instance, Olmsted wanted to site the house on the peak of a rise to take advantage of views and to command the site; Webb instead chose a spot near the edge of the lake. Olmsted wanted to plant an arboretum of hardy indigenous trees—an ambitious scheme that would have rivaled the Arnold Arboretum in Boston; but Webb wanted to include delicate ornamentals like rhododendron and tea roses. Before his departure, however, Olmsted did put his imprint on the overall landscape, most noticeably in the wooded entry drive that offers glimpses of Lake Champlain (mere tastes of the view) before plunging in back into woodlands. The handsome residential landscape around the house (now an inn) gives excellent views of the water, while the adjoining acreage has been restored to its original state, now operating as an agricultural museum devoted to conservation practices. Programs in sustainable

GARDEN OPEN: dawn–dusk daily, mid May–mid October. **ADMISSION:** free.

FURTHER INFORMATION FROM: 102 Harbor Road, Shelburne 05482. (802) 985-8686

NEARBY SIGHTS OF INTEREST: Shelburne Museum, Ethan Allen Homestead, Fleming Museum

The grand allée culminates in an effusion of color.

agriculture and landscape management take place throughout the farm. Around the manor house, Lila Webb planted formal parterre gardens until she came under the influence of English garden writer Gertrude Jekyll in the first years of the twentieth century and redesigned the gardens in a more flowing, informal, and beautiful style. A grande allée is the centerpiece of the design. A long central pathway divides two stunning border gardens. Jekyll's "clumps" are the predominant parti, which contemporary gardeners divide into three distinct color combinations: cool colors, hot colors, and a baby-doll section of blues and pinks. The allée culminates in a hosta and peony garden centered around a statue of cupid. A charming border of roses and lavender connect across a lawn to a radial herb garden framed on one edge by espaliered pears. This rose/lavender combination is carried over to the formal rose garden, which is designed with four square beds of hybrid tea roses around a fountain ringed with lavender. The delicate and diminutive herbs provide a subtle background for a provocative display of modern rose varieties. This carefully orchestrated romance is completed by a strict hedge of yew and climbing roses around the perimeter. It is a delight that the pleasures of a formal garden are retained at Shelburne Farms while the property at large remains devoted to its environmental mission. Too often these foci are divergent in America, but here one can delight in both.

16 Shelburne: Shelburne Museum

LOCATION: ROUTE 7, SEVEN MILES SOUTH OF BURLINGTON

In its thirty-five buildings, spread across a lilac landscape, the Shelburne museum houses an eclectic collection of Americana including everything from Shaker quilts to the steamboat Ticonderoga. The lilacs are an important component of the display, and by being situated close to the structures, echo colonial traditions. In late May they bloom in vivid purples, blues, and whites and transform the museum into a fragrant delight. Besides the lilacs, there is the reproduction of an old vegetable garden next to the Dutton House, an eighteenth-century structure relocated to this spot—like the rest of the buildings that comprise the museum—from its original site in a small town in southern Vermont. Notwithstanding the date of the house, the Dutton Garden represents nineteenth-century tastes gleaned from a popular book on horticulture and gardening that made the rounds of educated and "progressive" rural homeowners in the mid-to-late 1800s. Thus the garden contains red Russian kale, brought to this country by eastern European immigrants, as well as collard greens, tennis ball lettuce, and other "sallads" popular at that time. Two formal gardens also grace the grounds. The Pleissner Garden evokes the feeling of Vermont painter Ogden Pleissner's works, while the Bostwick Garden, named after the museum founder's daughter, is a small collection of annuals and perennials laid out like a painter's palette, with four colors—green, blue, yellow, and red—arranged around a circle. A mixture of plants strives to create season-long interest. Elsewhere, the museum also showcases a garden of medicinal herbs and herbs as well as plants used to create dyes.

GARDEN OPEN: 10am–5pm daily, late May–late October. ADMISSION: $17.50 adults, $7.00 children (includes the entire museum).

FURTHER INFORMATION FROM: P.O. Box 10, Shelburne 05482. (802) 985-3346 www.shelburnemuseum.org

NEARBY SIGHTS OF INTEREST: Ethan Allen Homestead, Fleming Museum, Shelburne Farms

Visitors to the Museum learn about colonial garden practices.

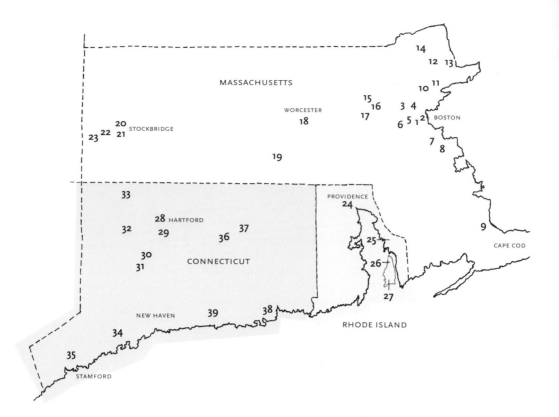

MASSACHUSETTS

WORCESTER

STOCKBRIDGE

BOSTON

CAPE COD

PROVIDENCE

HARTFORD

CONNECTICUT

RHODE ISLAND

NEW HAVEN

STAMFORD

SOUTHERN NEW ENGLAND:

Massachusetts, Rhode Island, and Connecticut

For many, Massachusetts represents the colonial past more than any other state in the Northeast. The Boston Tea Party, Paul Revere's ride, and other iconographic moments tend to paint the region in monochromatic strokes. To be sure, there is plenty of colonial history in the region—not only in Boston but in the small hill towns of Connecticut and the dark side streets of Providence. But interest in preserving the colonial past really began in earnest around 1876, during the first centennial when historians and laypeople began discovering that many historic homes and landscapes had been lost over time. A movement commenced, generally called the Colonial Revival movement, to preserve and restore these places. Due to a number of factors, not the least of which was a lack of strong historical methods or technologies (like today's magnetic resonance imaging), as well as an exuberance on the part of the historians, Colonial Revival tended to impose ideas from the Victorian world upon its subject rather than unearthing the facts of colonial life. Gardens, perhaps more than houses, were affected by this. Today a controversy rages over whether to dismantle Colonial Revival landscapes in order to unearth an earlier history or whether to retain them as historically valid in their own right. Some, such as the Mission House in Stockbridge (*page 52*) and the Longfellow House in Cambridge (*page 32*), were designed by important landscape architects working within the Colonial Revival style. Others, such as the Bellamy-Ferriday House in Bethlehem, Connecticut (*page 61*), offer interesting glimpses into the successive layers of history.

OPPOSITE: *Reenactors don Colonial era garb to tend gardens at Old Sturbridge Village.*

TOP: *Stately pergolas overlook a major new garden at Tower Hill in Boylston, Massachusetts.*

BOTTOM: *Ragna Goddard play tricks with perspective in the diminutive but infinitely interesting Sundial Garden in Higganum, Connecticut.*

It is hard to overestimate Boston's influence on the garden history of the region, or even the country. Mount Auburn Cemetery (*pages 29–31*), which receives extensive coverage here, was the first garden cemetery in the country, influencing Andrew Jackson Downing, Frederick Law Olmsted, and the parks movement of the late nineteenth century. At the turn of the century, Harvard University's landscape architecture department became a locus for many of the greatest landscape architects of the early twentieth century, including Arthur Shurcliff, a strong influence on the Colonial Revival style and designer of Colonial Williamsburg, as well as his son Sidney Shurcliff and other notable designers. One, Fletcher Steele is also prominently featured here; his lifelong work at Naumkeag (*pages 49–51*) surely stands as one of our greatest modern garden landscapes.

Of course garden history in America has often been propelled by the private vision of individuals as opposed to static traditions, and the smaller gardens of Rhode Island and Connecticut merit much attention. The excruciating detail and intellectual rigor of the Sundial Garden in Higganum (not to mention their fine tea, *pages 68–69*), the sensitive reworking of Shakespeare's Head (*page 55*), and the loving testament of Caprilands (*page 66*) are all worth the trip.

Boston: Isabella Stewart Gardner Museum

LOCATION: 280 THE FENWAY, BACK BAY

MUSEUM OPEN: Tuesday–
Sunday 11am–5pm. Closed
Thanksgiving, Christmas, and
New Year's Day. ADMISSION:
$10 adults, $7 seniors, and
$5 students. Children under
18 free.

FURTHER INFORMATION FROM:
280 The Fenway, Boston
02115. (617) 566-1401

NEARBY SIGHTS OF INTEREST:
Museum of Fine Arts,
The Fens

There is a lot of lore circulating in Boston concerning Isabella Stewart Gardner's eccentricities, such as the delightfully macabre myth that she frequently walked pet lions down Beacon Street. What is certain is that her meticulous care and discerning tastes bequeathed a most fascinating jewel to posterity: the Isabella Stewart Gardner Museum. Fronting on Boston's Fens, this fifteenth-century Italian palazzo was constructed in 1903 to house Mrs. Gardner's immense collection of European oil paintings and antiquities, which she arranged—along with priceless furniture, textiles, works of gold and silver, and rare manuscripts—to create the feeling that art is part of a living context. The experience is vibrant, blurring the perhaps fatuous divisions between the arts: Rembrandt's *Self-Portrait* and Albrecht Dürer's *A Man in a Fur Coat* are hung against an emerald green, silk damask wall covering, over an oak cabinet reproduced in the seventeenth-century Dutch style, which is flanked by Louis XIV upholstered Italianate side chairs. Just inches to the right of these highly wrought artifacts, the view opens to the splendor of the interior courtyard: a garden of hydrangeas and delphiniums and Greco-Roman statuary, a green tapestry of groundcover, and the slightest trickle of a great fountain—the light, sound, and quiet feel of which conjoin with one's perception of the artworks to form a single, sublime experience. This integrationist policy was carried out in the architectural ornamentation of the building itself. An array of artifacts collected from several different crumbling European estates were integrated into a single whole—the most impressive display of which is seen within the courtyard, where Gothic and Byzantine window arches alternate on each floor.

Ever since opening night on New Year's Day 1903, when Mrs. Gardner unveiled a Mediterranean display of palms—a miraculous sight in the depths of a Boston winter—the garden has served as the canvas for a perpetually changing floral display. A team of expert gardeners oversee the designs. Inside the confines of this small space, topiaries, hanging baskets, geometric beds, and single impressive specimens are employed within a vocabulary of gardening traditions derived from Mediterranean cultures. Beginning in 1989, under the auspices of museum director Anne Hawley, the displays began to take on a more regular, studied aspect. Early spring begins with orange and blue flowers; summer sees violet-blue (delphiniums) and white (hydrangeas) take over; and to lift spirits in winter, oranges, yellows, and reds (George Washington geraniums) make appearances. An effusive Easter display annually

Easter nasturtiums tumble toward the meticulously designed courtyard.

features orange nasturtiums cascading from the third-story balcony. Surrounding this ever-shifting pastiche lies the courtyard's Greco-Roman architecture, originally laid out by Isabella Stewart Gardner. The centerpiece is a large mosaic terrace featuring the head of Medusa. Standing around her (perhaps caught looking), are several stone statues, including a second-century statue of Artemis and several Greco-Roman figures. A path of gravel frames the scene, and beds of moss, vinca, and ivy complete the permanent, unchanging backdrop against which the superlative floral displays are overlaid. The garden is inaccessible, meant solely for viewing from the cloisters that surround it or from one of the windows above. This restriction is in fact a liberating element that creates unique perspectives not often achieved in a small garden. Depending on the mood of the display (which is highly dependent on the season) and from where the garden is viewed (which is highly influenced by the surrounding art and architecture), a hundred different experiences can be had in a single visit.

Outside the museum, the southern lawn, containing a short allée of *Katsura* and teak benches, gives way to the Monks Garden, so named for a friend of Mrs. Gardner, which is a more natural collection and fairly permanent. Nothing special is intended for this area other than to provide a comfortable place to relax and eat lunch. The restaurant has a terrace here. But the same accomplished garden staff that creates the courtyard displays also attends to this area, so its presentation is far above average. A few architectural elements dot the landscape, as well as some interesting plant material, such as a silk plant that produces delicate pink flowers in the spring.

GARDEN OPEN: Tuesday–Sunday, 10am–4pm. The garden is accessed from outside the museum.
ADMISSION: free.

FURTHER INFORMATION FROM:
465 Huntington Avenue
Boston 02115. (617) 267-9300

NEARBY SIGHTS OF INTEREST:
Isabella Stewart Gardner Museum, The Fens

2 Boston: Tanshin-En

LOCATION: AT THE NORTH END OF THE MUSEUM OF FINE ARTS, ON THE FENWAY

Throughout the twentieth century, American garden designers have looked to the East, the Far East, for guidance and inspiration. Fletcher Steele, designer of Naumkeag, spent much time in China studying garden design. Walter Beck at Innisfree, Beatrix Farrand and Mildred Bliss at Dumbarton Oaks, and even the quintessential Americanist Arthur Shurcliff at the Fuller estate in New Hampshire—all imbibed at the fountain of oriental traditions and translated them into occidental modes, with varying degrees of success. In recent years, interest in Eastern gardens has progressed to the point where garden designers from Japan, China, and other countries in the Orient are regularly receiving commissions from American

clients. In the 1980s, the Boston Museum of Fine Arts commissioned Japanese garden designer Kinsaku Nakane to create a garden on museum grounds to commemorate the first curator of the Asiatic collection, Okakura Tanshin. Nakane responded with a contemplative viewing garden, a still and carefully controlled environment intended for passive thought rather than active perusal. A single platform containing a single bench from where the garden is viewed strictly regulates the experience. There are no paths, no opportunity for strolling; rather, one sits and meditates. The garden is in the *kare sansui* style, which literally translates as "dry mountain water," and attempts to approximate or re-create the spiritual experience of a water landscape using stones, gravel, and plant material. A large swath of raked, white gravel, which gives the impression of a salt flat or a dry desert lake, extends before the viewing platform. Several rock groupings planted with perennials and herbaceous shrubs, connected by elegant granite bridges, give focus and anchor the garden architecturally, while mounds of layered plantings step up a rocky hillside in the background to give depth and emotion. Impressed by the natural beauty of the New England landscape, Nakane employed many native species in his design and there is a noticeable lack of conifers. Symbolically, the garden is intended to represent a coastal landscape in miniature. The gravel bed serves as the ocean. The stone outcroppings, islands, while the hillside represents a mountainous landfall. To achieve the illusion, perspective is manipulated to great effect. Views are limited to what can be perceived from the platform, which has the effect of "flattening" the landscape onto a seemingly two-dimensional canvas. A slight hint of the third dimension is infused into the painting by drawing some of the plantings onto a small portion of the platform—a Japanese maple and a quiet marble bubbler are located near the benches. But even these fail to compete with the rest of the landscape, a living still life every bit as enigmatic as a Dutch oil painting.

At Tanshin-En the view is everything.

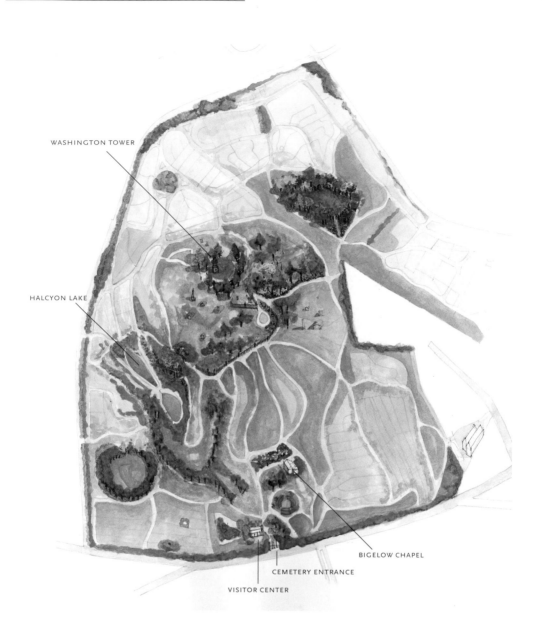

WASHINGTON TOWER

HALCYON LAKE

BIGELOW CHAPEL

CEMETERY ENTRANCE

VISITOR CENTER

3 Cambridge: Mount Auburn Cemetery

LOCATION: MOUNT AUBURN STREET, ONE MILE WEST OF HARVARD SQUARE

Like other cultural values, attitudes toward death have evolved over time. In the seventeenth and early-eighteenth centuries, American cemeteries were dark places that no one dared to venture into except on funereal occasions. Nowhere was this attitude more stringently ensconced than in Puritan New England. But in 1831, a handful of enlightened Bostonians, led by Harvard professor Jacob Bigelow, set out to transform this attitude by creating a cemetery on the western edge of town that would celebrate life through the presentation of nature and art: a pleasure ground for eternal rest. Bigelow was an outstanding figure. A botanist, a Unitarian, a physician, and an architect, Bigelow spearheaded the drive for Mount Auburn, convincing Boston brahmins of its necessity and actually designing most of its road system and architecture, not to mention selecting many of the cemetery's tremendously diverse trees. In many ways Mount Auburn was inspired by Paris's great cemetery, Père LeChaise. Narrow roads and footpaths create a sense of enclosure as they weave a serpentine web between monuments, giving the landscape a sense of surprise and wonder. Like Père LeChaise, the hilly topography of the site heightens the effect. But this is where comparisons end. Where the Parisian inspiration can often look like a glimmering sea of marble, Mt. Auburn is an awe-inspiring fabric of

CEMETERY OPEN: 8am–5pm daily; open until 7pm during daylight saving time.

ADMISSION: free. AUDIO TOUR RENTAL (about 1 hr): $5, with $7 deposit.

FURTHER INFORMATION FROM: 580 Mount Auburn Street Cambridge 02138. (617) 547-7105

NEARBY SIGHTS OF INTEREST: Harvard Square, Longfellow House, Arnold Arboretum

ABOVE: *The experience of the landscape is carefully controlled by topography, planting, and architecture at Mt. Auburn Cemetery.*

OPPOSITE: *Mt. Auburn was conceived as a pleasure ground that celebrates life rather than broods about death.*

green. In 1997 an inventory counted over 5,000 trees, many of which were over one hundred years old. Some of the largest and oldest specimens predate the cemetery, but overwhelmingly the majority were added by Bigelow during his reign as director. There are many state- and regional-champion trees, including a smooth-leaf elm that stands almost a hundred feet tall.

Once convinced to support the cemetery, Boston's aristocracy flocked to be buried there. Notable figures contained within its depths include art doyenne Isabella Stewart Gardner, U.S. Supreme Court Justice Oliver Wendell Holmes, Harvard art historian Charles E. Norton, and city mayor Josiah Quincy. Writers Bernard Malamud, Henry Wadsworth Longfellow, and Julia Ward Howe, as well as artist Winslow Homer and illustrator Charles Dana Gibson (famous for his "Gibson girl") are also buried here. Perhaps attributable to Bigelow's interests, several luminaries in botany and landscape architecture also found their way to Mount Auburn, including Louis Agassiz, Asa Gray, Charles Eliot and his son Charles W. Eliot—and, of course, Bigelow himself. The monuments, in their own silent way, tell the story of Boston's great renaissance in the nineteenth century, and the city's enduring legacy in the twentieth century. The gravestones are also magnificent works of public art in their own right. And viewing the different aesthetic interpretations and styles can consume an entire afternoon, especially when considering how the sculptural and architectural effects work against the natural backdrop.

At the center of the cemetery, the earth rises to a promontory topped by Washington Tower, designed by Bigelow to honor the first president. From here there are excellent vistas of Boston, neatly framed by the canopy of trees that are at eye level. From the tower, which is accessible, a 360-degree, unhindered panorama is achieved. Halcyon Lake, located in the lower elevations of the cemetery, casts a tranquil atmosphere over the monuments that border it, such as the glistening marble tomb of Mary Baker Eddy, founder of the Church of Christ, Scientist, and the *Christian Science Monitor*. The Gothic revival Bigelow Chapel, with its bulky, gingerbread house-like pinnacles, was also designed by Bigelow and stands beside a road near the entrance as if watching over its charges in the rest of the cemetery. Nearby, a stone sphinx—a memorial to the

TOP: *Washington Tower provides panoramic views of Boston.*

BOTTOM: *Architectural details become part of the landscape fabric.*

"strength" and "duration" of the Union, created by Martin Milmore—responds with stoicism.

Arborists from around the country conduct their research at Mount Auburn, which, among other things, possesses more than three dozen rare and unusual specimens of trees. A garden commemorating Asa Gray, near the entrance, boasts a pyramidal dove tree (*Davidia involucrata*) and a thundercloud cultivar of cherry plum (*Prunus cerasifera* Thundercloud) with dark purple foliage that explodes with pink petals in summer. In the spring, thousands of bulbs planted throughout the landscape in a carpetlike pattern ignite in snaking curves that underlay the lush canopy of trees to offer a strong design counterpoint. And in the late fall and winter, when the garden sheds its softness for sheer architectural grandeur, the monuments can seem to shimmer, especially during the first minutes of dusk. Visitors should be reminded that Mount Auburn Cemetery is still an active, working cemetery and not a recreational public park.

Bigelow envisioned a secular Eden, where the beauty of nature was tangible.

GARDEN OPEN: dawn–dusk,
Wednesday–Sunday, mid
March–mid December.
ADMISSION: $2 adults.

FURTHER INFORMATION FROM:
105 Brattle Street, Cambridge
02138. (617) 876-4491
www.nps.gov/long

NEARBY SIGHTS OF INTEREST:
Harvard Museum, Gore Place

*A modern Colonial Revival
garden blends bold plantings
with Victorian structure.*

4   # Cambridge: Longfellow House

LOCATION: **105** BRATTLE STREET, JUST OFF HARVARD SQUARE

Poet Henry Wadsworth Longfellow—a lover of both history and
nature—may have been equally motivated to purchase this
colonial house in 1837 by the simple, yet magnetic, reason that
George Washington established his headquarters here while
planning the siege of Boston in 1775, or by virtue of the wonderful meadow that sloped down to the glistening Charles River
behind the house, creating a bit of the country in the middle of
the bustling city. During his tenure here, until 1882, the house
served as an intellectual locus for the Massachusetts literati;
Nathaniel Hawthorne, Ralph Waldo Emerson, and Julia Ward
Howe were counted among the frequent visitors. After his
death, the nine-acre property was divided among Longfellow's
children, all of whom built new houses on their plots, except
for his daughter Alice, who moved into the main house. In the
early twentieth century the meadow was transferred to the town
of Cambridge, and Charles Eliot was hired to design a park
landscape with some fairly formal features. A long, almost rectangular oval of grass, marked by a drive, lies over the slope. At
the bottom the space culminates in a natural terrace that hosts
a cast of Saint-Gaudens's Longfellow bust and an exedra framing steps down to the river. Alice Longfellow hired landscape
architect Martha Brooks Hutchinson to design a colonial garden surrounding the house. Hutchinson's design is very much
in the Colonial Revival style. A central boxwood parterre outlines flower beds, while a variety of shrubs and lilacs and a line
of chinoisserie fencing conspire to create a border. Architectural elements like a brick walkway and a Victorian pergola give

the space a strong, formal anchoring. Twenty years after Hutchinson's work, Ellen Biddle Shipman devised a planting plan for the garden in a lusher, looser style, using vertical masses of delphinium, phlox, and thermopsis that spill over the edges of the beds. In bold recognition that history contains many layers, the entire garden is currently undergoing a massive restoration, not to Longfellow's time but to the Colonial Revival garden of Hutchinson and Shipman. Such a development would have pleased Longfellow, who understood that artistic expression far outlived the flesh of the body when he wrote: "Art is long, and time is fleeting."

5 Brookline: Fairsted

LOCATION: BOYLSTON STREET (ROUTE 9) TO WARREN STREET,
FIVE MILES WEST OF BOSTON

From this perch in suburban Boston, landscape architect Frederick Law Olmsted generated many of his major designs, including those for the U.S. Capitol Grounds in Washington, D.C., Boston's Emerald Necklace, and the Biltmore Estate in Asheville, North Carolina. When he wasn't consumed with work, he also cast his eye upon his surroundings and neatly arranged these grounds, covering under two acres, into a microcosm of his landscape ideas. Today the office houses an Olmsted museum as well as an archive of his work, while the landscape has been preserved and offers one of the best maintained examples of Olmsted's residential work. The largest portions of the landscape are given over to the kind of grand park lawn that one will find in most of his compositions. A variety of deciduous trees are carefully arranged to visually anchor the space and to lead the eye over the terrain. Within this overarching scheme, there are several "rooms" designed on a more human scale and which offer places of perspective and contrast with the larger landscape. At the corner, a slight hillock conceals a narrow path as it cuts through laurel and other shrubbery at the wood's edge. The Hollow, near Olmsted's office window, offers a comfortable refuge from the expanse of handsome lawn. Both of these spaces are uniquely intimate, and critics have seen here connections to other nodes in Olmsted's landscapes, such as the Ramble in New York City's Central Park. Photographs from the 1890s show the house completely covered in wisteria, a "wildness" that Olmsted continually referred to in his writings, and which he postulated would knit man to his surroundings. Today the National Park Service has cleaned the place up a bit, but a current investigation of its natural heritage may bode some significant changes.

GARDEN OPEN: 10:00am–4:30pm, Friday–Sunday, year-round except federal holidays. ADMISSION: free.

FURTHER INFORMATION FROM: 99 Warren Street, Brookline 02146. (617) 566-1689 www.nps.gov/frla/index.htm

NEARBY SIGHTS OF INTEREST: John F. Kennedy Historic Site, Arnold Arboretum

Jamaica Plain: Arnold Arboretum

LOCATION: ARBORWAY, FOUR MILES WEST OF DOWNTOWN BOSTON

ARBORETUM OPEN: dawn–
dusk daily. Visitor's center
open: 9am–4pm Monday–
Friday; noon–4pm weekends,
except holidays.
ADMISSION: Free. **MAPS:** $1.

FURTHER INFORMATION FROM:
125 Arborway, Boston 02130.
(617) 524-1718

NEARBY SIGHTS OF INTEREST:
Fairsted, Mount Auburn
Cemetery

The Arnold Arboretum is the geographical and symbolic center of Boston's Emerald Necklace, the system of greenways and public parks designed by Frederick Law Olmsted that encircle the city. Geographically, it is in the middle of the system as it bends its way back toward downtown. Symbolically, the arboretum's internationally significant collection of hardy trees recall the idealism and intellectual vigor that fueled public parks projects in the late-nineteenth century. The garden was the brainchild of Charles Sprague Sargent, brother of the painter John Singer Sargent and a passionate horticulturist. Sargent envisioned the arboretum as a fusion of botanical garden, where wide variety of species would be on display for the intellectual edification of scholars, and a public park, where weary city dwellers could connect with nature—a *rus in urbe* as Parks Movement boosters quipped. Sargent's selection of trees focused on native species and exotics that could survive in the New England climate. Over a forty-year period, Sargent and a coterie of Harvard botanists, including the intrepid Ernest Henry Wilson, traveled to Japan, China, and Korea, as well as parts of Northern Europe and southern Chile and Argentina, gathering specimens from similar climes. Under Sargent's direction the trees were planted in Olmsted's landscape according to genus and family. The contrasts are extraordinary, both horticulturally and in terms of design. For example, next to an American sugar maple, one will find a Japanese maple and a Chinese maple—a combination that would never occur in nature, but that allows for interesting comparisons between the form of each species. The focus here is on trees. Each specimen is meticulously labeled, while the abundant herbaceous plants that act as filler are not. Those searching for abundant floral color will be disappointed at the arboretum (except during the lilac festival, and of course in autumn). Instead the emphasis is on the abundant yet subtle texture and architecture of trees.

The splendid architecture of the historic tree collection

Just gaze for a while at the knotted trunks of the Amur cork trees or enter the spirited grove of metasequoia, with its strangely Euclidean branch system, and the point won't be lost.

Unfortunately, today the arboretum is not managed as well as it might be. A scourge of undergrowth threatens large swaths of woodland, while eroded pathways have thinned some of the canopy and prove unsightly in the greater vistas. Beneath a general appearance of unadorned nature, however, there are many vestiges of Olmsted's artful design, including an exquisite roadway system, which heightens

the experience as well as several well-designed vistas. In addition to the collection of trees, there are some flowering shrubs, such as mountain laurel, lilac, and viburnum. In mid-May, the arboretum sponsors its annual Lilac Sunday for viewing some 250 different varieties. There is also a bonsai and dwarf conifer collection. While the trees are all labeled, the arboretum is not. The only map is located at the Arborway gate entrance.

7 Quincy: Adams House

LOCATION: HANCOCK STREET, OFF DIMMOCK, TEN MILES SOUTH OF BOSTON

According to certain historians, John Adams was uncomfortable with the presidency. While his predecessor, George Washington, was absent from office 181 days during eight years, Adams missed 385 in only four. This was partly due to the disdain he felt from Philadelphians. But when the seat of government relocated to Washington, D.C., another excuse was found in the uncomfortable, half-erected White House. Reading between these lines, one might discern the real reason for Adams's absences: homesickness for the little house in Quincy, Massachusetts, where he'd been born and raised. Today a compound of twelve buildings set on twelve acres comprises the Adams National Park. In addition to the birthplace of John and his son John Quincy, the sixth president, the park also contains the family church and a cultural landscape that tells the story of this indefatigable family. Around the "old house," Abigail Adams, the second first lady, created a

GARDENS AND HOUSE OPEN: 9am–5pm daily, April 19– November 10. **ADMISSION:** $2; children under 16 free.

FURTHER INFORMATION FROM: 135 Adam Street, Quincy 02169. (617) 773-1177

NEARBY SIGHTS OF INTEREST: John F. Kennedy Library

Brooks Adams' flower garden flanks the "Old House."

luxurious garden for which she drew upon her frequent travels to Europe with her husband on diplomatic missions, and planted it with many exotic species not commonly used in New England gardens at the time. After her death, four successive generations of Adamses put their imprint on the flower garden, and it is currently restored to the last owner, the Brooks Adams family. An eight-inch dwarf boxwood hedge encloses the small rectilinear garden arranged around a classic lawn. Chinese balloon flower, phlox, peonies, and many colorful annuals fill the space in four successive layers. It is an early-twentieth-century (Brooks Adams died in 1926) experiment with more relaxed and unusual combinations set within eighteenth-century "bones," which reflect a taste for classical regularity. The landscape also contains many other historical features, such as an orchard of pears, apples, and quince thought to have been originally planted by John Adams, a Yorkshire rose planted by Abigail, and John Quincy's stately black walnut tree.

GARDENS OPEN: continually year-round. **MUSEUM OPEN:** 1:30pm–4:30pm Tuesday–Saturday, June–September. Old Ship Church holds services Sunday mornings and is open to visitors. Interpretive guide to Old Ship Memorial Garden available only inside the church.

FURTHER INFORMATION FROM: Old Ordinary Museum Hingham. (781) 749-0013

NEARBY SIGHTS OF INTEREST: Abigail Adams birthplace

8 Hingham: Old Ordinary Garden and Old Ship Memorial Garden

LOCATION: ONE BLOCK NORTH AND ONE BLOCK EAST, RESPECTIVELY, OF THE SQUARE IN HINGHAM, FIFTEEN MILES SOUTHEAST OF BOSTON

According to local history, this garden was designed by the Olmsted Brothers firm in 1922 as an approximation of a late colonial garden circa 1770. But in actuality, the adjacent ordinary—a New England term for a tavern that served "ordinary food to ordinary travelers"—dates to a period much earlier than that. The garden reflects a Victorian sensibility rather than a strict interpretation of history. It includes a parterre of boxwood and romantic brick paths that converge on a lovely sundial, and beds of perennials that serve to balance an extremely large tulip tree over 150 years old. Behind the ordinary, a garden club has recently restored a terraced hill, designed by a minister who occupied the house around 1900 as a relaxing place to sit and observe his surroundings. The same garden club also manages the Old Ship Memorial Garden, located only a few blocks away. This small plot is situated on the western end of the Old Ship Church, a magnificent example of early American civic architecture and where services have been held continuously since its construction in 1684. This garden is a truer example of what would be found in a typical colonial garden, down to the deep red geraniums—heartier than their fairer cousins and favored by Puritan pioneers. Many of the plants are actually descendants of nineteenth-century plants, including a lilac tree traceable to 1770.

9 Sandwich: Heritage Plantation

LOCATION: EXIT 2 OFF THE MID-CAPE HIGHWAY (ROUTE 6),
BACKTRACK TO GROVE STREET

Josiah Lilly, scion to the Eli Lilly fortune, was an avid collector of Americana whose interests ranged from cars to carousels to military miniatures. In 1967, he purchased the rhododendron farm of Charles O. Dexter, a famous hybridizer who collaborated with Charles Sprague Sargent of the Arnold Arboretum on atypical varieties. Here Lilly established his Heritage Plantation, a museum of cultural artifacts that reflect their collector's eclectic tastes. Lilly also had a passion for plants, perhaps owing to a brief stint as owner of a holly farm in nearby Falmouth, and augmented the seventy-six acre property with a variety of trees and woody plants. He added to the rhododendron collection and planted a forest of evergreens, lilacs, and viburnums that rolls through the grounds like a green connector between the disparate museum collections. Daylily-lined paths lead to several gardens, including a significant sampling of day-lilies overseen by the American Hemerocallis Society. Many perennial and annual gardens are interwoven into the arboretum, some of which are planted in a formal style. Like the museum itself, the gardens are diverse—jumping from formal to informal without much rhyme or reason other than simple attractiveness and the peculiar eye of their creator. Other notable gardens include a hosta garden, a holly garden planted beside the Military Museum, and an herb garden that graces the administration building.

GARDEN OPEN: 10am–5pm
daily, May 10–October 18.
ADMISSION: $9.00 adults,
$8.00 seniors, $4.50 children.

FURTHER INFORMATION FROM:
67 Grove Street, Sandwich
02563-2147. (508) 888-3300

NEARBY SIGHTS OF INTEREST:
Sandwich Glass Museum,
Yesteryears Doll and Toy
Museum

ABOVE: *Daylily trails connect
a variety of specialty gardens.*

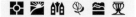

10 # Danvers: Glen Magna Farms

LOCATION: CENTER STREET EXIT OFF ROUTE 1, FIFTEEN MILES NORTH OF BOSTON

GARDENS OPEN: 9am–dusk Monday–Friday; 9am–noon Saturday–Sunday; year-round. House open to tours. Glen Magna Farms is closed on certain weekends during the summer for weddings.

FURTHER INFORMATION FROM: Ingersoll Street, Danvers 01923. (978) 774-9165

NEARBY SIGHTS OF INTEREST: Page House, Putnam House

An esplanade of annuals leads through the garden.

The original farm at Glen Magna was purchased during the War of 1812 by Capt. Joseph Peabody, who enlarged the farmhouse into a summer estate. The Peabody Gardens, directly behind the house, were designed and planted by George Huessler, an Alsatian gardener who designed several gardens in Salem in 1912, although the floral additions might have been the work of Charles Eliot. Sometimes called the Old-Fashioned Garden, the space is oriented around a walkway lined with annuals and trained rose trees that once led to an enormous tulip tree. After this venerable specimen came down in the 1920s, several others were planted near the house. An octagonal gazebo installed in 1840 marks the end of the path; however, its aspect of a complete structure from afar is proved an illusion up close when we discover that the entire building is contorted into a flattened shape. Beyond this area is "lover's walk," composed with an allée of arborvitae. From here a path leads back in the general direction of the house and into the canopy of one of the most impressive weeping beech trees in the world. The branches reach to the ground in a full circle, through which three "doorways" are cut. The living cave is dark, smelling distinctly organic, and creates its own musky microclimate that is particularly enticing on a hot, humid day. One of the paths from the beech cave leads to the rose garden, designed by Herbert Browne in 1904. The collection contains mostly old-fashioned roses arranged in radial beds. Besides the unusual, but visually interesting practice of training climbers to dead cedars, a handsome brick wall capped in marble that surrounds the space, the perennial borders, and the attractive, tiled pools filled with lilies add a touch of grace to an otherwise unimaginative garden. The high point of the rose garden is the unique summerhouse at one end. The 1794 McIntire Tea House, as the structure is called after its architect, is an excellent example of late-Federal-period architecture. The house is now a National Historic Landmark and is maintained in wonderful condition.

The last garden of note at Glen Magna is the Chamberlain Garden, designed by landscape architect Joseph Chamberlain, who is better known as the father of British prime minister Neville Chamberlain. The garden is a traditional Italian-style perennial garden that has been planted in a more contemporary vein. Contemporary tastes are reflected in the plantings of hosta and the succulent sedum. At the end of the garden, a columned arbor bedecked with magnificent wisteria provides an anchor along one end. The gardens are situated within a landscape designed by the Olmsted firm in the 1890s, which includes a splendid allée of paired pin oaks.

II Beverly: Sedgwick Gardens at Long Hill

LOCATION: ON MILE NORTH OF ROUTE 128 AT EXIT 18 (ESSEX STREET),
TWENTY MILES NORTHEAST OF BOSTON

GARDENS OPEN: 8am—sunset
daily. ADMISSION: free.

FURTHER INFORMATION FROM:
572 Essex Street, Beverly
01915. (978) 921-1944

NEARBY SIGHTS OF INTEREST:
Gloucester, Salem Witch
Museum

*A lawn terrace connects
the manor to the
surrounding woods.*

Long Hill was the home of Mabel Cabot Sedgwick and her husband, Ellery Sedgwick, editor of the *Atlantic Monthly*. Mabel, the author of a book on home gardening, laid out the original gardens beginning in 1916 when the couple first purchased the property. After her death in 1937, Ellery married Marjorie Russell, a distinguished gardener in her own right, who expanded on the first Mrs. Sedgwick's vision. Each woman had a distinct approach to gardening that is faintly perceptible throughout. The original approach to the house passes between two white posts and along a path flanked by a delicate blend of mountain laurel and sassafras culminating in a circular drive that winds around an enormous copper beech tree. Behind the house, a series of intimate lawn gardens, testimony to the discerning eye of Mabel Sedgwick, flow into one another. Several iron architectural features, such as a Venetian pavilion called Mount Sam, as well as artfully placed cedars and hedges outline and demarcate the gardens and create a sense of enclosure and protection from the wilds beyond. The Little Garden contains climbing trellises for clematis, a Chinese terrace, and a profusion of astilbe, rose, and foxglove packed into a tight composition. Beyond this lies a precious lotus pool, not bigger than a square yard, that blooms white in August. Several paths progress along the southwestern face of the house, the nearest of which enters a formal terraced lawn. The plantings here are intended to accentuate the house, which is a reproduction of an early-nineteenth-century Southern mansion that Mr. Sedgwick discovered on a journey through the South, and include wisteria and boxwood. Descending away from the house, the garden evolves into a more botanically interesting and natural landscape, leaving behind the intricate design of the lawn gardens and embracing the surrounding woods. Marjorie Sedgwick shared a love of unusual flora with Charles Sprague Sargent of the Arnold Arboretum, and like that maverick botanist, imported many unique specimens to Long Hill. The Sargent hemlocks at the edge of the Fan Steps are stately trees, made more so by the architecturally subtle steps. Farther along, these juxtapositions become less intriguing. A Chinese pagoda sits incongruously beside Carolina allspice, an unusual shrub remarkable less for its form than its aroma. Nearby, a forlorn split-leaf maple—a nod, perhaps, to the Orient—adds to the confusion. A grove of mountain laurels culminates the tour, giving the entire garden a sense of unity despite the various hands and minds that have been at work here.

GARDEN OPEN: continually
year-round. **ADMISSION:** free.
HOUSE OPEN: 10am–4pm
Wednesday–Saturday;
1pm–4pm Sunday. **HOUSE
TOUR ADMISSION:** $5 adults,
$2 children.

FURTHER INFORMATION FROM:
Heard House, 54 South Main
Street, Ipswich 01938.
(978) 356-2811

NEARBY SIGHTS OF INTEREST:
Castle Hill, historic towns of
the North Shore

12 Ipswich: John Whipple House

LOCATION: JUST SOUTH OF THE VILLAGE GREEN IN IPSWICH ON ROUTE 1A,
THIRTY-FIVE MILES NORTHEAST OF BOSTON

Puritan settler John Whipple made a comfortable living in
Ipswich in the seventeenth century exporting textiles from New
England mills to England. In 1655, befitting his status, Whipple
built what for the period was considered an exquisite townhouse and is today a perfectly preserved remnant of colonial
Yankee architecture—a brown plank box, its arrow-straight
roofline adorned with only the slightest irregularity in two
diminutive dormer windows. The house was originally located
near the mills in town, but was removed to its present five-acre
plot by the preservation society that restored it in the 1920s.
Arthur Shurcliff, Boston-based landscape architect of Colonial
Williamsburg, was retained to design grounds in the 1950s,
and produced a grandiose Colonial Revival scheme. Little of his
plan was implemented beyond the placement of the garden—
which adorns the entranceway to the house rather than the
backyard, which would have been the placement of a true New
England colonial garden—and the symmetrical division of the
beds. The plant selection is typical of a housewife's garden and
was created by garden historian Ann Leighton in the 1980s,
based upon her meticulous research of seventeenth-century
New England kitchen gardens. The plant palette includes old
varieties of sweet William, old velvet, and lilacs arranged in
an informal, but pleasing, manner in raised wooden beds, also
typical of colonial kitchen gardens. Leighton also designed a
heritage rose garden adjoining the property and a pear orchard
nestled behind a lilac hedge. The roses are of the shrub variety,
including yellow Harrison's and apothecary roses, whose high
oil content gives them a deep fragrance. Although the garden
was laid out in a semi-formal manner—balancing beds around
a quaint summer seat and trellis, which gives views of the village green of Ipswich—the negligence of the gardeners and the
naturally rambling, wild architecture of the plants themselves
have conspired to re-create a less rigidly Victorian aesthetic.
Nearby, climbers are trained to a helix-shaped trellis, a curious
feature common to colonial rose gardens farther north in
Portsmouth, New Hampshire. Horticulturists will be dismayed
at the lack of labeling, although the house staff are very knowl-
edgeable about both the garden and the roses and on slow days
will give brief tours.

13 Ipswich: Castle Hill

LOCATION: ROUTE 133, FIVE MILES EAST OF THE IPSWICH TOWN CENTER,
THIRTY-FIVE MILES NORTHEAST OF BOSTON

Chicago industrialist Richard T. Crane made his fortune providing America with "a better bathroom." Valves, piping, and fixtures comprised the empire of Crane Co. They also financed Crane's summer estate at Castle Hill. In 1924, the original Italian villa that stood on the site was razed and replaced by the reproduction of a seventeenth-century English great house designed by architect David Adler, whom Crane imported from his native Chicago. The architecture, within and without, is all original, however much of the furnishings are replacements purchased during over the last twenty years in an effort to replicate, according to photographs and reminiscences, Cranes' lifestyle. During their lifetime, the Cranes enjoyed several luxurious gardens, including a sunken Italian Garden designed by the Olmsted firm and a circular rose garden designed by budding landscape architect Arthur Shurcliff in a classical mode. At one time, each of these gardens boasted Italianate columns and extensive wooden arbors, filled luxuriously with a profusion of flowers. Today, however, only the underlying architectural structure of the Italian Garden has been restored—the flowers replaced by lawn that merely hints at the former glory of the space. The Rose Garden is in ruins, which seems oddly befitting its Roman roots. And yet by observing the "bones" of these spaces we get a palpable sense of the formal beauty that once adorned the estate. The real treat at Castle Hill is the landscape, largely designed by the Olmsted firm, which tumbles off the hill in surprising ways. Of particular interest is a grande allée, designed by Shurcliff in 1915 and consisting of a 160-foot wide swath through the canopy that runs nearly two-fifths of a mile down a valley and up to the crest of a hill that finally overlooks the bay of Ipswich. Lined by a naturalistic woods predominated by stands of sugar maples, it is a grand statement that provides ample context for the house and the views.

OPEN: 10am–4pm Wednesday and Thursday, May 27–Oct 8. Thursday guided garden tours: 11:00am and 1:30pm. ADMISSION: $7 adults, $5 children and seniors.

FURTHER INFORMATION FROM: 290 Argilla Road, Ipswich 01938. (978) 356-4351

NEARBY SIGHTS OF INTEREST: Gloucester, Essex Shipbuilding Museum

Grand vista and maple allée

GARDENS OPEN: 8am–5pm
daily, mid April–June; 10am–
5pm daily, July–mid September. **ADMISSION:** $5 adults, $2
seniors and children.

FURTHER INFORMATION FROM:
65 Orchard Street, Byfield
01922. (978) 462-1144

NEARBY SIGHTS OF INTEREST:
Cushing House Museum,
Custom House Maritime
Museum

ABOVE: *A perennial border
relaxes the formal lines of the
Summer Garden.*

14 Byfield: Newbury Perennial Gardens

LOCATION: ORCHARD STREET, OFF CENTRAL STREET (INTERSTATE 95 EXIT 55), FIFTEEN MILES NORTHEAST OF LAWRENCE

According to Rich Simkins, proprietor of the Newbury Perennial Gardens, his efforts at garden design are just a gimmick to get people to visit his nursery. Honesty is blessed, but so is humility, and Simkins's gardens, designed in conjunction with his wife, Pat, are truly beautiful. Begun in 1974 the gardens, which grace the grounds of their private home as well as their garden center, now contain twenty-four theme areas. Ornamental grasses, shade plants, fruit trees, heathers, and vegetables are combined with the usual perennials and annuals in wonderfully diverse displays. Some of the gardens stray toward the predictable experiments with color: a white garden, a hot garden of red and yellow annuals, and so one. Others reflect the sensibilities of the Simkinses, sometimes whimsical, sometimes touching. The Weeping Garden marks a graveyard for past pets, the tombstones of which are interplanted with weeping varieties of evergreens, wisteria, cherry, larch, and beech. A grotto garden, under construction, promises to be a cross between an "Italian romantic garden and Tom Sawyer nostalgia." The oldest garden on the property, the Summer Garden, gives the slightest nod to formal gardening traditions—a central axis is marked by evergreens and rectilinear borders—but is executed with a flourish of color and an eye for irregularity, surprise, and modern pleasures. The garden center, of course, sells all of the plants that are on display. But proof of purchase is by no means necessary to enter the gardens, which the Simkinses offer to the mutual enjoyment of all.

15 Lincoln: Codman House

LOCATION: CODMAN ROAD, OFF ROUTE 126, FIFTEEN MILES WEST OF BOSTON

In the 1790s, much of the western edge of Boston was res-
olutely farmland. However, John Codman, influenced by several trips to England, desired to transform his tract of land into
an English landscape park. He set about constructing some
typical country estate features, including a ha-ha wall (a retaining wall that prevents livestock from encroaching on the house)
and a winding drive that manages the entry experience to the
house. In the 1860s Codman's descendant, Ogden Codman
Sr., steered the estate in a different direction when he imposed
a series of formal terraces immediately surrounding the house.
Oriented to a strong axis, with symmetrical plantings and architectural features, such as a balustrade that defines the upper-
most terrace, the gardens display an Italian influence.
Fortunately these new additions complemented the existing
landscape plan by providing vistas from which to view the original arrangements (which were always meant to be compre-
hended from a distance). Ogden Codman's son, the architect
Ogden Codman Jr., enlisted the help of his friend Edith
Wharton in the late nineteenth century to design a sunken garden. A series of terraces descend to a reflecting pool that is now
planted with water lilies. Symmetrical pathways and a semicircular apse were designed as formal elements; however the garden has a decidedly personal and informal style, owing both to
design and neglect. A green garden from its inception (with the
exception of some forsythia defining an edge),
even the terra-cotta pots were planted with non-
flowering, herbaceous plants. A rough jumble
of stone defines the edge of the rectilinear
pool—an odd juxtaposition of natural grotto
and European formalism that seems primeval
or Shelley-esque. Although most Italianate gardens (of which this is one) are meant to be
observed like a painting, this garden is secreted
into a low part of the landscape, which often
floods, and can be easily missed. A sculpture of
Bacchus occupies one of the nooks, a testament to the perhaps mischievous intent of the
siting, while the tangle of vines and dense
shrubbery of the surrounding wilderness seem
to ever encroach. Ogden Codman Jr.'s garden
appears pushed aside, as if wanting to hide
itself. According to estate curators the later
generations, in stark contrast to the first
Codman, were reclusive and secretive people—
characteristics evidenced, as well they should
be, in their garden.

GARDEN OPEN: sunrise–
sunset Wednesday–Sunday,
June 1–October 15.
ADMISSION: $4.

FURTHER INFORMATION FROM:
Codman Road, Lincoln 01773.
(781) 259-8843
www.spnea.org

NEARBY SIGHTS OF INTEREST:
Walden Pond, DeCordova
Museum and Sculpture Park

*Waterlillies and ferns adorn
a sunken garden.*

16 Waltham: Lyman Estate,
or The Vale

LOCATION: ROUTE 20 AND TOTTEN POND STREET, EIGHT MILES
WEST OF BOSTON

GARDEN OPEN: 9am–5pm
Monday–Saturday, year-
round. **GREENHOUSES OPEN:**
9:30am–4:30pm, Monday–
Saturday, year-round.

FURTHER INFORMATION FROM:
185 Lyman Street, Waltham
02452-5642.
(781) 891-4882, ext. 244
www.spnea.org

NEARBY SIGHTS OF INTEREST:
Charles River Museum,
Gore Place

The 1790s were good for Theodore Lyman, a Beacon Hill merchant who made a fortune trading with China. Among other
interests, Lyman belonged to the Massachusetts Agriculture
Club, an association of wealthy Bostonians (mostly Harvard
alumni, though Lyman was not one) that, much in the spirit of
George Washington's writings, advocated the propagation of
agricultural knowledge as a means of enhancing democracy. In
1793, with pockets bulging, Lyman purchased 400 acres of
farmland outside the city and set about testing his ideas through
the construction of a gentleman's farm. The English gardener
William Bell was hired to fashion a working farm, separated
from the house by a woodland garden underplanted with ornamental shrubs. A "peach wall" also serves to demarcate the living space from the farmland. Recessed into a slope and facing
south, the wall was planted with espaliered peaches, nectarines,
and plums—plants that normally wouldn't grow here but, due
to the amount of heat retained in the wall after a sunny day,
thrived. An imminent restoration project aims to repair the wall
and to replant the fruit trees that have succumbed to the ravages
of time. The main horticultural attraction at The Vale, as Lyman
called his country home, is the greenhouse complex, which
includes an ancient structure (as greenhouses go) that dates
back to 1800. The structure is in need of repair and closed to the
public, but it presents a venerable appearance. Lyman was
enthusiastic for the strange combination of camellias, orchids,
and grapes, each of which continues to thrive in the three newer
greenhouses that are open to the public.

*The greenhouse
tradition continues at
the Lyman estate.*

17 South Sudbury: Garden in the Woods

LOCATION: FOLLOW RAYMOND ROAD SOUTH FROM ROUTE **20**, THREE MILES
NORTH OF FRAMINGHAM

GARDEN OPEN: 9am–5pm
daily, April 15–June 15;
9am–5pm Tuesday–Sunday,
June 16–October 31; extended
hours to 7pm in May.
ADMISSION: $6 adults, $3 children (6-16 years), $5 seniors.

FURTHER INFORMATION FROM:
180 Hemenway Road
Framingham 01701.
(508) 877-6574
www.newfs.org/~newfs/

NEARBY SIGHTS OF INTEREST:
Walden Pond, DeCordova
Museum and Sculpture Park

In 1931, while following a brook through the woods from
Framingham to Sudbury, landscape architect Will Curtis came
across a wet valley of hemlocks. Inspired by the natural conditions, he set about planting a wild flower garden with his friend
Dick Stiles. More than sixty-five years later, that woodland
garden is now Garden in Woods, a forty-five-acre naturalistic garden containing some 1,600 varieties of flowers and shrubs and
managed by the New England Wild Flower Society. New England
natives are featured, however, many hardy plants from other
regions of the country that can become acclimated to the harsh
New England climate and acidic soils have been imported as
well. The garden is arranged as a series of rooms beside a mile-
long trail. The tour begins in a woodland grove in which the
canopy has been engineered to allow light to filter down to a collection of wild flowers including phlox, maidenhair fern, and one
of the largest collections of trillium anywhere. Each plant wears
a label that includes information on its native habitat. Dotting the
path are also several narrative signs that explain some aspects of
naturalistic garden cultivation. While botanical interest is the
main focus, notice the artful management of the woods themselves. Soils and irrigation have been adjusted to accommodate
fussy rare species, while the canopy and understory have been
carefully pruned to admit just the right amount of light. The
result is not only healthy flowers but a perfectly layered context
for the garden. Further along the trail are several display gardens
that illustrate different attributes and uses of native plants, such
as a lily pond ringed by water grasses and a well-drained rock garden planted with alpine plants. The Tufa Rock Garden and
Northern New England Acid Slope illustrate how plant selection
can accommodate soil conditions endemic to the region. A
swamp and bog are juxtaposed along with an excellent description of the differences between the two types. Further along
there are displays of fly-eating pitcher plants, a New Jersey pine
barrens, and sunny meadow plants. The managed gardens
comprise just seventeen of the 45 acres. The remaining tract is
left to nature and acts as a buffer against the encroaching suburbs. The unmanaged woods also provide one of the best visual
demonstrations of the difference between tended nature and
"wild" nature—the view from the pristine gardens into a tumble
of rotting logs, swampland, and colorless woods argues silently,
but well, for the value of gardens. At the end of the garden trail is
a new display of rare and endangered plants native to New
England, created in 1997. Unlike the rest of the garden this display is immature and thus, at least for a few years less attractive.

*Yellow lady's slipper and
blue wood phlox define this
woodland.*

18 Boylston: Tower Hill Botanic Garden

LOCATION: EXIT 29 OFF INTERSTATE 290, TEN MILES NORTH OF WORCESTER

GARDEN OPEN: 10am–5pm Tuesday–Sunday and Monday holidays. Closed Thanksgiving, Christmas Eve, Christmas, and New Year's Day.

ADMISSION: $7 adults, $5 seniors, $3 children.

FURTHER INFORMATION FROM: 11 French Drive, Boylston 01505. (508) 869-6111

NEARBY SIGHTS OF INTEREST: Gardner Museum, Cook's Canyon

Tower Hill was purchased in 1986 by the Worcester Horticultural Society as a base for their operations and as the site for the organization's new public garden. In garden terms, it is still considered "new"; however, there are a few areas that have seen enough growing seasons to provide plenty of interest. The highlight of the garden is the Davenport Collection of historic apple trees, which were originally housed in a service area at Old Sturbridge Village but were relocated a few years ago to occupy a more prominent position here. The orchard contains 119 rare varieties that contrast widely in terms of architecture. Some trunks split at the base and grow haphazardly through space, while others effect a pristine demeanor, as if to disassociate themselves with their randy brethren. An intriguing design brings the orchard across the entry drive at an oblique angle to wrap gently around a lawn garden and the Secret Garden, both of which were planted in 1990. The former features an informal bed of perennials and groundcover beneath a sparse woodland of specimen trees and surrounded by a brick wall designed in a herringbone pattern. A pergola anchors this space on one end and overlooks the intimate Secret Garden, which contains a display of pastel flowers. North of the visitors center is Pliny's allée, a double row of oaks named in honor of a garden donor as well as Pliny the Elder and Pliny the Younger, two Roman statesmen who also wrote about gardening. A trail system winds through the rest of the meadow and woodland property, passing by a wildlife garden containing bat houses and birdhouses and butterfly-attracting plants that ascend up Tower Hill itself. From the belvedere located halfway up, there are wonderful views of Mount Wachusett in the distance. This area of Massachusetts has historically contained some of the most pristine meadows and open space in the region, although that heritage has been seriously threatened in recent years. One of the central goals of the Worcester Horticultural Society is to retain the character and beauty of its 132-acre tract of land. Although a relatively small plot, in 50 years it should look pretty spectacular.

Overflowing Spanish urns in Autumn at Tower Hill

19 Sturbridge: Old Sturbridge Village

LOCATION: ROUTE 20, ONE MILE FROM EXIT 9 OFF THE MASS PIKE (INTER-
STATE 90), FIFTEEN MILES SOUTHWEST OF WORCESTER

Old Sturbridge Village is a working museum of American history that includes over forty different structures moved here from all over New England. Alongside the cooperage and historic houses lie several gardens, which fall into two categories: kitchen gardens and pleasure gardens. Typical nineteenth-century vegetable gardens adorn the Fenno and Freeman Farms and the Bixby House. Because colonist pioneers subsisted largely on a heavy meat and grain diet, the gardens feature surprisingly few green vegetables. However, White Dutch runner beans, student parsnips, lady's finger potatoes, and Boston marrow squash are mainstays of each of these gardens, and are planted in unimaginative rows. The last vegetable garden demonstrates a new trend in nineteenth-century American gardening: At the parsonage of Reverend Richardson museum curators have planted a "progressive garden" in which American vegetable gardens were being influenced by English advice manuals that advocated a far broader selection of "sallads," peppers, and other exotic veggies. Raised beds were filled with manure and compost, and a makeshift greenhouse was built over a portion of the garden to house early melons and to start tomatoes. The beds were surrounded by a border of crocuses, tulips, and other spring bulbs, which added life and variation to the space. This trend was carried further in English texts that made their way through the upper classes in the 1830s, and could possibly have influenced the pleasure garden found beside the house of Salem Towne and his wife, Sally. Towne was a man of politics in Charlton, Massachusetts, and built an impressive Federal-style house there in 1796 (it was moved to Old Sturbridge Village in 1955). A symmetrical garden of encircling walks presents a visually stimulating picture from the windows of the sitting room and parlor. A summerhouse and grape arbor provide places to rest within the garden and to view and smell the old roses, peonies, and foxgloves. Behind the Fitch House is a formal garden based upon the writings of late-nineteenth-century Boston horticulturist Joseph Breck, who advocated planting a garden for the education of children. The plan of the garden is circular, with the inner circle containing tulips and daffodils, and the outer heartease (*Viola tricolor*) and crocus. A smattering of exotics, which appealed to Victorian tastes, are also planted throughout the garden, including coreopsis, which had only been brought to New England from the West recently by the naturalist writer Thomas Nuttall. Besides these house gardens, there is a major herb garden at Sturbridge that features medicinal and household herbs in a lovely semiformal setting of country stone terraces and potted flowers.

VILLAGE OPEN: 9am–5pm daily, April–November; 10am–4pm daily, November and December (closed Christmas Day); 10am–4pm weekends, January and February; 10am–4pm Tuesday–Sunday, February and March. ADMISSION: $16 adults, $15 seniors, $8 children (includes entire museum).

FURTHER INFORMATION FROM: 1 Old Sturbridge Village Road Sturbridge 01566. (508)347-3362

NEARBY SIGHTS OF INTEREST: Stone House Museum, American Antiquarian Society

"Colonists" still tend the massive herb garden at Old Sturbridge Village.

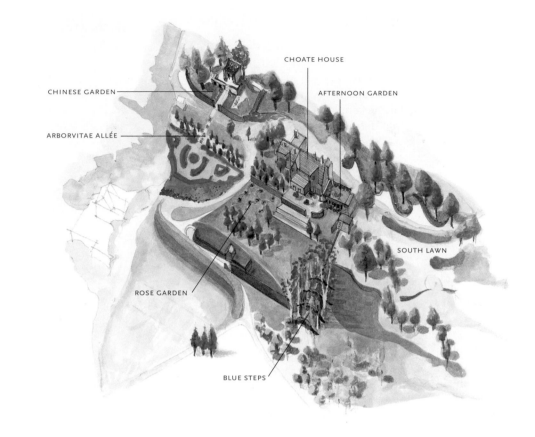

CHOATE HOUSE

CHINESE GARDEN

AFTERNOON GARDEN

ARBORVITAE ALLÉE

SOUTH LAWN

ROSE GARDEN

BLUE STEPS

20 Stockbridge: Naumkeag

LOCATION: PROSPECT HILL, TWO MILES NORTH OF STOCKBRIDGE

Attorney Joseph Hodges Choate and his family first came to the Berkshires in the 1870s to escape the summer heat of New York City. According to legend, the family picnicked beneath the same old oak tree on a side of Prospect Hill each year until Mr. Choate decided to purchase the land. Here, in 1884, he erected his summer mansion, which he called Naumkeag, after the Indian name for his birthplace in Salem. The house was designed by Stanford White in 1885, and its handsome orna-mentation, shingled roof, and broad eaves are reminiscent of the architect's creations at Newport, Rhode Island, East Hampton, New York, and elsewhere in the Northeast. The hilly terrain was first terraced in 1889 by Nathan Barrett, who also designed a perennial garden and a topiary garden on the north-ern end of the house. All that remains of Barrett's design today is an overgrown allée of arborvitae that joined the topiary gar-den to the house. In 1926 Choate's daughter, Mabel, attended a lecture by the landscape architect Fletcher Steele. Inspired by his bold ideas, which drew on European traditions but in a dis-tinctly original and client-driven manner, she commissioned him to create a garden room off the library on the southern end of the house. Steele's Afternoon Garden revolves around what he termed "a giddy carpet," formed by a parterre of boxwood vaguely knotlike in its layout. In the center is a black-glass reflecting pool surrounded by four scalloped fountains. Weaving together these disparate geometries are beds of chipped coal, which, combined with the black pool and deep green parterre, give the whole area a cool appearance in the afternoon sunlight. Supposedly this effect was calculated in response to Miss Choate's complaint that certain flowers were looking wilted in the sun. Beyond this area is the South Lawn, a stretch of grass leading down to the woods. Because of its situation at the southern end of the house, this lawn provides a visual accompaniment to the view of Bear Mountain beyond. Perceiving this effect, Steele consciously shaped the lawn in a large arc, which reflects and echoes the distant peak. Curvaceous plantings—a hedge of hemlock on the eastern edge mirrored by a curving line of globe locusts on the western edge—contribute to a sense of gentle undulation. The judicious use of these linear features accents the natural topography and pulls the eye into the far reaches of the space, to where a Japanese pagoda sits in a stand of Japanese maples, and then beyond, to the beginning of a linden walk, constructed in the 1890s on the instructions of Mabel's mother. The walk shoots into the forest to a statue of the huntress Diana, who mischievously awaits visitors. Anchoring the south lawn and somewhat encircled by the globe locusts is the 200-year-old

GARDEN OPEN: 10am–5pm daily, Memorial Day–Columbus Day.
ADMISSION: $5 for gardens; $7 for the house tour.

FURTHER INFORMATION FROM: P.O. Box 792, Stockbridge 01262. (413) 298-3239 www.berkshireweb.com/trustees/naumkeag.html

NEARBY SIGHTS OF INTEREST: Norman Rockwell Museum, Tanglewood

OPPOSITE: *A Chinese temple, inspired by visits to the Orient, gives magnificent views of the Berkshires.*

Steele's Rose Garden was supposedly inspired by a Chinese mushroom.

oak that the Choate family once picnicked under. Its broad canopy unifies several rooms in the landscape that seem to prefer their own individuality in lieu of the larger community. Descending from the South Lawn is one of Steele's greatest creations, the Blue Steps, constructed in 1938. Initially, the steps were prompted by a utilitarian concern: to transport Mabel Choate effortlessly down to her cutting garden at the bottom of the hill. But Steele progressed far beyond that stated purpose and created an architectural wonder: concrete block steps descending from square terraces. Countermanding this rigidity, Steele carved graceful arcs into the facade of each terrace and then painted them blue. A simple, steel railing echoes the voluptuousness of these forms with congruent curves that wind through the architecture of the stairs. Rather than two separate forms—the curvilinear and the rectilinear— the stairs meld into a single gesture, a unity that is given palpable measure by a rill bringing a slight flow of water from the Afternoon Garden down the brick path to the top of the steps. The water then pours into a small opening at the top of the first step, reemerges in a pool on a lower terrace, only to disappear then reemerge again, and so on. Steele arranged brick and concrete in just such a way as to create a slight gurgling, rather than a rush of water. Around the stairs, he planted a stand of birch trees and lines of taxus. The white trunks of birch are a perfect extension of the architectural themes of the steps. In color they contrast with the blue arcs, but in form they contribute to the overall unity of graceful vertical movement.

Like many great collaborations, Naumkeag is the result of many years of discussions between a tasteful and educated client and her visionary designer. Although Steele designed many other commissions throughout his career, Naumkeag remained a touchstone, and he continued to modify and create new designs for Mabel Choate until her death in 1958. The last of these was the Rose Garden. Designed in 1952, Steele's rose garden defies all expectations of this familiar component in

American gardens. Three wave-like beds of pink gravel, edged in steel, cut through the lawn of a sunken garden like pulsating serpents. Set at intervals, four scalloped beds, also edged in steel, break up the monotony and add rhythm. Each is filled with a single hybrid tea rose, which varies in color from bed to bed. The design is said to be inspired by Chinese mushrooms; however another theory involves cocktail hour on the porch above, where the view of the garden is more spectacular. Moving beyond this garden, but back in time, we come to Mabel Choate's Chinese garden, separated from the rest of the gardens behind its own imposing, stone-and-brick wall. The garden reflects Choate's passion for the Orient and includes architectural ornaments that she brought back from her many trips there, such as the blue tile roofs of the temple and The Devil's Screen. Steele designed a marble rill that divides the center of the room from its outer edge and creates the slightest trickle of water—a serene element typical of oriental gardens. Chinese tree peonies, ginkgo trees, and large-leafed *Petasites* complete the scene. But the garden is as much western as it is eastern, most notably in the situation of the temple, which is raised in order to give magnificent views of the distant mountains. In traditional Chinese gardens, such a plinth would be focused on the garden instead. Entrance to the garden is gained by stepping around the Devil Screen, a tricky passage designed to prevent evil spirits from entering. The exit is through a moon gate, a perfectly round oculus designed by Steele according to photographs of the gardens at Chieh Tai Su in China, which he visited in 1934.

On the Blue Steps, Steele choreographed a dance of natural and architectonic forms that remains a classic in garden design.

Several paths wind through the terraced fields and gardens of lesser interest, such as the Evergreen Garden arranged around Barrett's original arborvitae allée. The veranda directly behind the mansion provides more spectacular views of the valley and the Berkshires. The intricate stonework that combines granite, bluestone, and marble into a sublime combination, as well as the seemingly ancient espaliered apple on the bleached wood railing beneath the view, speak of the tremendous care and enjoyment that both Mabel Choate and her esteemed colleague Fletcher Steele took in the creation of Naumkeag. While the individual elements are notable for Steele's nascent modernism, which still retained the spirit of his Beaux-Arts education, Naumkeag is a singular experience in exquisite taste.

Stockbridge: Mission House

LOCATION: SARGEANT STREET, ONE-HALF MILE WEST OF
STOCKBRIDGE TOWN CENTER

HOUSE AND GARDEN OPEN:
10am–5pm daily, Memorial
Day–Columbus Day.
ADMISSION: $5.00 adults,
$2.50 children.

FURTHER INFORMATION FROM:
P.O. Box 792, Stockbridge
01262. (413) 298-3239

NEARBY SIGHTS OF INTEREST:
Naumkeag, Chesterwood

*Fletcher Steele's twists
on tradition*

In the 1920s Mabel Choate, doyenne of Naumkeag, removed this seventeenth-century home of missionary pastor John Sargeant from the hillside near her home to this plot in town in order to preserve it as a museum. Fletcher Steele, landscape architect at Naumkeag, was enlisted to design a small, colonial-style garden around the house as an extension of the museum within. Steele did not attempt a painstaking reconstruction; indeed, it is not known whether Sargeant had a garden at all, or if he did, what it might have looked like. Rather, Steele's was an artistic interpretation based on an appreciation of what he called "the dignity and simple beauty of the past." Signaling this approach is the fact that the entire garden is divided into distinct rooms—a Steele trademark. The first room, the Orchard Garden, is a wild space of vegetables, herbs, and flowers commonly grown in the seventeenth century, such as bee balm, climbing beans, and phlox, mixed in with a few exotics from Steele's palette, such as Japanese *astilbe*, a wispy, wild flower that contrasts with the strict confines of the space. A row of apple trees along the central spine provides a visual anchor, while a short loop path through the southwestern quadrant gives the garden a playful asymmetry. Behind the Mission House, Steele constructed a grape arbor that partially winds around an antique well adorned with a large well sweep. The entry garden is laid out as a semiformal perennial garden of two balanced ellipses filled with narcissi, primroses, and several peony bushes which rise above the fervor. By utilizing his own planting patterns Steele introduced a new vocabulary of form into the rather staid and stuffy Colonial Revival style.

MISSION HOUSE
MUSEUM
The House of the
REV. JOHN SERGEANT
First Missionary
to the Stockbridge
Indians.
BUILT IN 1739

A PROPERTY OF THE
TRUSTEES OF
RESERVATIONS

22 Stockbridge: Berkshire Botanical Garden

LOCATION: ROUTE 102, TWO MILES WEST OF STOCKBRIDGE TOWN CENTER

GARDEN OPEN: 10am–5pm daily, May–October. Greenhouse and gift shop open year-round.

ADMISSION: $5 adults, $4 seniors, $3 students, free for children under 12.

FURTHER INFORMATION FROM: P.O. Box 826, Stockbridge 01262. (413) 298-3926

NEARBY SIGHTS OF INTEREST: Tanglewood, Norman Rockwell Museum

The first sight that greets visitors to the Berkshire Botanical Garden is the mystifying horticultural curio "ash-on-the-rock," a sizable ash tree that has tenaciously perched itself on top of a boulder near the parking lot. The garden occupies a wooded area that stretches across busy Route 102; however, the rush of cars is soon forgotten by entering the first garden rooms. Formal collections include: a garden of old roses set amid a grove of apple and *Katsura* trees and traversed by paths planted in aromatic thyme, a 1937 ornamental herb garden containing over 100 species organized by use and character, and what might be called a Berkshire-style informal border garden, containing a mixture of trees, shrubs, and perennials combined to create a pastel of pinks and blues. Near the parking lot, a solar greenhouse has been embedded in the side of a hill. During the winter months, fuchsias and geraniums fill its interior. The boulders removed in the excavation provide the setting for an array of sedum, which has evolved into a general display of drought-tolerant and alpine plants that enjoy well-drained soil. In early spring, a primrose garden recasts the wetland glade as a carpet of color, while hyacinths, ferns, and bluebells provide drama throughout the rest of the season. An arboretum separates the northern portion of the garden from the road. Within its confines are several varieties of beech, hawthorn, linden, and honey locust. The Berkshires—and Stockbridge especially—are populated by garden enthusiasts; this heavily used facility is animated throughout the season by a plethora of events and the continual propagation of plants. Several greenhouses are located near the main building, including the Rice Greenhouse of desert and tropical plants.

ABOVE: *A Berkshire herb garden offers hidden surprises.*

HOUSE AND GARDEN OPEN:
10am–5pm May–November.
ADMISSION: $7.50 adults,
$4.00 seniors, $2 children.

FURTHER INFORMATION FROM:
4 Williamsville Road
Stockbridge 01262
(413) 298-3579

NEARBY SIGHTS OF INTEREST:
Norman Rockwell Museum,
Tanglewood

*From the foyer of his
studio French gazed
upon his gardens.*

23 Stockbridge: Chesterwood

**LOCATION: ROUTE 183, TWO MILES SOUTH OF ROUTE 102, SIX MILES WEST OF
STOCKBRIDGE TOWN CENTER**

Chesterwood was the home of Daniel Chester French, the
successful early-twentieth-century sculptor best known for his
iconographic statue of Abraham Lincoln sitting inside the
Lincoln Memorial in Washington, D.C. His collaborator on that
commission, the architect Henry Bacon, also collaborated
on the construction of this summer home and studio. In addition to magnificent works of statuary, French also designed
the grounds and gardens of his estate, including the survey and
engineering work for roads and bridle paths through the
wooded property. The main garden area is located adjacent to
his studio, where French spent most of his time, compulsively
working, receiving visitors and patrons, and gardening. A
gravel path, traveling almost due east-west, forms a central axis,
transecting a smaller, minor path, from the entrance to the
studio leading to a semicircular courtyard. Off the western arm
of the main axis is a balanced, rectangular lawn. Together
these elements speak directly of a formal Italianate scheme,
with which French was familiar from his numerous travels
to Europe to study the masters. But the interest in the garden
lies in the areas where he departed from this rigid scheme.
The rectangular lawn should really be a long, narrow reflecting
pool, instead French built a square marble basin and filled it
with water lilies, almost as a tongue-in-cheek assent to the
form. Along the northern edge of the axis, which in an Italian
garden would be left sparse and architectural, French planted
a traditional perennial border vaguely English in character.
Today, certain annuals are mixed in to maintain continual
color, as well as to approximate some of the plants that French
used in a now-destroyed cutting garden elsewhere on the property. According to the estate gardener, French ritually capped
a twelve-hour day of work with a few more in the garden.

French's leisurely sense of fusion finds further expression
in the courtyard. The semicircular space is bounded along
one side by a curved marble seat, called an exedra. In the center
is a marble cement (a money-saving innovation) fountain
designed in collaboration with Bacon, who handled the architecture of the base and the basin while French designed the
prancing putti in relief around its middle. Here again, the
effect is vaguely Italian, except for its distinctly Gilded Age
material and diminutive scale. Extending beyond the fountain,
the transverse axis is carried into an elevated lawn by a walk
of peonies and pollarded hydrangea trees. In addition to the
formal garden, there is a woodland walk, which French regularly used to clear his mind.

24 Providence: Shakespeare's Head

LOCATION: MEETING STREET, JUST OFF BENEFIT STREET

GARDEN OPEN: 9am–5pm
Monday–Friday, year-round.
ADMISSION: free.

FURTHER INFORMATION FROM:
21 Meeting Street, Providence
02903. (401) 831-7440

NEARBY SIGHTS OF INTEREST:
Historic properties along
Benefit Street

Benjamin Franklin's influence in Providence extended beyond his design for the Boston Post Road (Route 1), which runs through town on its way from Boston to New York City and Philadelphia. Franklin was also mentor to young John Carter, who returned to Providence after studying with Franklin and set up a printing shop on Meeting Street. Over time, the house evolved into a post office and bookstore—two other Franklinian passions—but the basement remained dedicated to printing Carter's newspaper, posters, and revolutionary broadsides. To advertise his literary endeavors, which included publication of the *Providence Gazette,* Carter hung a bust of Shakespeare near the door, and in time his home and shop became known as Shakespeare's Head. In the 1930s the house was restored, and a minor excavation of the backyard revealed the existence of a garden pattern. James Graham, a landscape designer who later taught at the Rhode Island School of Design, constructed a small Colonial Revival garden on the spot, using boxwood to mimic the original pattern, planting fruit trees around the perimeter, and setting a trademark sundial in the middle. In 1996 local landscape architect Lala Searle, who studied under Graham, replanted the garden in a more faithfully colonial manner, replacing Victorian mainstays like lily of the valley with more truly colonial plants, such as monkshood, columbine, and bee balm. Besides a restoration to historical accuracy, the garden needed a complete redesign as it had evolved over the years from a predominantly sun-filled garden to a shaded enclosure dominated by surrounding maples and quince trees. Spring is an excellent time to visit, when the blossoms of a silverbell tree cover the landscape with a milky white sheen.

*A moss-covered stone walk
sets the quiet tone.*

GARDEN OPEN: 10am–5pm daily. **ADMISSION:** $5 adults, $1 children. **HOUSE TOURS:** mid April–mid October. **ADMISSION:** $8 adults, $6 seniors, $4 children.

FURTHER INFORMATION FROM: P.O. Box 716, Bristol 02809-0716. (401) 253-2707

NEARBY SIGHTS OF INTEREST: Newport mansions, Green Animals Topiary Garden

The water garden connects us to the surrounding context.

25 Bristol: Blithewold Gardens

LOCATION: OFF ROUTE 114, FIFTEEN MILES SOUTH OF PROVIDENCE

Just a few miles north of the opulent summerhouse of Cornelius Vanderbilt, another coal tycoon, Augustus Van Wickle, built an entirely different estate. While the Newport mansions are recognized for their grandeur, accentuated by Italian and French formal gardens, Blithewold owes its expression as much to American naturalism as to English country estates. The thirty-three-acre landscape at Blithewold gracefully tips toward the Narragansett Bay, passing through a romantic assemblage of trees, all arranged by John De Wolf, the landscape architect supervising Frederick Law Olmsted's plan for Prospect Park in Brooklyn, New York. Throughout its history Blithewold has retained an association with the Arnold Arboretum in Boston, to the effect that many botanically significant trees dot the property. These include the intriguing Chinese Toon tree (*Cedrela sinensis*) and a ninety-foot giant sequoia, the largest such specimen on the East Coast, which was planted here after it outgrew De Wolf's greenhouse. Within the landscape are several garden features, such as a water garden designed with Asiatic species and a rock garden containing alpine plants. A profusion of daffodils flank the north end of the mansion, while a rose garden, planted in 1912, still contains many of the original varieties, including a David Austen and many climbers. The house is limned with a formal garden. The original parterres are long gone, but a perennial border that mixes blues, yellows, and purples frames the manor and makes for a lovely scene in early summer.

GARDEN OPEN: 10am–5pm daily, April 26–October 31. **ADMISSION:** $6.50 adults, $3.50 children.

FURTHER INFORMATION FROM: Newport Preservation Society 424 Bellevue Avenue Newport 02840. (401) 847-2251

NEARBY SIGHTS OF INTEREST: Newport Mansions, Herreshof Marine Museum, Blithewold

26 Portsmouth: Green Animals Topiary Garden

LOCATION: OFF ROUTE 114, TEN MILES NORTH OF NEWPORT

George Mendonça is a self-effacing, quiet man who has spent his life creating one of the greatest treasures among American gardens. Green Animals began as the small country estate of Thomas Brayton, located on scenic Narragansett Bay, only a few miles north of Newport. In the early part of this century, Brayton's daughter Alice enlisted the talents of her gardener, Joseph Carriero, to beautify the vegetable garden with perennials. Inspired by the site and Ms. Brayton's enthusiasm Carriero began peppering the estate with playful topiary forms that delighted his employer. What began nonchalantly soon blossomed into a love for "green animals." In the 1940s, when

Carriero's son-in-law, Mendonça, took over the garden, there were some thirty different living sculptures. However, due to the nature of topiary, today's garden is largely the vision of Mendonça, who has lovingly tended the grounds for fifty years. The main topiary garden is laid out according to a formal scheme of parterres filled with annuals. Set upon privet hedges are some of the oldest animal forms on the property, including a monumental giraffe and a ninety-year-old camel, as well as several playful spirals and other geometric forms. Further along, the gardens become more informal, and such muted sculptures as the tubby teddy bear created by Mendonça in 1970, strike theatrical poses on a grass lawn, some as if asking questions, other as if casting a watchful eye over the rest. Creating and maintaining topiary requires Herculean patience, and Mendonça has had to rebuild most of the animals several times because of hurricane damage and the unyielding progression of time, which is their greatest adversary. As the privet grows, its branches become larger until wood, not foliage, begins to show through the leafy exoskeleton. In order to cut away the older branches, the gardener must anticipate the problem several years in advance and begin weaving a new branch into position to take the place of the older wood. The process is a meticulous dance with father time and requires a devotion unusual in our ten-second world. Mendonça uses hand shears, and although he works almost exclusively with privet, a fast-growing hedge, most of his work is the result of years of painstaking manipulation and gradual pruning. Regardless, well-heeled visitors regularly offer to fly Mendonça to their estates for a few days to "make animals," at whom this ninety-year-old artist laughs incredulously.

The gardens also include an herb collection, a display of annuals, a gourd arbor, and stimulating views of the bay. Especially invigorating are late fall afternoons, when a cool breeze picks up on the water, the haunted foliage of the deciduous canopy provides shadows to the evergreen topiary, and the song of Mendonça clip-clip-clipping fills the air.

A parade of fanciful figures at Green Animals

GARDENS OPEN: 10am–5pm
daily, April–October, and various weekends during winter.
THE BREAKERS ADMISSION:
$10 adults, $6 students, $4
children. **THE ELMS AND ROSE-
CLIFF ADMISSION:** $8.00
adults, $5.00 student, $3.50
children. Combination tickets
available.

FURTHER INFORMATION FROM:
The Preservation Society of
Newport County
424 Bellevue Avenue
Newport 02840
(401) 847-1000
www.newportmansions.org

NEARBY SIGHTS OF INTEREST:
Chateau-sur-Mer, Marble
House, and other Newport
mansions, historic Newport

*Bedded annuals on the
terrace of The Breakers*

27 Newport mansions: The Breakers, The Elms, Rosecliff

LOCATION: DOWNTOWN NEWPORT

America's Gilded Age peaked and diminished in Newport, Rhode Island, the summer home of coal magnates and robber barons that fueled and were fueled by the Industrial Revolution. The so-called "cottages" constructed on this spit of land are some of the country's most outlandish displays of wealth, calculated less to house families than to impress friends.

The French neo-classical palace, The Elms, was designed by Philadelphia architect Horace Trumbauer (designer of James Duke's residences in New York City and Somerville, New Jersey) for Edward Berwind, who owned the largest coal company in the United States at the time. The landscape was designed by Ernest Bowditch, a protégé of Frederick Law Olmsted, and Charles Miller. The formal drive is graced by an impressive collection of gingkos, beeches, and lindens. Behind the cottage, a terrace overlooks a great lawn that was the sight of lavish parties, including one held during the height of Newport decadence when the Berwinds unleashed a troupe of pet monkeys that scurried through the crowd and into the New England night. At the base of the lawn stands a marble tea-house which hides a sunken Italian garden. Here, a central fountain flanked by two rectilinear pools anchors a formal lawn garden framed in boxwood.

Rosecliff was the home of Teresa Fair Oelrichs, the grande dame of Newport society, who also presided over its decline in the second decade of the twentieth century as she herself drifted into madness. During its height, the mansion was encircled by ornate rose gardens, of which only one has been restored. (Years of neglect have required years of restoration; and the gardens are last on the list.) Five beds lined with boxwood and separated by brilliant white gravel are planted in individual colors—a powerful effect that only hints at the strength that must have pervaded the entire grounds back in their heyday.

The Breakers, arguably the most opulent of the Newport mansions, also showcases a few gardens, although the main features here

are the extravagant interiors, designed by various architects, including Richard Morris Hunt (who constructed the building) and Ogden Codman Jr. A verdant lawn terrace, designed by Bowditch as well, adjoins the west side of the house and contains a fleur-de-lis parterre of bedded annuals in bright pink and white. Yew and juniper cut in strict lines accentuate the formal balustrade and architecture of the house.

28 West Hartford: Elizabeth Park Rose Garden

LOCATION: PROSPECT AND ASYLUM AVENUES, FIVE MILES WEST OF HARTFORD

GARDENS OPEN: dawn–dusk daily. ADMISSION: Free.

FURTHER INFORMATION FROM: Friends of Elizabeth Park West Hartford 06119. (860) 242-0017

NEARBY SIGHTS OF INTEREST: Wadsworth Atheneum, Mark Twain House

Set in an open field, as if it were yet another baseball diamond, is the Rose Garden in Elizabeth Park and its stunning array of All-America Roses. The garden was designed and planted in 1904 by horticulturist Theodore Wirth when the 100-acre park was donated to the city by industrialist Charles Pond. The design is a traditional radial scheme on a large scale, with multiple beds of lavish hybrid tea roses extending out like the rays of a star. Four passageways defined by arches covered with red and white ramblers meet in the middle and give the garden its overall geometry. In the center of the garden sits a gazebo surrounded by a rambler called Caroline Testout, an audacious and romantic flower that hugs the architecture. The garden is one of 23 All-America Rose test sites nationwide, and thus contains some of the best-tended and most unusual roses around. Not all of the roses are labeled, although there is an extensive plan mounted at the entrance. Across a park road, noted horticulturist Fred McGourty designed a perennial garden in similar fashion with a central gazebo and concentric beds of flowers. Hidden in a corner is an intimate copse of historic varieties of roses. Although less dramatic than fussy hybrid teas, heritage roses offer much fuller fragrance and a glimpse of a time before pesticides. This area also features a rock garden, adorned with a magnificent kousa dogwood and designed to lead the eye through a variety of landscapes in miniature, much like some of the oriental traditions of garden design. This garden, however, concludes with an annual garden laid out in psychedelic stripes that lead back to the main attraction. The best time to visit is in June, when the roses are at their best. Some prefer slightly later, as the bigger buds die—perhaps even on a rainy afternoon, when the place empties of people. It is then that the entire garden takes on a fermented, after-the-fact appearance that is quite delightful.

GARDEN OPEN: dawn–dusk daily. **ADMISSION:** Free.
HOUSE OPEN: 10am–5pm daily in the summer; 11am–4pm daily in the winter. **TOURS:** $6 adults, $5 senior, $3 children.

FURTHER INFORMATION FROM:
35 Mountain Road
Farmington 06032. (860) 677-4787

NEARBY SIGHTS OF INTEREST:
Wadsworth Atheneum,
Mark Twain House

29 Farmington: Hill-Stead Museum and Gardens

LOCATION: OFF ROUTE **6,** FIFTEEN MILES WEST OF HARTFORD

Iron magnate Alfred Atmore Pope built this country house in 1901 primarily as a place to store his growing collection of Impressionist artworks. The Colonial Revival farmhouse designed by the New York architectural firm of McKim, Mead & White now houses works by Monet, Manet, Whistler, and Cassatt, as well as a handful of engravings by Dürer and an extensive collection of period furniture. Pope's daughter, Theodate Pope, was a successful architect who had a hand in designing the house. After her death in 1946, the estate was converted into a museum, with the rooms left as they were at the time. The grounds at Hill-Stead were designed by Warren Manning, a protégé of Frederick Law Olmsted. Like the architects of the house, Manning was directed to imitate the aesthetic of a colonial farm carved from the wilderness. Ostensibly, his design achieves this: no gardens surround the house; rather, meadows cut with dry-set stone walls slope gently toward the woodlands, which comprise the majority of the 150-acre estate. But the contrivance is evident in the careful arrangement of elements. The construction of the drive to shield the house until the last moment, the siting of the house on top of the hill, and the bucolic pond immediately below the view all demonstrate a concern with nineteenth century theories of landscape architecture: the beautiful and the picturesque, carefully and painstakingly arranged.

Across the drive from the portico lies a hexagonal sunken garden, originally designed by Beatrix Farrand in 1916. Whether the garden was ever built according to her plan is unclear, but in the forties the area was grassed over, leaving only a summerhouse, a hedge, and the general earthen depression to guess at. Over the last decade, a restoration of Farrand's plan has been conducted. A brick walk transects the garden, running through a long summerhouse that, in its finials, hints at the Orient. Flower beds separated by belts of lawn radiate from the house and are planted with a variety of peonies, lilacs, and ferns. According to the estate's historian the garden represents Farrand's study of Gertrude Jekyll, whom she admired for her use of color. But in execution, today's garden presents a striking contrast to the Glebe House garden only 20 miles away. Here, Jekyll's impressionism, her tight knitting of plants, is absent, resulting in a much more pedestrian, formal style that focuses on the individual specimen, isolated from its fellows, rather than masses of plants treated as an abstract form.

Oriental accents on a Connecticut garden house

30 Bethlehem: Bellamy-Ferriday Garden

LOCATION: INTERSECTION OF ROUTES 6 AND 132, TEN MILES
NORTHWEST OF WATERBURY

HOUSE AND GARDEN OPEN:
11am–4pm Wednesday,
Saturday, and Sunday, May–
October. ADMISSION: $5,
house and garden tours.

FURTHER INFORMATION FROM:
9 Main Street, Bethlehem
06751. (203) 266-7596

NEARBY SIGHTS OF INTEREST:
Antique shops of Bethlehem,
Lorenz Studio

The Right Reverend Joseph Bellamy came to Bethlehem in 1744 to establish a theological school and to settle his family. He couldn't have chosen a more bucolic nook in the New England woods. The farm and manse have been improved since that time, largely by New York industrialist Henry Ferriday and his family, who purchased the place in 1912. Ferriday's wife, Eliza, restored the estate in the Colonial Revivalist manner, augmenting it with her own tastes. Behind the house she added a formal garden designed to imitate an Aubusson carpet that once lay in the front hall of the family's New York townhouse. Like that French design, the garden is arranged in a system of radial geometry—strong lines created with boxwood parterres and overlaid with a pastiche of pastels, taupes, beiges, and white hues. Against the strong evergreen presence of the hedge, Mrs. Ferriday planted white roses, peonies, and herbaceous plants like gray-blue lambs ears. The exiguous space can be accessed by stepping carefully into the maze, where one gets the sense of entering an unusually miniaturized, precious world, a bit like Carroll's portrayal of Alice's wonderland. But to appreciate the entire design, one must ascend the second story to view it, where, from the bay windows installed in the Ferridays' daughter's room on the back of the house, one can take in the full scene.

Beyond the formal garden lie Mrs. Ferriday's rose and lilac collections, a handful of mature plants that were meticulously cared for and augmented by her daughter, Caroline, until she turned the house and property over to the nonprofit trust that currently administers it. Further into the property, a line of magnolias conceals a path that meanders around the edge of the estate, past a rich fern meadow with wildflowers and a number of mature specimen trees, such as a gigantic Paulowinia that flowers in mid-May. A number of eighteenth- and nineteenth-century outbuildings constructed by Bellamy's descendants, as well as some additional structures built by the Ferridays, are well preserved on-site, including a small schoolhouse, a barn, and two "necessaries" (outhouses). Although contemporaneous with other private gardens designed by well-known landscape architects and garden designers, the Bellamy-Ferriday Garden is decidedly an expression of Ms. Ferriday and her daughter's personal aesthetic, and as such, provides a noteworthy view of the common person's enthusiasm for the Colonial Revival.

A carpet of flowers and patterned boxwood re-create French carpet design.

31 # Woodbury: Gertrude Jekyll Garden at Glebe House

LOCATION: OFF ROUTE 67, TEN MILES WEST OF WATERBURY

GARDEN OPEN: continuously.
HOUSE OPEN: 1pm–4pm
Wednesday–Sunday,
April–November, or by
appointment.
HOUSE ADMISSION: $4.

FURTHER INFORMATION FROM:
P.O. Box 245, Woodbury
06798. (203) 263-2855

NEARBY SIGHTS OF INTEREST:
Antique shops of Bethlehem,
Lorenz Studio

*Masses of perennials in
the June Garden*

In the early part of the twentieth century, British garden designer Gertrude Jekyll (pronounced JEE'kul) bucked the Victorian tide of formal geometry and neatly clipped parterres with her impressionistic mixture of flowers and other herbaceous plants. Jekyll actually began her career as a painter, but as her eyesight deteriorated in middle age, she gave up the canvas for gardens, where she created artistically sensitive, yet revolutionary, work. Jekyll's work is distinctive for two reasons. The first is her wonderfully diverse and sensitive plant palette and her ability to combine colors and forms much like her painterly colleagues Monet and Renoir. But she is also known for bringing clarity and force to the idea of a garden border, which she designed in strictly straight, long, and narrow rectangles defined by a wall or hedge. The rigid geometry has the effect of heightening an awareness of her "wild" plantings, which are at once unfettered and domesticated. At Glebe House, the only extant garden designed by Jekyll in the United States, she decided to emphasize the diminutive size of the garden with evergreen hedges and holly that ring the entire property in a continual band and convey a sense of enclosure and privacy. At the back of the plot is a delightful herb garden set in a quadrangle of brick beds, and an arbor hung with climbing roses, both of which lovingly cradle the modest house (c. 1750). At the end of the walk, the comforting cottage feel is extended into the lawn, where a vibrant border of shade plants extends the length of the property. Here Jekyll worked in bunches and clumps, like a painter using a palette knife rather than a brush, to create a single, undulating gesture. Along the northern extremity of the property, the effect ripples: flowering spirea, icicle veronica, seashell paeonia, and other varieties of white flow into a conical, almost-yellow sorrel tree and large conglomerations of blue thistle and soft-pink virginiana roses. The garden consists of two borders: one around the outside of the lawn, pushed against the fence; and another beside the house. Viewed from almost anywhere within the garden a dialogue becomes apparent between this austere, uncomplicated scheme and the complexity of the plantings.

This glebe house (an English term for church property reserved for the use of the parish priest) served as the residence of John Rutgers Marshall, the first Episcopal minister of Woodbury. A group of church clergymen gathered here in 1783 and elected Dr. Samuel Seabury to travel to Scotland in order to be consecrated bishop (the Scottish church did not require an oath of loyalty to England) so that American ministers might be ordained as such in the United States. When he returned, this glebe house became known as the birthplace of the Episcopal Church in America. In 1925 a group of preservationists rescued the house from demolition, and one of the group visited Jekyll (then in her eighties) to commission a garden design for the site. Although Jekyll obliged the restorationists, her design was never implemented. The original document disappeared for several decades, until the 1980s, when researchers discovered it among the papers of Beatrix Farrand at the University of California. When a suggestion was made to construct the garden according to the Jekyll plan, many on the board of the preservation society dissented, recommending that the colonial house should have a proper colonial garden. In the early 1990s, the board finally decided to implement the Jekyll design as a way of acknowledging the entire history of the site. The house was returned to its original blue (for which the plan was developed) and a few minor alterations were made. But in essence, Jekyll's hand is evident throughout. The garden is lovingly tended by the preservation group that owns it. Observing the lawn mowed by hand on a summer's morning is not uncommon.

32 Litchfield: Laurel Hill

LOCATION: OFF WIGWAM ROAD, FIVE MILES SOUTHWEST OF LITCHFIELD TOWN CENTER. TAKE ROUTE 118 EAST FROM LITCHFIELD TO ROUTE 254; AFTER THREE MILES, TURN RIGHT ONTO WIGWAM ROAD. THE GARDEN IS ON THE LEFT ONE MILE FURTHER.

GARDEN OPEN: daily.
ADMISSION: Free.

NEARBY SIGHTS OF INTEREST:
Historic Litchfield

Unpretentious Laurel Hill sits beside a little-traveled country road in the northwestern corner of the state, a treasure among enlightened garden aficionados. The garden is actually a lovingly tended landscape of daffodils, which transforms a typical meadow into an effusion of color that undulates through the spring. In April the scheme is dark, evolving into yellow and then white by late May. A path takes visitors from the road through a glade of ferns and into the meadow. From here, energetic souls can continue on the rest of the mile-long circuit around a lake and back to the road. The first daffodils were planted in 1941 by a couple living across the street. Since then the site has been maintained by the Laurel Hill Foundation. There is no gatehouse, or trash can, or bench; just a sign prohibiting dogs. Because it is so decidedly informal Laurel Hill, can be an extremely subtle experience, requiring a different sensitivity to topography, texture, and color than is required in more formal gardens.

33

Norfolk: Hillside Gardens

GARDEN OPEN: 9am–5pm
daily, May–Sept. 15. After Sept
15, by appointment or by
chance. **ADMISSION:** free.

FURTHER INFORMATION FROM:
515 Litchfield Road, Norfolk
06058. (860) 542-5345

NEARBY SIGHTS OF INTEREST:
Winchester Museum

LOCATION: LITCHFIELD ROAD, THIRTY-FIVE MILES NORTHWEST OF HARTFORD

Good nurseries are usually known less for their artistic beauty
than for their scientific acuity. Hillside Gardens thankfully
bucks this trend. It is the creation of proprietors Fred and Mary
Ann McGourty, who are emphatically gardeners rather than
nurserypeople. The garden was begun in 1963 as a hobby while
Fred McGourty was working at the Brooklyn Botanic Garden.
But it became an abiding obsession in the early seventies when
he removed himself to this isolated location permanently
and began the nursery in order to support his habit. The garden
is primarily a showcase for perennials, about which the
McGourtys have published several books. Border gardens featuring a subtle and carefully studied combination of flowers
adorn the house. Attention has been given to plant combinations and flowering longevity; the blooming season is measured out to early September, a feat in this northernmost part
of Connecticut. Primulas, columbines, peonies, irises, and
many other selections swirl together in unusual combinations
that are sometimes unified by color, other times by texture or
contrasting form, and still other times in eclectic massings that
highlight species differentiation. The nursery proper extends
beyond the gardens but continues the same theme of juxtaposition. The garden is surrounded by pristine woodland, including
a state park, which provides a dramatic, green backdrop to the
floral displays.

34

Redding: Highstead Arboretum

GARDEN OPEN: 8:30am–
4:30pm Monday–Friday;
suggest calling ahead.
ADMISSION: free.

FURTHER INFORMATION FROM:
P. O. Box 1097, Redding
06875. (203) 938-8809

NEARBY SIGHTS OF INTEREST:
Aldrich Museum of
Contemporary Art

LOCATION: ROUTE 107, TWELVE MILES NORTH OF FAIRFIELD

The delicate mountain laurel (Connecticut's state flower) is
rarely a featured element in the landscape, and yet for a woodland garden, there are few understory shrubs that are as graceful. At the Highstead Arboretum, botanist Richard Jaynes has
developed one of the most outstanding collections of mountain
laurel throughout New England—a region in which it is indigenous. Taking advantage of an existing stand, Jaynes began
experimenting with cross-hybridization in the early 1980s. The
results are colorful drifts set into a bucolic woodland that range
far beyond the typical white flowers. Some of Jaynes's specimens bloom in full pink, whereas others inch toward violet and
burgundy. In one unusual creation, dubbed *Kalmia petalov*, the
petals themselves have been replaced by five, macabre-looking
stamens. The collection is laid out within a verdant and

well-designed 36-acre woodland that traverses several
habitats, including an alpine
ledge, a swamp, and a
meadow. In May a large collection of deciduous azaleas colo-
nize a major portion of the
garden, giving an infusion of
color in an otherwise elaborately green place, while witc-
hazel, blueberry, winterberry,
and delicate sassafras fill out the rich and diverse understory.
A recent collaboration with Garden in the Woods in South
Sudbury, Massachusetts (*page 45*) has resulted in a wild flower
garden, which will require several years to achieve the level of
horticultural complexity the rest of the garden displays, though
an impressive beginning has been made.

A world of mountain laurels,
Connecticut's state flower

35 Stamford: Bartlett Arboretum

LOCATION: ROUTE 137, SEVEN MILES NORTH OF STAMFORD CITY CENTER

This outpost of the University of Connecticut is nestled into
the quiet woodlands of southwestern Connecticut only a half-
hour from the bustle of New York City. The grounds serve as a
working laboratory for the university's horticultural research
division, particularly in the area of arboriculture. Stunning
specimen trees and cultivars dot the property near the visitors
center in somewhat anarchical fashion. Owing to the institution's academic bent, most of the trees are well labeled, to
appeal to our Linnaeusean fancies. But for the more romantically inclined, there is a conifer garden, a small area devoted to
the display of an exotic variety of cone-bearing and needle-
leaved trees. Early in the morning or late in the evening, when
the sunlight enters the space at an angle, the informally
arranged display of textures and shades can be truly sublime.
Other curiosities include a small garden of pollarded hedge
maples, chestnuts, and plane trees, as well as a collection of nut
trees chosen by the arboretum's founder, the renowned
arborist Dr. Frances Bartlett. The flowering gardens, which
include a display garden of annuals, a wild flower garden, a
perennial border, and an azalea and rhododendron garden, are
all fairly mediocre when compared with the magnificence of
the trees displays; however, the serenity of the setting, enforced
by a stroll along any of the paths that wind through the full 63
acres of woodlands surround the educational center and garden, makes all observation joyous.

GARDENS OPEN: 8:30am–
sunset daily. Visitor's center
open: 8:30am–4:30pm,
Monday–Friday, except
holidays. ADMISSION: free.

FURTHER INFORMATION FROM:
151 Brookdale Road, Stamford
06903. (203) 322-6971

NEARBY SIGHTS OF INTEREST:
Silvermine Guild Arts Center,
Hoyt Barnum House

North Coventry:
Caprilands Herb Farm

GARDENS OPEN: 10am–5pm
daily, except holidays. Lecture
and lunch on Friday and
Saturday by reservation.
ADMISSION: free

FURTHER INFORMATION FROM:
534 Silver Street, North
Coventry 06238
(860) 742-7244

NEARBY SIGHTS OF INTEREST:
Strong-Porter House,
University of Connecticut

**LOCATION: SILVER STREET, SOUTH OF ROUTE 44, TWENTY MILES
EAST OF HARTFORD**

Caprilands is the brainchild of Adelma Simmons, a patron saint
of herb gardeners everywhere. Miss Simmons inherited this 55-
acre worn-out dairy farm from her parents. And after failing to
turn a profit with goats (there are still several on-site, and the
name Caprilands is derived from the Italian word for goat), she
began converting the land into a vast herb garden, consisting of
some 29 different rooms. Herbs love it here. The soil is well
drained; there's plenty of sun. But mostly there's been plenty of
love and imagination put into this plot. Each garden is planted
according to a theme: a fragrance garden, a cook's garden, a
salad garden, and gardens of herbs from the eighteenth and
nineteenth centuries. Other themes are more creative. In the
Shakespeare garden, hyssop encircles a slate sign painted with
Iago's refrain from *Othello*: "So that we will plant nettles, or sow
lettuce, set hyssop and weed up thyme." Small statuettes and
narrow brick pathways leading into knotted, absolutely tiny garden spaces give Caprilands the feel of a constant adventure and
discovery: a journey on which you never feel the guiding mis-
tress is too far afield. The homey sense of the place is heightened by the garden shop, which sells dried flowers, barrels of
lavender, potted plants—and cups of free hot tea. From Miss
Simmons's house, still private and around which the entire garden wraps itself, big band jazz gently wafts. Only a year ago, visitors might happen upon her at work in the garden or strolling
the grounds and ask her a question about these enchanting
lands, but Miss Simmons passed away in 1997 at the age of 93,
a loss to the entire gardening world.

ABOVE: *Vegetables, orna-*
mentals, and plenty of herbs
fill the Identification Garden
at Caprilands.

37 Woodstock: Roseland Cottage

LOCATION: ROUTE 169, OFF ROUTE 44, SEVEN MILES NORTHWEST OF PUTNAM

Henry Bowen left rural Woodstock for New York City when he was a young man seeking his fortune. His travels led him to abolitionism, and in his twenties he founded the antislavery newspaper *The Independent*. But rural life beckoned, and Bowen and his wife, Lucy, returned to Woodstock and commenced the construction of a Gothic Revival house, called Roseland for the strawberry-colored planking that still adorns it. Bowen improved the property with larches, willows, and tulip trees; he constructed a fence along one side; planted an orchard of apples, quinces, grapes, and currants; and even built a small bowling alley, one of the first of its kind. In 1850 he hired local nurseryman and garden designer Henry Dyer to fashion a formal flower garden in front of the house. Dyer created an overlarge parterre garden, one of the oldest in New England. The paths and boxwood parterres are narrow and filled to the brim with celosia, foxglove, geraniums, lilies, hollyhocks, and hundreds of roses (Bowen's favorite)—a selection based in large part on the recommendations of Andrew Jackson Downing, whose writings were influential at this time. The lines of the garden also reflect Downing's influence. Laid out as a neatly trimmed carpet, the garden is best viewed from the second floor of the house. Every summer Bowen mounted a fervently patriotic display of fireworks, to which he invited all the leading figures of the day, including the president, who sometimes showed up. (An apocryphal story holds that when Grant visited, he bowled a strike on his first shot, only to be told later that he had to remove himself outside to smoke.) The eccentric displays, patriotic and rooted in family values, were part of what writer Alan Emmet called the "mixture of the conservative and avant-garde that characterized [Bowen's] entire life." The garden itself, a formal arrangement overlaid with an eccentric tapestry of color, continues that legacy today.

GARDEN OPEN: 11am–4pm Wednesday–Sunday, June–October 15.
ADMISSION: $4.

FURTHER INFORMATION FROM: Route 169, Woodstock 06281.
(860) 928-4074
www.spnea.org

NEARBY SIGHTS OF INTEREST: New Center for Contemporary Art, Prudence Crandall Museum

Historic boxwood encloses an eccentric garden.

Waterford: Eolia,
the Harkness House

LOCATION: EXIT 80 OFF INTERSTATE 95 TO ROUTE 1 TO AVERY LANE (ROUTE 213), THREE MILES SOUTHWEST OF NEW LONDON

GARDEN OPEN: 8am–dusk daily. **HOUSE OPEN:** 10am–3pm Saturday–Sunday.
PARKING: $5 weekdays, $8 weekends.

FURTHER INFORMATION FROM:
275 Great Neck Road,
Water-ford 06385.
(860) 443-5725

NEARBY SIGHTS OF INTEREST:
Eugene O'Neill Theatre

Mary Stillman's sister built this Italianate mansion on the windswept coast of Connecticut in 1909 but soon abandoned it to Mary, when the weather proved to her disliking. Stillman and her husband, Edward Harkness, heir to his father's Standard Oil fortune, occupied the estate and made several subtle changes to soften the harsh formalism of the house—an extension of the facade to meet some freestanding columns, the enclosure of two loggias in glass to create a sunny breakfast room, and in the 1930s, a commission for Beatrix Farrand to design several gardens around the house. The West Garden and its superb view of Long Island Sound, framed by a grand, sloping lawn and clumps of copper beech, yellow rue, pachysandra, and rugosa roses, were designed by the Boston firm of Brett and Hall. The garden is formal Italian in structure, with two large rectangles of turf surrounded by boxwood and yew. A fountain anchors the space in the center, while a pergola stands back at the far end, contemplating the sea. Throughout the garden, statuary from Mrs. Harkness's travels to Europe and the Orient stand in silence; a most absorbing display of the Seven Wonders of Womanhood occupies one flank. In the 1920s, the Harknesses hired Beatrix Farrand to soften the formal lines of the West Garden with an arc of perennials massed in impressionistic clumps. Farrand also designed a rock garden to provide a buffer against the lawn and to soften the stone walls of the terrace when viewed from a distance. Two streams ramble through the garden, twining themselves about a fountain. One path takes visitors down into the heart of the garden where the central fountain is situated, whereas another climbs the rock ridge along one boundary. Eastern red cedars and pines provide a vertical element, while an informal carpet of perennials and spruce climb up the boulders toward the West Garden. The East Garden was designed by Mrs. Harkness alone to showcase her statuary and is composed of two granite terraces. The upper terrace is planted with delphinium and lilies, while silvers and white artemisia dominate the lower terrace. A geometric border of catmint and teucrium surround beds of bushy heliotrope. The final garden at Harkness, a cutting garden, was recently restored. Snapdragons, gladiolas, and hundreds of dahlias flood the area in the height of summer. The windy, picturesque environment of the estate had a strong attraction for the Harknesses, who named their home Eolia, after the Greek god of wind. On a brisk October day, looking out over the Sound from above Farrand's rock garden, intimations of that original force are still very much alive.

39 Higganum: Sundial Garden

LOCATION: HIDDEN LAKE ROAD, TWENTY-FIVE MILES SOUTH OF HARTFORD

Americans love flowers. But the European gardens, from which American gardens are derived, traditionally paid little attention to flowers. These were architectural spaces, conceived to frame space in artistic ways—and to perhaps show us the world in a new way. This philosophy underlies Ragna Goddard's Sundial Garden. On a historic site tucked into the Connecticut River Valley, Goddard has designed a traditional quadrant garden upon perfectly described axes. The first quadrant is occupied by the eighteenth-century cottage. The second quadrant, a knot garden, lies on axis with this and creates, essentially, an extension of the house—an outdoor room. Narrow paths wind around a ribbon-like parterre of herbs. When viewed from the steps up to the house, the first in a series of excellent vistas is achieved. The eye travels across the knot, through an arch, across a meadow, and into the woods, where a small statue has been placed to create perspective and a sense of space. The second vista occurs within the knot garden proper, where the eye travels through an arbor of pleached (woven) pears into an eighteenth-century formal garden. The progression of the sight line from light to shade to light, as well as through an interior space, gives the gardens an extended field, as if they were far larger than they really are. But in fact the gardens are quite small. Including the last garden, a topiary garden of trimmed hedges and architectural details, the entire plot measures only about 150 feet square. Yet Goddard's sensible eye—she is a graphic designer by training—has discerned a wealth of interest within this small space. Narrow paths are lined with intricate parterres, pots of specimen trees, long gestures of arbor, and arches crafted in false perspective frame views and carefully manage the experience of the entire garden.

Goddard and her husband host a formal tea in their teahouse on the property, complete with cucumber sandwiches, world-famous homemade scones (of a "civilized size and refined taste" quips Goddard), and exotic teas from around the world that put American "tea dust" to shame. The meticulous detail of the gardens, the formal teas, the country teahouse, and even peerless Goddard herself are rooted in ancient ideas—that humans have a distinctive, cultured connection to the world, one that can and should be artfully expressed in everything we do.

GARDEN OPEN: 10am–5pm Saturday–Sunday, except holidays. Reservations required for tea. ADMISSION: $1 (gardens only). daily.

FURTHER INFORMATION FROM: 59 Hidden Lake Road Higganum 06441. (860) 345-4290

NEARBY SIGHTS OF INTEREST: Goodspeed Opera House, Historic Chester

Even in winter the Sundial Garden's spirit stirs.

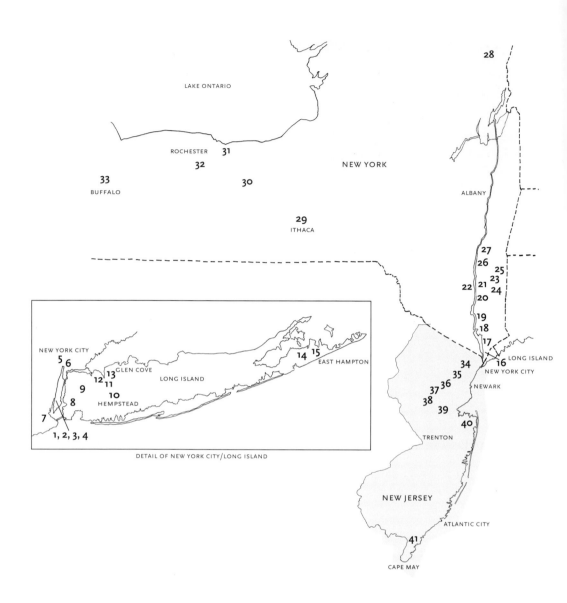

DETAIL OF NEW YORK CITY/LONG ISLAND

MID-ATLANTIC NORTH:

New York and New Jersey

I n the mid-nineteenth century, New York's Hudson River Valley was witness to a revolution in American aesthetics. Painters such as Frederick Church, Thomas Cole, and other members of the Hudson River school translated English romantic notions into their particular region, revealing the sublime aspects of the bucolic, picturesque, and sometimes haunting American landscape. A similar, if not more far-reaching, revolution took place in landscape design as well when Andrew Jackson Downing published his influential and widely read *Treatise on Landscape Gardening and Rural Architecture.* Downing translated the perceptions of the painters into a set of prescriptives for a new American taste in landscape gardening. The result was the landscape-park style of rolling lawns and conspicuously placed trees that frame views and create a sense of scale, all set against wooded enclaves that offered seclusion and a sense of mystery.

With the great accumulation of wealth in the latter part of the century, the Hudson Valley region became home to families who created palatial estates and gardens, most of which were designed in this new style. The greatest expressions of these ideas are in the romantic landscapes at Cedarmere (*page 87*) Kykuit (*pages 92–93*), Locust Grove (*page 95*), and Montgomery Place (*pages 101–02*)—each linked by its preoccupation with the Hudson River. In the twentieth century, many of these estates were retrofitted with flower gardens and formal terraces. Although today we don't classify the nineteenth-century landscape as a garden in the strict sense (in large part because it lacks flowers), in the most basic sense it was. Like any garden, these landscapes attempted to beautify nature through artful

*Leaming's Run showcases
Jack Aprill's unusual
collection of annuals.*

arrangement and to knit humans to their natural sur-

roundings. Experiencing these two wildly different approaches to the same end

makes many of these gardens excellent and worthy trips.

Another great tradition that influenced the character of gardens in this

region was the botanical garden movement in the late nineteenth and early twen-

tieth centuries—a natural outgrowth of the parks movement that began in the

1860s and the advances in horticultural research that occurred around the turn of

the century. Although based on British precedents, these gardens are quintessen-

tially American in that they seek to classify, calculate, and inventory nature's

bounty in a spirit of eternal curiosity. The expression of this spirit is most aptly

experienced in the New York Botanical Garden (*pages 79–81*) and the Brooklyn

Botanic Garden (*page 83*), both of which were created around this time and which

combine the seemingly disparate goals of science and art.

Off the beaten path, there are several gardens of unusual flavor in the

Mid-Atlantic North region—most of which are located quite a distance from New

York City. Robert Dash's Madoo (*page 89*), Leonard Buck's garden (*page 112*), and

Jack Aprill's Leaming Run (*page 115*) are all exciting, and highly original gardens

that are rarely included on garden club circuits.

New York City: Liz Christy Garden and other community gardens

LOCATION: BOWERY AND HOUSTON STREETS, AND THROUGHOUT MANHATTAN

According to an apocryphal story, Liz Christy was pushing a baby carriage through her Lower East Side neighborhood one afternoon back in 1973 when the carriage struck an obstruction, lurched forward, and tossed the child into a garbage-strewn, abandoned lot. The trauma of the experience opened Christy's eyes to the sordid conditions of the area—the abandoned lots that were plentiful in the area were host to drugs, crime, and vandalism. So she canvassed her neighbors, put together a group of activists and set about turning the dangerous corner into a verdant garden. A quarter of a century later the Liz Christy Garden still thrives: a wrought iron fence keeps out vandals, while a handful of mature trees including a stately metasequoia provide tranquillity and shade. Several active gardeners maintain separate plots arranged around a common area, which includes a slender crescent of grass, a turtle pond, and a small covered deck. The plots, although expressive of individual tastes, form a cohesive whole—one that reflects the strong character of the East Village, traditionally a radical and activist section of Manhattan. The makeshift scarecrow lends an eclectic, artsy air, even if it has an ameliorative effect on the pigeons.

The small group of activists that rallied around Christy evolved into the Green Guerrillas, an organization that continues to help Manhattanites till the ground on abandoned lots. Punctuating the grid like bright stars, these gardens are an important part of local neighborhoods, often reflecting the cultural heritage of New York City's immigrant populations. On the Lower East Side, for instance, Puerto Rican immigrants harvest corn and tomatoes and decorate their plots with flags and signs of national identity. Many of these small gardens also boast covered decks and small houses, called *casitas*, where people can play music and socialize on summer evenings.

The Avenue B and Sixth Street Garden is perhaps one of the best-maintained gardens in the city. Several mature trees provide shelter to an abundance of small plots that intermix to form a lush floral tapestry. Many member gardeners have also set up structures here—benches, small lean-tos—the most conspicuous of which is Edward Boros's "Garbage Can," a tower of artifacts (couches, two-by-fours, pictures, toys, stuffed animals, balloons) rescued from the streets of New York and piled within his four-by-eight-foot plot; the lurching structure reaches higher than most of the surrounding trees. All of these community gardens are planted and tended by local residents, and are therefore considered private. However, all of them are also open to the public at some time during the week.

LIZ CHRISTY GARDEN OPEN: 12pm–4pm Saturday, year-round; 6pm–dusk Tuesday, May–September. **AVENUE B GARDEN OPEN:** summer evenings. **ADMISSION:** free.

FURTHER INFORMATION FROM: The Green Guerrillas 625 Broadway, 2nd floor, New York 10012. (212) 674-8124

NEARBY SIGHTS OF INTEREST: Bowery, Little Italy, Lower East Side Tenement Museum

Edward Boros's "Garbage Can" in the East Village

GARDEN OPEN: 8:00am–
3:30pm Monday and Tuesday;
8am–6pm Wednesday–
Friday; 12 noon–6pm
Saturday and Sunday.
ADMISSION: free.

FURTHER INFORMATION FROM:
400 East 34th Street, New
York 10016. (212) 263-6058

NEARBY SIGHTS OF INTEREST:
United Nations,
Empire State Building

2

New York City:
Enid A. Haupt Glass Garden

LOCATION: 34TH STREET AT 1ST AVENUE

In the 1960s and 1970s, researchers were intrigued with the
notion that contact with nature might have therapeutic bene-
fits, not only nourishing the minds and souls of patients but
also lowering health costs. The hypothesis held under scrutiny.
Several key studies produced data to suggest that even passive
contact, like viewing a garden from a window, had an ameliorative effect on patient recovery rates even shortening hospital
stays by as much as twenty percent. Since then, horticultural
therapy has fallen out of favor, and few hospitals have continued to expand, or even to maintain, their gardens. One major
exception to this is the Enid A. Haupt Glass Garden, a 17,000-
square-foot glass house appended to the New York University
Medical Center (named after the great benefactress of gardens
and chairperson of the American Horticultural Society). There
are several different horticultural therapy programs at the garden, some involving actual planting and maintenance, as an
alternative to typical physical therapy, others involving passive
contact with nature. The facility is wheelchair accessible and
serves the entire hospital population. Plant beds are raised and
angled to provide the wheelchair-bound with the full garden
experience—touching and smelling, as well as seeing. The collections include primarily hardy plants acclimated to the low-
light environment caused by the towering adjacent skyscrapers.
A lovely pond garden containing shade-loving Boston ferns,
philodendron, and ripsala offers a tranquil respite from the
city. Many of the displays are educational, aimed at visitors
whose contact with nature is not only presently curtailed by a
hospital stay but may generally be limited by life in the city. The
grocery garden showcases plants that can be grown on a win-
dowsill from pits and seeds gathered from foods purchased at
the market, such as macadamia nuts. The garden also provides
a multisensory experience. Some 100 caged birds are arranged
throughout. Their singing and cawing, mixed with the humidity caused by misting machines, creates a tropical and serenely
natural experience. Outside the conservatory lies a perennial
garden planted with shade plants and containing an arbor. A
recently constructed children's garden provides youngsters visiting a relative a place to play, as well as pediatric patients a
place to get away from the hospital atmosphere. Although the
glasshouse is strongly oriented toward patient care, it is open
to the public and encourages visitors, of which there were
100,000 last year. It is a wonderful place to step outside the
bustling world of Manhattan and to see how gardens can
fulfill a need beyond the simply aesthetic or environmental.

3 New York City: The Conservatory Gardens

LOCATION: 105TH STREET AND 5TH AVENUE, UPPER EAST SIDE

GARDEN OPEN: 8am–dusk daily. ADMISSION: free.

FURTHER INFORMATION FROM: 830 Fifth Avenue, New York 10021. (212) 397-3156

NEARBY SIGHTS OF INTEREST: Museo del Bario, Museum of the City of New York, Spanish Harlem

Wrought iron gates from a Vanderbilt mansion at 58th Street mark the entrance to one of the jewels of Central Park. The original plans for the park drawn up by Frederick Law Olmsted and Calvert Vaux in 1857 specify this area for an arboretum or horticultural collection; however, it wasn't until 1899 that a conservatory was erected on the site. In 1934 Robert Moses, who built most of New York's highway system, had the structure demolished to alleviate maintenance costs and organized a Works Project Administration project to build the garden that exists today. Set off from the traffic on Fifth Avenue by a row of stately elms, the gates, and a thin woodland, are three formal gardens stitched seamlessly together by two major perimeter paths and a recognizable geometry. The Central Garden is a perfect set piece: a large, rectangular lawn edged by a deep-set hedge that frames a view of a dynamic, spurting fountain. A semicircular, iron pergola covered with a bough of wisteria and set atop a bluestone terrace caps the space much like the apse of a Roman basilica. Lining the lawn are two parallel allées of crabapple that date back to the 1930s. To the south are arcing beds that surround the Secret Garden, a quiet copse designed to accommodate a statue of Mary and Dickon, the protagonists from Frances Hodgson Burnett's classic children's story *The Secret Garden*. The water lily pool and the canopy of a magnificent crabapple imbue the space with serenity. The surrounding garden hosts a protean display of perennials, including astilbe, geranium, alyssum, and veronica arranged in clumps of varying color. In the center of each bed is a serpentine gesture of hedge that provides a bold backdrop for the flower display and creates a sense of structure to an otherwise fluid performance. The North Garden, on the other side of the lawn, hosts seasonal plantings of annuals. In October the garden perimeter comes alive with the blooming of a rare variety of chrysanthemums that the garden staff grow from seed. In the center of the garden are duotone parterres in the French, fleur-de-lis tradition, which are typically designed with diminutive, delicate plants of boldly contrasting colors, such as vivid red alternanthera and spruce-green teucrium. Few such well-designed and well-managed gardens are open to the public within Manhattan that the Conservatory Gardens can truly be called an urban oasis.

A fall display captures the last, energetic gasp of the season.

4　New York City: The Cloisters

LOCATION: FORT TRYON PARK, WASHINGTON HEIGHTS

MUSEUM AND GARDEN OPEN:
9:30am–5:00pm Tuesday–
Sunday. ADMISSION: $8
adults, $4 seniors and
students, free for children.

FURTHER INFORMATION FROM:
Fort Tryon Park, New York
10040. (212) 923-3700

NEARBY SIGHTS OF INTEREST:
Harlem, Washington Heights
Museum

Although Nelson Rockefeller is usually considered the member of that influential family most active in the arts, it was his father, John D. Rockefeller Jr., who created The Cloisters museum. He donated much of the architecture and ornamentation for this re-creation of medieval cloisters, as well the awe-inspiring mountain it sits upon on the northern tip of Manhattan. Cloisters built in the middle ages were centered on a courtyard to form the heart of a monastery and a place where resident monks could gather for communal events, to study, or simply to enjoy gardening. The Cloisters Museum was assembled from the ruins of many different monasteries spanning several centuries and now houses the The Metropolitan Museum of Art's vast medieval collection, including the famous Unicorn Tapestries. Surrounding the museum are three medieval gardens. A garth (lawn) garden graces the facade of the Cuxa Cloister, a structure composed from a twelfth-century French Benedictine monastery. The Mediterranean courtyard, in a geometrically composed pattern of crossed paths and a central fountain, would have provided the monks with a sunny, south-facing outdoor room. Modern updating has meant the inclusion of flowers, both of medieval and contemporary varieties, including Easter lilies and crocuses. The surrounding ornaments include a vast array of animistic imagery set against traditional Christian iconography. An herb garden occupies the Bonnefont Cloister, a Cistercian abbey from the south of France. Raised beds are arranged around a wellhead containing over 250 different herbs commonly found in medieval gardens, many of which were mentioned by Charlemagne in his wish list for the imperial gardens at Anchen. The espaliered fruit trees

Medieval Cloister gardens link nature's forces with internal meditation.

and wattle fencing are also typical features. The last cloister, the Trie Cloister is composed of marble arches from a fifteenth-century convent; it combines depictions of Biblical scenes from the lives of the saints with grotesque symbolism. The garden has traditionally been planted with species depicted in the Unicorn Tapestries, however in recent years the palette has been expanded to include other medieval plants. The Cloisters sit atop some of the most spectacular land in the city, with excellent views of the Hudson River and New Jersey beyond.

5 Bronx: Wave Hill

LOCATION: INDEPENDENCE AVENUE AND W. 249TH STREET, ONE MILE NORTH
OF MANHATTAN (ON THE HUDSON LINE OF METRO NORTH)

GARDEN OPEN: 9:00am–
5:30pm Tuesday–Sunday
(Fridays until dusk), mid
May–mid October; 9:00am–
4:30pm, mid October–mid
May. ADMISSION (March
15–Nov. 14): $4 adults, $2
seniors and students, free
for children; free the rest of
the year.

FURTHER INFORMATION FROM:
675 West 252nd Street, Bronx
10471-2899. (718) 549-3200

NEARBY SIGHTS OF INTEREST:
The Cloisters, Van Cortlandt
House

Wave Hill's glorious views of the Palisades are partly the reason
the cliffs were saved from development in the 1940s. Throughout its 150-year history, Wave Hill has been influenced by this
view more than anything else. In the late-nineteenth century,
when publishing scion William Henry Appleton owned the
estate, he brought Thomas Henry Huxley for a visit, and the
renowned naturalist declared the Palisades one of the world's
greatest natural wonders. But it wasn't until the twentieth century, when George Perkins, a partner in the J. P. Morgan
Company, purchased the house, that Wave HIll began to take
shape. Perkins sculpted the slopes, developed gardens, and
planted trees to frame the views that exist today. The gardens
fell into disrepair in the early 1960s, but were revitalized in
1967 by Marco Polo Stufano, a young horticulturist from
the New York Botanical Garden. He transformed the rose garden into a flower garden that includes many plants popular
in the early nineteenth century, to reflect the site's heritage—
these include *Hydrangea paniculata* and tobacco flower—but
also many exotic variations that give the garden an untamed
presence. The Herb Garden, arranged simply to delight, takes
advantage of each plant's visual or aromatic character, and
also features many quite strange additions, such as the curious
"curry plant" (*Helichrysum angustifolium*), which possesses
the aroma of spiced lamb. Passing through a dry garden and
past an alpine house, the path enters the Wild Garden, an
assemblage of floral diversity that proves a different experience
for each visitor. An abundance of narrow paths traverse a rocky
slope planted with spiky succulents, meadow perennials, hor-
monal evergreens that pose in the ether as if suspended by
strings, and a thousand other odd inclusions. Here the effect is
distinctly American, induced partly by the picturesque setting
and harsh slope and partly by Stufano's bold approach. In stark
contrast, this wild garden is fronted by a formal garden area that
includes a pool of aquatic plants surrounded by a lawn and two
stately pergolas shaded by an abundance of vines. The Monocot
Garden, which balances the pool, features ornamental grasses
that create an intriguing architectural foundation to the area.
The landscape of Wave Hill slopes away from the gardens in a
lulling, harmonic manner, carrying visitors either back to the
Great Lawn, where lawn chairs set beneath an Italian-style pergola host the vista across the Hudson, or down into the wooded
lower portions of the property on a network of trails. The 1843
residence and other structures at Wave Hill house sundry art
and horticulture organizations. In the winter there is an annual
jazz festival, and in the summer Wave Hill hosts a dance series.

*Autumn overlooking
the Hudson River and
the Palisades*

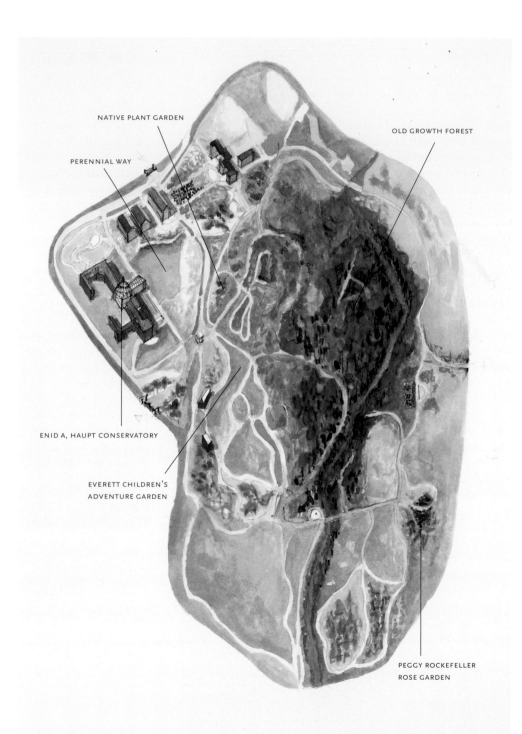

NATIVE PLANT GARDEN

OLD GROWTH FOREST

PERENNIAL WAY

ENID A, HAUPT CONSERVATORY

EVERETT CHILDREN'S
ADVENTURE GARDEN

PEGGY ROCKEFELLER
ROSE GARDEN

6 Bronx: New York Botanical Garden

LOCATION: FORDHAM ROAD AND BRONX RIVER PARKWAY (ON THE
NEW HAVEN LINE OF METRO NORTH RAILROAD)

The New York Botanical Garden is at once a major public garden and a leading research institution. To combine these seemingly disparate foci takes tremendous resources—botanical, capital, and human. This botanical garden has all of these. It was founded by Columbia University botanist Nathaniel Lord Britton who, along with his wife, Elizabeth, was impressed with London's public botanical gardens at Kew and returned to New York with the desire to establish an equivalent on these shores. With the help of local financiers with names like Vanderbilt, Morgan, and Carnegie, the garden opened its doors in 1891. The original vision for the institution was to provide a forum for the development of the botanical sciences, and to extend that knowledge to the general public. Today, behind the scenes, in the Plant Studies Center, thirty doctoral candidates in residence from programs around the country employ the latest technology in molecular science and climatology to their contemporary studies. A major focus of their work lately has been on biodiversity issues, which the garden as a whole has taken as a primary research goal.

Outside the laboratories, 250 acres of gardens await. After a four-year restoration, the architectural centerpiece of the garden, The Enid A. Haupt Conservatory, is once again open. Named for a great benefactress of gardens and the chairperson of the American Horticultural Society, this Lord and Burnham steel-framed glasshouse, constructed in 1902 for $177,000, is the largest Victorian conservatory in the country. During the $25 million restoration, more than 17,000 panes of glass were replaced, and the exhibits were completely redesigned. The

GARDEN OPEN: 10am–6pm Tuesday–Sunday and Monday holidays, April–October; 10am–4pm, November–March. ADMISSION: $3 adults, $2 seniors and students, $1 children; free Wednesdays and Saturdays, 10am–noon. EVERETT CHILDREN'S ADVENTURE GARDEN OPEN: 1pm–6pm, April–October; 10am–6pm, July and August; 1pm–4pm, November–March. ADMISSION: $3 adults, $2 seniors and students, $1 children. ENID A. HAUPT CONSERVATORY ADMISSION: $3.50 adults, $2.50 seniors and students, $2.00 children

ROCK GARDEN AND NATIVE PLANT GARDEN ADMISSION: $1.00 adults, $0.50 seniors, students, and children.

FURTHER INFORMATION FROM: 200th Street and Kazimiroff Boulevard, Bronx 10458-5126. (718) 817-8700 www.nybg.org

NEARBY SIGHTS OF INTEREST: Bronx Zoo, Poe Cottage

A three-year restoration rejuvenated the conservatory originally built by Lord and Burnham in 1902.

structure is accessed through the central atrium, which houses the largest collection of American palms under glass. Within the transverse wings there are eleven, computer-controlled ecological zones, including a tropical rain forest and an African desert. The exhibits are designed to create an "immersion experience." Rather than highlight one particular species or plant, the displays are designed according to ecosystems, as one might find them in nature. Mosses and lichen cover tree trunks; understories are crowded and seemingly arranged by the hand of anarchic nature. At one point in the walkway, the large fern-covered limb of a kapok tree creates a low archway over the path, forcing visitors beneath its subterranean form and giving them the feeling of crawling through the tropical rain forest. Elsewhere there are ramps and causeways that raise the visitor above the displays to create unusual perspectives. Within the enclosed outdoor space created by the rectangular wrapping of the conservatory is a courtyard containing two water lily pools.

Perennial Way cuts across the front of the conservatory. Along here are several perennial gardens designed to contrast "hot" and "cool" plants. There is also a garden of fall perennials that illustrates atypical floral species. An herb garden nearby was designed by Penelope Hobhouse in the style of a traditional Renaissance garden, with two flower-shaped parterres set within a rectangle. Pots anchor the space, ringed in turn by a modern border of perennial herbs and shrubs to creates a sense of enclosure and intimacy. There are hundreds of unusual herbs here, including four different kinds of hops and the macabre-sounding and strongly fragrant bigroot cranes bill. Also nearby is the Chemurgic Garden containing plants used in industry.

Proceeding away from the entrance and the conservatory, the botanical garden becomes progressively less formal, transitioning in the center to a 40-acre tract of old-growth forest that is the last remnant of the forest that once covered the entire New York metropolitan area. A few major paths loop through the edges of the woods, however the interior is left untouched except by the hand of natural succession. A "leave it where it fell" management strategy ensures that this civic treasure will continue to exist for posterity. At the edge of the forest is the educational Native Plant Garden, containing several different plant habitats: a meadow, a bog, a barrens, a limestone formation, a coastal prairie, a southern rockery, and small woodlands. Each space transitions almost seamlessly into the next, giving a sense of wonder and enchantment. Wildflowers of diverse stature continually bloom from March to November. Adjacent to this area is the lovingly restored Rock Garden, a two-and-a-half-acre tract of alpine meadow plants, arranged within an invigorating setting.

In appreciation for the philanthropy that sustains the botanical garden, most gardens bear the name of their benefactor. David Rockefeller dedicated The Peggy Rockefeller Rose Garden in 1988 in honor of his wife. Designed originally in 1916 by Beatrix Farrand, the garden was not built until the 1980s due to lack of funding. The garden contains 2,700 plants of 290 varieties, including many All-America Roses. In an Americanization of an English tradition, old roses crawl around the perimeter of the space, while modern tea hybrids fill the interior. The newest addition to the botanical garden is the Everett Children's Adventure Garden (funded by philanthropists Henry and Edith Everett), a corridor of garden rooms that are emphatically programmed to complement the New York State educational curriculum for kindergarten through sixth grade. The Adventure Garden is also meant to be fun, and features a boulder maze, a hedge maze, and a bird's-nest-making exhibit, where kids create their own nests with handfuls of reeds and cattails. A pristine wetland slinks along the edge of this garden, and a small dock is equipped with a tubular bucket used to retrieve salamanders and plantlife from the water. Collections of lilacs, magnolias, crab apples, and daffodils planted into a romantic hill are just some of the features that complete the botanical garden. At the edge of the Bronx River, which strolls lazily through the forest, is Snuff Mill, an architectural artifact that describes—as does the entire garden—another side of New York City.

TOP: *Springtime on the tulip walk*

BOTTOM: *A mock lumber camp tells the story of Adirondack life in the Everett Children's Adventure Garden.*

Staten Island: Staten Island
Botanical Garden

LOCATION: SNUG HARBOR, STATEN ISLAND

GARDEN OPEN: 9am–5pm
daily. ADMISSION: free.

FURTHER INFORMATION FROM:
1000 Richmond Terrace
Staten Island 10301.
(718) 273-8200

NEARBY SIGHTS OF INTEREST:
Newhouse Center for
Contemporary Art, Staten
Island Ferry, Garibaldi-Meucci
Museum

Opened in 1973, the Staten Island Botanical Garden is the
youngest botanical garden in the city. However, considering
its splendid location and growing collections, it should not
be overlooked. The jewel in the crown is the new Chinese
Scholar's Garden, to open in May 1999. Forty artisans from
China—as well as a cargo ship of wooden beams, columns,
and hand-crafted ornamentation—were employed in the construction of the garden which includes three major rooms: a
Billowing Pine Court, the Wandering-in-Bamboo Courtyard,
and the Court of Uncommon Reeds, each ringed by pavilions.
Although Japanese gardens, based on the Victorian interpretation, are fairly ubiquitous in America, the equally ancient
Chinese art is practically unknown here. Designed by the
Chinese landscape architect Gong wu Zou in the style of a
scholar's garden—a traditional place for meditation and
intellectual pursuits dating back to the Ming Dynasty (1368–
1644), the garden incorporates many elementary principles
of Chinese tradition, such as Feng Shui, the art of juxtaposing
and blending elements like water and hills into a balanced
harmony. Besides this remarkable new addition, the Staten
Island Botanical Garden contains a significant collection
of Siberian irises, a hothouse full of the exotic phalenopsis
and cattleyas orchids, and a white garden, inspired by the
famous gardens at Sissinghurst in Britain. The arboreta
exhibits include both freshwater and saltwater wetlands, a
forest of dogwoods, and a recently commenced 750-acre "tree
plantation" of which about 450 specimens have been planted.
The botanical garden is located on the grounds of Snug
Harbor, once a retirement community for sailors but which
now houses an artist colony. As with any place in this borough,
the Gardens are accessed from Manhattan by the historic ferry
that believe it or not, is free—the best buy in the city.

ABOVE: *A pastel garden
overlooks the duck pond at
the Staten Island Botanical
Garden.*

8   Brooklyn: Brooklyn Botanic Garden

LOCATION: EASTERN PARKWAY AND FLATBUSH AVENUE, ON THE SOUTHERN
EDGE OF PROSPECT PARK

GARDEN OPEN: 8am–6pm
Tuesday–Friday and
10am–6pm weekends and
holidays, April–September.
Garden closes 4:30pm in the
winter. CONSERVATORY OPEN:
10:00am–5:30pm Tuesday–
Saturday, April–September;
10am–4pm Tuesday–
Saturday, October–March.
ADMISSION: $3.00 adults,
$1.50 seniors, $0.50 children.

FURTHER INFORMATION FROM:
1000 Washington Avenue,
Brooklyn 11225.
(718) 622-4433
www.bbg.org

NEARBY SIGHTS OF INTEREST:
Brooklyn Museum,
Prospect Park

In 1897 Brooklyn was Manhattan's political rival. Immigrant workers bolstered its census, industry and shipping terminals lined its extensive waterfront, and the Brooklyn Bridge stood as a symbol of American empire to the entire world. In the midst of this great time, local visionaries earmarked a neglected parcel of land, just beyond the confines of Prospect Park, to make the vision a reality. In 1910 philanthropist Alfred T. White raised $25,000 to establish a botanic garden to rival the New York Botanic Garden a few miles, and several rivers, away. Today, the botanic garden features numerous exciting landscapes and plant displays woven into a park-like setting. Although there is an admission charge, Brooklynites treat it like a park, and the lawns and esplanades are often filled with people sleeping, reading, or having a picnic.

The central spine of the garden is a meandering progression of plants called the Plant Family Collection, which tells the story of plant evolution. Few signs make this clear, but the "tour" begins in the northern reaches of the garden, at the edge of the pond in the Japanese Garden. Here are found the ferns and fungi that are at the beginning of the evolutionary chain of species. Next come the gymnosperms, or conifers, and then flowering shrubs and deciduous trees that, roughly, proceed from magnolias (a transition plant) to daisies, believed to be the most recently evolved of the herbaceous flowers. It is a subtle, ingenious, and unique exhibit that consumes a large percentage of the garden in rolling naturalistic displays. Elsewhere, four conservatories are linked by underground tunnels and feature habitat exhibits: a desert room of unusual succulents and plants from the Sonoran Desert in the Southwest and North African deserts; a humid tropical room, where coffee plants, citrus trees, and the very cool yellow shrimp plant coalesce around a circular path; a bonsai collection, a sparse aquatic collection, and temperate zone greenhouse are also located here. Outside the greenhouses, fronting the original palm house building, which was designed by Penn Station architects McKim, Mead & White, lies a formal garden walk. Two rectangular pools and a fountain define the space, while an annual border reaches along one side and a perennial border the other. The Japanese Garden is a major focus, but it combines the traditionally separate Japanese forms of a view garden and a stroll garden, to strange effect. The illusion of seeing a landscape in miniature is often marred by figures strolling around the overlarge lake. A second spine of the botanic garden, and perhaps the most popular feature, is the Cherry Esplanade, a magnificent sloping lawn lined by double rows of cherry trees that burst forth in spring.

Conifers, Japanese maples, and a garden gate form the Japanese Hill-and-Pond Garden.

9 Flushing: Queens Botanical Garden

LOCATION: CORONA PARK, QUEENS

GARDEN OPEN: 8am–6pm
Tuesday–Friday; 8am–7pm
Saturday and Sunday, April–
October; 8:00am–4:30pm
Tuesday–Sunday, November–
March. ADMISSION: free.

FURTHER INFORMATION FROM:
43-50 Main Street, Flushing
11355. (718) 886-3800

NEARBY SIGHTS OF INTEREST:
Queens Museum of Art,
Flushing Meadows,
U.S. Open

ABOVE: *The Wedding
Garden attracts visitors
throughout the summer.*

Like most things in this area of Queens, the original botanical garden was a byproduct of the historical world's fair that took place here in 1939–40. The current twenty-acre garden was developed in 1960, just in time for another world's fair. And from many places within the garden the imposing Unisphere, a leftover of that event, can be seen. Significant trees dot the landscape of this garden, although a campaign to label all of them has only just begun. The entry is marked by two blue atlas cedars that date to the first world's fair. Behind the administrative building lie an impressive allée of oaks that frames a succession of lawns and perennial beds. A great lawn encircled by Kwanzan cherry trees adorns the west facade of the building. All the usual botanical garden suspects are here, including an herb garden, a rose garden containing some 4,000 plants, a neatly organized woodland garden, and an all-American display garden of popular annuals and perennials. Besides a bird garden, planted to attract such native species as blackbirds, finches, and cardinals, there is a particularly well-designed bee garden, which is continually active due to the presence of several hives. Adjacent to all this buzzing is the Victorian Wedding Garden, designed with pretty footbridge, a babbling brook, and cute gazebo. The abundant perennials and cherry trees (a staple in this area of New York) virtually explode with color in May and early summer, making this a very popular spot for tying the knot. Recently, the botanical garden received a large donation of dahlia roots, which have been planted beyond the rose garden and will create a symphony of color in the late summer and fall. An arboretum of rolling lawns and specimen trees, including a collection of crabapple, drifts off the property to the north linking the garden with the rest of Corona Park and Queens beyond.

10 Old Westbury:
    Old Westbury Gardens

LOCATION: EXIT **39** OFF THE LONG ISLAND EXPRESSWAY, TWENTY MILES
EAST OF NEW YORK CITY

GARDEN OPEN: 10am–5pm
Wednesday–Monday,
April–Christmas, except
Thanksgiving. GARDEN ADMIS-
SION: $6 adults, $5 seniors,
$3 children. HOUSE ADMIS-
SION: $10 adults, $8 seniors,
$6 children.

FURTHER INFORMATION FROM:
P.O. Box 430, Old Westbury
11568. (516) 333-0048

NEARBY SIGHTS OF INTEREST:
Old Bethpage Restoration

In the first years of this century, millionaires flocked to the
towns of western Long Island. Although subdivisions have
since replaced those grand estates, Old Westbury still stands.
Old Westbury was the home of John Phipps, son of an original
partner in the Carnegie Steel Company, and his wife Margarita,
from a well-to-do family in Sussex, England. Owing to Mrs.
Phipps's background, the estate, which was cobbled together
from several farms in 1901, is designed with a distinctly Angli-
can flair. The house contains European furnishings and oils by
Gainsborough, Reynolds, and Constable. Several different garden experiences are offered at Old Westbury, a testament not
only to the wherewithal of Phipps but his unflagging interest in
nature and landscape. A walled garden is the highlight. A handsome brick wall with limestone quoining, punctuated by iron
gates, encloses a traditional English border garden. Gravel
walks, narrow strips of grass, and generous beds of perennials
are situated in perfect proportion. In the spring, 2,000 bulbs
come alive in curvaceous ribbons of color. A water lily pond sits
at one end, sheltered by an ornate blue pergola. Under the central pavilion, a marble statue stares wistfully over the scene. Old
Westbury provides a tutorial in the art of spatial transition. We
exit the Walled Garden by way of an overly-narrow romantic
path that descends to a lovely sunken rose garden.

*A cottage garden relaxes the
atmosphere.*

A great lawn frames the rear face of the house with harmo-
nious symmetry. An allée of linden and yew hedge extends the
strong axis of this space into the landscape, whereas at the
other end, the wall of the rear terrace forms an architectural
backdrop for a gathering of helical topiaries. The obvious formal thrust of this garden is tempered by the presence of a
dense forest just beyond the boundaries of the outer linden, a
mixture that is echoed in the Boxwood Garden nearby. Two-
hundred-year-old English boxwood, imported from Virginia in
1928 when they were already 125 years old, frame a rectangular
lawn. A small central reflecting pool, adorned with a bronze
nymph, and a colonnade covered with climbing roses complete
the Italianate scheme. However, the boxwoods are pruned in
Southern fashion—in undulating, irregular clumps, which
gives the area a warm, informal feeling. The eclectic nature of
the garden continues down a woodland path that takes us deep
into the forest where the Temple of Love lies hidden just
beyond a lake. Six scrolled columns support a delicate dome of
iron filigree. Although no effigies of Venus are visible, a semicircular bench is romantically oriented toward the naturalistic
lake surrounded by beech, birch, and sycamore. From here, or

anywhere within the garden, one is treated to an exquisitely tasteful experience. Its as if one spiraled backwards through time to a warm summer evening only to be surprised on the path by a Gatsby or some other bon vivant, and in the distance a band plays, glasses clink, and the conversation is eternally interesting.

GARDEN OPEN: 11am–5pm Tuesday–Sunday.

ADMISSION: $4 adults, $3 seniors, $2 children.

FURTHER INFORMATION FROM: 1 Museum Drive, Roslyn Harbor 11576. (516) 484-9338

NEARBY SIGHTS OF INTEREST: Castlegould, Falise, and Hempstead House

Allen Bertoldi's Wood Duck *(1979) sits enigmatically above an autumn pond.*

11 Roslyn Harbor: Nassau County Museum of Art and Sculpture Garden

LOCATION: NORTHERN BOULEVARD (ROUTE 25A), EXIT 39 OFF THE LONG ISLAND EXPRESSWAY (INTERSTATE 495), FIFTEEN MILES EAST OF NEW YORK CITY

When the poet and newspaper editor William Cullen Bryant first moved out to the gold coast of Long Island, in 1843, he purchased a little farm on Roslyn Harbor to build a Gothic Revival cottage designed by Calvert Vaux. At the end of the century, this was replaced by a Georgian manor designed by Ogden Codman Jr. The house finally fell into the hands of Childs Frick, heir to the Frick steel empire and a paleontologist who made several adjustments to the landscape, including the construction of two ponds and the planting of a pinetum that once contained over 400 species of rare and exotic conifers. Frick's wife, Frances, employed the landscape architect Marian Coffin, known best for her work with Henry du Pont at Winterthur, to design a formal garden. A hedge of privet and trellised roses encloses the garden, which is cut by central and transverse axes into quadrants, each of which is lined with hedge and accessed through a narrow passage. After passing around a central pool, the main axis culminates in a teak trellis designed as a classical dome. The garden and landscape are now employed as backdrop for the Nassau County Art Museum's significant collection of sculpture, which includes works by Alexander Calder, Roy Lichtenstein, and Auguste Rodin, as well as Barnett Newman, Tony Smith, and multiple works of Allen Bertoldi. For many of these pieces, landscape seems to be a natural component, such as Bertoldi's *Red Bank 31*, a series of square partitions that walk across an empty lawn toward one of Frick's ponds; or Richard Serra's *Equal Elevations-Plumb Run*, that stands apart from the surrounding forest as if abandoned to its own self-contemplation. Elsewhere, groves and enclosures of foliage echo different sentiments: Reuben Nakian's *Moonlight Goddess*, a gnarled, sensual form, is embraced by a grove of maple and other woodland plants. Coffin's formal garden, an impressive space in itself, now hosts works by Xavier Corbero and Chaim Cross, among others.

12 Roslyn Harbor: Cedarmere

LOCATION: BRYANT AVENUE, EXIT 39 OFF THE LONG ISLAND EXPRESSWAY
(INTERSTATE 495), 20 MILES EAST OF NEW YORK CITY

William Cullen Bryant spent much of his life trying to get out of New York City, purchasing several homes on Long Island before finally retiring to Massachusetts. Cedarmere was his second residence in Roslyn and the house in which he spent a large part of his life. A relentless promoter of city parks (his editorials in the *Evening Post* influenced the creation of Central Park), Bryant designed the gardens and landscape at Cedarmere himself. Today, they have been carefully restored according to his plant journals and several historic photographs. An engaging geometric composition provides the outline for the main garden. Constructed in boxwood parterres, four rectangular beds surround a conjunction of circles and triangles. The lawn-filled square provides a solid frame for the flowerbeds containing Bryant's selection of perennials and annuals, among which are found heirloom roses, hollyhocks, and foxgloves. Curiously, late bloomers are predominant, a preoccupation with Bryant. Tripods occupy some of the beds, providing structure not only for sweet peas and trumpet vine (*Campsis grandiflora*) but also for the eye of the beholder. Across the lawn is the second formal garden, designed in 1916 by Bryant's grandson, Harold Godwin, an artist by trade. A round of masonry walls forms the edge of this sunken garden, situated several feet below grade. At the surface the wall is planted around with a thin border of violas and pansies. However, the garden proper has always remained a finely manicured lawn, a refreshingly original idea that seems ever more thought-provoking at a time when gardens are increasingly being redefined as exercises in flower arrangement. At one end of the space lies a masonry fountain, and at the other a bronze bas relief of Bryant sculpted by Godwin himself—elements that both frame the space and seem to expand it. Like the main garden, this garden has also recently been restored using photographs dating to 1920. Although sparse to the modern eye, the gardens and landscape at Cedarmere exert a powerful hold on the mind. Indeed, they physically manifest the "sense of beauty, the grateful perception of harmony, of color, and of grace, and fair proportion of shape" which Bryant wrote would cause the garden to "enter the mind and wean it from grosser and more sensual tastes."

GARDEN OPEN: 10:00am–4:45pm Saturday and holidays; 1:00pm–4:45pm Sunday, May–November.
ADMISSION: free.

FURTHER INFORMATION FROM:
225 Bryant Avenue, Roslyn Harbor 11576

NEARBY SIGHTS OF INTEREST:
Museum of Science, Castlegould, Humes Japanese Stroll Garden

Bryant's idyll at Cedarmere

13 Mill Neck: Humes Japanese Stroll Garden

LOCATION: CHICKEN VALLEY ROAD, AT EXIT **39** OFF THE LONG ISLAND EXPRESSWAY, TWENTY MILES EAST OF NEW YORK

GARDEN OPEN: 11:30am–4:30pm Saturday and Sunday, April 25–October 18.

ADMISSION: $5. Call for periodic tours of the garden and interpretation of the tea ceremony.

FURTHER INFORMATION FROM: P.O. Box 671, Locust Valley 11560. (516) 676-4486

NEARBY SIGHTS OF INTEREST: Museum of Science, Castlegould, Cedarmere

Vistas and views create a narrative experience.

Ambassador John P. Humes and his wife constructed this garden in 1960 after returning from Japan. The original design was created by noted Japanese landscape designers Douglas and Joan de Faya; however, today the garden is managed by Stephen Morrell, who has made his own alterations. The central idea of the garden is a narrative experience. The stroll is a carefully arranged walk along stepping stones set into a gravel path. Subtle twists and turns focus views on certain objects in the landscape, both architectural and natural, and often along diagonals off the main movement of the path—a common element in traditional Japanese garden design. The composition of the garden is derived from gardens constructed in Kyoto during the Edo period (1603–1867); however, a major component of those gardens is a response to existing topography and climatic conditions. So here, the plant composition includes rhododendrons, snowbells, red oak, American beech, and other Long Island natives that don't seem Japanese at all. A few Japanese maples, stewartia, gingko trees, kousa dogwoods, and other hardy Asiatic species are also included, and combined

with a bamboo grove give the garden an authentic feel. Architectural ornamentation has been placed throughout the landscape to capture the eye's attention. A teahouse provides the most visible object, while several types of stone lanterns and climbing arbors also make appearances. Unlike a traditional European garden, where the message (if there is one at all) is communicated structurally, the Japanese stroll garden contains a highly developed system of individual symbols, such as the tortoise, created by a moss mound set within a pond with stones set about for its feet, head, and tail. Farther along lies an arrangement of three stones representing heaven, man, and earth. Water symbolism pervades the rest of the garden as well. The paths represent rivers, stone edging the coastline, a pond the sea. But even if the narrative remains ineffable, the garden's main purpose, to provide a place of beauty and solitude where one might embark on a walking meditation, remains inescapable.

14 Sagaponack: Madoo Conservancy

LOCATION: SAG MAIN STREET, OFF ROUTE 27, EIGHT MILES EAST OF
SOUTHAMPTON, LONG ISLAND

Madoo Conservancy, derived from a Scottish word meaning
"my dove," exudes a similar kind of familial love and affection.
As well it should. It is the construction of one man, Robert
Dash, an artist who moved here in the late 1960s. Under his
tutelage, the gardens have evolved into an eclectic admixture of
plantings and sculptural elements, often shockingly painted. A
formal vocabulary has been twisted and turned by Dash to curious effect. An allée of laburnum, a blueberry garden interpenetrated with roses, topiary privet, and a chinoiserie bridge are all
assembled together in a hodgepodge that, far from disconcert-
ing, draws the visitor into a world apart. The unifying elements
are Dash's plantings, which tend toward the impressionistic
but indicate a deep understanding of texture and form; extravagant color serves as a secondary element. Views often focus on
elements within the garden, a technique that serves to heighten
the eclectic contrasts and anchor the visitor in the immediate
experience. For instance, from the bright purple gazebo, one
looks down on a grove of fastigiated gingkos and boxwood, an
unusual combination that the Conservancy literature likens to
"boules or hedgehogs." A map takes visitors through, but often
the amiable artist is in the garden on sunny days and ready to
answer questions and provide pointers.

GARDEN OPEN: 1pm–5pm
Wednesday and Saturday,
May–September.
ADMISSION: $10.

FURTHER INFORMATION FROM:
618 Sag Main Street,
Sagaponack. (516) 537-8200

NEARBY SIGHTS OF INTEREST:
De Salvo Museum,
Montauk Lighthouse

ABOVE: *Robert Dash's*
new canvas: the gardens
at Madoo

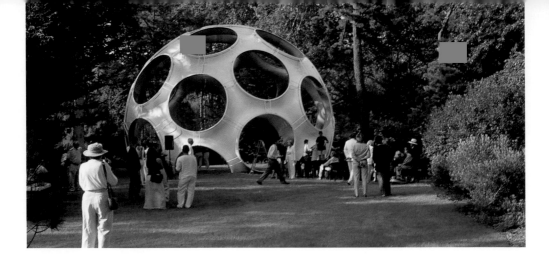

GARDEN OPEN: 2pm–5pm
Wednesday and the first and
third Saturday of the month,
April 25–September 12.
ADMISSION: $10 for gallery
and garden.

FURTHER INFORMATION FROM:
133 Hands Creek Road, East
Hampton. (516) 329-3568

NEARBY SIGHTS OF INTEREST:
Montauk Lighthouse,
De Salvo Museum

15 East Hampton: Long House Reserve

LOCATION: TAKE STEPHEN HANDS PATH OFF THE MONTAUK
HIGHWAY (ROUTE 27) TO HANDS CREEK ROAD, THREE MILES
NORTH OF EAST HAMPTON TOWN CENTER

A flood of immigrants (mainly wealthy Manhattanites) to the eastern tip of Long Island over the last decade threatens some of the best landscape in the region. Except for those in parts of southern New Jersey, the rare pine barrens here are all we've got. Bucking the slash-and-burn trend is textile artist Jack Lenor Larsen, who moved out to East Hampton in 1975 and constructed a beautiful, eco-friendly house designed by architect Charles Forberg. Larsen promptly set about designing his 16-acre property as a rolling series of garden rooms that showcase sculptures by Dale Chihuly, Grace Knowlton, and others (including even a *Diana* by Augustus Saint-Gaudens). In 1992 Larsen created the Long House Foundation, converted his home into a gallery, and opened the gardens to the public. The entrance drive lined with the delicate foliage of cryptomerias sets the stage. Manicured lawns wrap around groves of trees and shrubs in an informal, irregular manner to impart mystery to the landscape—a motif brought to its fullest expression in the Secret Garden. Ornamental grasses, perennials, even stands of bamboo are planted in woven strands that seem to translate Larsen's milieu into landscape. Often the plant material serves to frame major spaces for artwork, but just as often they act as works of art in themselves. A canopy of second-growth trees arches over much of the property, a residual blessing from history. Larsen's enthusiasm for cultural preservation is also exemplified by the long berms that cut through the site. They are reminiscent of the boundaries of the farms that once thrived in this area, but in their serpentine meanderings and modern boldness, they evince less traditional ideas and embody what Larsen calls "a considered lifestyle at the end of the millennium." The gallery exhibits the work of leading textile crafters and sponsors periodic art and gardening events.

ABOVE: *Buckminster Fuller's Fly's Eye Dome will be on view until September 2001.*

16 Tarrytown: Lyndhurst

LOCATION: BROADWAY (ROUTE 9), HALF-MILE SOUTH OF INTERSTATE 87 AND
THE TAPPAN ZEE BRIDGE

The "bones" of Lyndhurst were constructed in 1838, when
former New York City Mayor William Paulding engaged
the architect Andrew Jackson Davis to construct a Gothic
Revival mansion on this tract of Hudson River farmland. A
friend and, in landscape affairs, a protégé of landscape architect
Andrew Jackson Downing, Davis also set about sculpting the
landscape to incorporate Downing's ideas of the beautiful—
nestled lawns and soft copses of trees—and the picturesque—
rocky crags, large vistas, and other natural irregularities. This
concept was refined after the Civil War, when Lyndhurst's new
owner, railcar entrepreneur George Merritt hired Ferdinand
Mangold, a German horticulturist. Mangold infused into this
American landscape the "gardenesque" aesthetic of English
writer J. C. Loudon, which advocated a more artistic placement
of trees within the parklike setting to create specific areas of
interest, rather than a single experience of the landscape. Many
of Mangold's ideas were carried out by Lyndhurst's next and
final owners, financier Jay Gould and his children. Today the
landscape contains an impressively diverse selection of trees,
arranged in some places to frame views and impart atmosphere, and in others, as botanical specimens themselves.
Behind the mansion, a garden path leads to the Rockery, original to the era of Mangold, where wooden garden seats situated
in a forest setting, with views of dark conifers and harsh geological formations, provide an excellent example of a compro-
mise hatched between Downing's picturesque and Loudon's
gardenesque. Two of the most magnificent greenhouses in the
Hudson River valley once stood on the northern edge of the
property. The first, built around 1870, burned to the ground.
The second, constructed on the same foundation, contained
fourteen different rooms of orchids, camellias, and other
exotics that were the passion of Gould. Unfortunately, the
greenhouse remains a shell of its former self, most of its glass
missing, like a haunted ruin in the landscape
waiting for a restoration that should progress
well into 2000. Adjacent to the greenhouse,
however, is the most lovingly restored rose garden, originally planted by Gould's oldest
daughter, Helen, in 1911. The garden now contains a selection of old roses and modern
hybrids, arranged in concentric, arbor-dotted
circles around a central gazebo. Although not
original to the estate, this modern addition
extends the general unfettered romantic feel of
the entire property.

GARDEN OPEN: 10am–5pm
Tuesday–Sunday, mid
April–October. Closes at 4pm
in the winter. ADMISSION: $9
adults, $8 seniors, $3 children
(a 45-minute house tour is
included).

FURTHER INFORMATION FROM:
635 South Broadway
Tarrytown 10591.
(914) 631-4481

NEARBY SIGHTS OF INTEREST:
Sleepy Hollow

*Romantic inspiration in the
Helen Gould rose garden*

17 Tarrytown: Kykuit

LOCATION: TOURS BEGIN AT PHILIPSBURG MANOR, ROUTE 9, TARRYTOWN, THIRTY MILES NORTH OF NEW YORK CITY, NEAR THE TAPPAN ZEE BRIDGE

GARDEN OPEN: 10am–4pm Wednesday–Monday, May–November. **ADMISSION:** $18 garden; $18 house.

FURTHER INFORMATION FROM: 150 White Plains Road, Tarrytown 10591. (914) 631-0089 www.hudsonvalley.org/ kykuit.htm

NEARBY SIGHTS OF INTEREST: Philipsburg Manor, Van Cortlandt Manor

The Rockefeller legacy is resplendent at Kykuit, the family's palatial estate that seems to hover over the Hudson River from its lofty perch. John D. Rockefeller Jr., the scion of industrialist John D. Rockefeller and father of Nelson Rockefeller (governor of New York from 1958 to 1974), built the mansion in 1913. All three generations lived here, as well as numerous children and grandchildren, until 1979 when the mansion, gardens, and outlying buildings that comprised the "family park" were entrusted to the National Trust for Historic Preservation. The original landscape was designed by William Welles Bosworth, a protégé of Frederick Law Olmsted, who translated Junior's nineteenth-century tastes into a series of Beaux-Arts gardens that highlight the Italianate and English formal roots of that style. What the gardens lack in size, they make up for in painstaking detail. In the Inner Garden, on the south side of the house, fountains, pools, pathways, and a sculptural allée of lindens artfully frame delicate lawns. Although the space is attractive in itself the intricate ornamentation of the marble fountains and the bronze sculptural accents fashioned by New York craftsman F. M. L. Tonetti beg a closer examination. On the northern end of the house Bosworth designed a romantic Rose Garden ringed with pink rhododendrons in an axial layout. A colonnaded pergola nearest the house covers an intricately tiled terrace, crafted by the Mercer family in Doylestown, Pennsylvania. True to his training, Bosworth focused much effort on fashioning the landscape, which flows down the hill in a pleasing assortment of venerable trees and rolling lawn, like a cloak. From the western terraces, views of the Hudson River are carefully framed and give the estate its name, which means "lookout" in Dutch. Abundant wisteria, which gives the house an organic, fluttering feel, ties the architecture to the landscape in a manner that accentuates the gardens' role as an extension of the interior space.

In the 1940s Nelson Rockefeller transformed the estate into his personal art museum, filling the basements of the house with paintings by Picasso, Lautrec, and Leger, and littered the gardens with over seventy works of modern sculpture. (Much of his collection was used to build the Museum of Modern Art in New

Kykuit, the Rockefeller estate stretches along the Hudson River's east bank.

York City.) Rockefeller continually moved sculptures around, often with the aid of a helicopter, in an evolving obsession with achieving the perfect placement for the work. In many cases he showed hints of genius, such as with *Triangular Surface in Space* by Max Bill, which fills the oculus at one end of the pergola on the north side of the house. The careful framing translates the work into a new mode. Several other gardens ring the house, including a Japanese garden and the naturalistic Brook Garden, all of which are only accessible via a carefully controlled two-hour tour of the grounds.

18 Garrison: Boscobel Restoration

LOCATION: ROUTE 9D, ONE MILE SOUTH OF COLD SPRING

Boscobel was the home of States Dyckman, a wealthy Tory who returned to the United States after the Revolutionary War to settle in the Hudson River Valley, where he held over 1,000 acres. The house was originally constructed on a lot nearby, but when the property was bought by the government in the 1940s and the house threatened with destruction, Lila Wallace of Reader's Digest fame purchased the historic house, had it taken apart in sections, and reassembled in its current location overlooking the Hudson River and West Point. The landscape was designed in the classic Beaux-Arts style, with such highly accentuated features as the long, formal entry drive and the enclosed courtyard, by the firm of Innocenti and Webel. Their design provides both a strong complement and a strong contrast to the house and its rare collection of furnishings, which are both Federal era, and subtly beseeches the visitor to consider the permutations in American wealth over the intervening century and a half. The formal rose garden follows a strict geometric composition, but is arranged in a highly original manner. Although divided into quadrants, the roses are planted around the edge as a border rather than focused within the center. The interior beds each contain a large weeping cherry tree, which segregates each quadrant into hybrid teas and grandiflora roses, delineated by candytuft (*Iberis*). A fountain and pool, rimmed by boxwood, occupies the center of the garden. In a small nook nearby sits a compact colonial orangerie and herb garden lined with an overabundance of tulips that explode in a vibrant display of yellows and reds, in striking contrast with the yellow structure. On the other side of the house, a great lawn balances the rest of the landscape and provides a palette upon which to consume the excellent panoramic views of the New York highlands across the river. A path leads to a belvedere at the edge, pulling the eye, and hopefully the body, further.

GARDEN OPEN: 9:30am–5:00pm Wednesday–Monday, April–November. Closes at 4pm during March, November, and December. Closed January and February. ADMISSION: $7 adults, $6 seniors, $4 children.

FURTHER INFORMATION FROM: Garrison-on-Hudson 10524. (914) 265-3638

NEARBY SIGHTS OF INTEREST: U.S. Military Academy at West Point

A vibrant spectrum enshrouds the orangerie and herb garden.

GARDEN OPEN: 10am–4pm
Tuesday, Wednesday, Friday,
and the first Saturday of the
month, mid April–mid
October. **ADMISSION:** $5.

FURTHER INFORMATION FROM:
RR 2, Box 371, Cold Spring
10516. (914) 265-2000

NEARBY SIGHTS OF INTEREST:
West Point Military Academy,
Washington's Headquarters

19 Cold Spring: Stonecrop Gardens

LOCATION: OFF ROUTE 301, BETWEEN ROUTE 9 AND TACONIC PARKWAY, ABOUT FIFTY MILES NORTH OF MANHATTAN

Frank and Anne Cabot began cultivating their gardens on this exposed hill in 1959, and so far the Hudson River Valley wind hasn't blown them away. Next to the country house are two very different formal gardens. The first is an English border garden enclosed by a cedar fence covered on one side with espaliered apples and pears and on the other, with clematis. The beds are planted with a variety of perennials that change every year but are regularly arranged in rectangular beds transected by two major axes, one of which leads to a fountain at the far end of the garden, the other of which deadends against the wall of espaliered fruit in a lovely arbor seat. Although the construction of the space follows a strict and discernible geometry, details such as this seat gives the space a reassuring, human scale. From this room, a lawn path proceeds through a small shade garden containing several distinctive trees, such as a paper birch and shad bush (*Amelanchier canadensis*), to the Enclosed Garden, the second formal space. The beds are designed in the form of a lattice carpet, mimicking the original fence that once surrounded them. Vegetables, flowers, and fruit are planted in an overflowing manner, much like the traditional English kitchen gardens that inspired Gertrude Jekyll. Imaginative combinations of color and form offer continual interest throughout the summer. For instance, trellis structures raise golden hops high above a patch of annuals, whereas in another part of the garden, a "cat's cradle" of espaliered little-leafed lindens creates a natural arbor over a path. The estate becomes increasingly naturalistic beyond the walls of the formal gardens. A stream, hostas, and the canopy of a single white oak combine to create a bucolic hillside garden. A wisteria pavilion, an informal lake, and a grove of awesome metasequoia provide different "rooms" farther down the hill. Stonecrop has ambitions to become a major horticultural center, providing public education along the model of Longwood Gardens and other public botanical gardens. As a start the many greenhouses, cold frames, and compost pits generate most of the organic materials on-site.

Stone ledge at Stonecrop

20 Poughkeepsie: Locust Grove and Springside

LOCATION: ROUTE 9, 11 MILES NORTH OF INTERSTATE 84

After Thomas Jefferson, Andrew Jackson Downing is considered the father of American landscape architecture. His writings on "landscape gardening" affected an entire generation of designers and rural landowners, and had a major formative impact on Central Park and the parks movement of the 1870s. Downing was so revered that President Millard Fillmore commissioned a plan, for the public grounds in Washington, D.C., in 1852. But his work on that project was cut short when the steamer *Henry Clay,* on which he was traveling down to New York City, caught fire and sank in the Hudson River. Although wildly influential and a prolific writer, there are few extant landscapes attributable to Downing. Springside is one. Downing designed this small estate for Poughkeepsie businessman Matthew Vassar, founder of the college that bears his name. Like most historic gardens, it was lost to the ravages of time and barely escaped total destruction. Condominiums have encroached on most of the property (Vassar's house is long gone), but there are still some interesting features to be seen: most particularly, the curving roads that cut through the site, which were borrowed from Mount Auburn cemetery in Boston. Connected to Springside by a greenbelt of woods is Locust Grove, the estate of painter and inventor Samuel F. B. Morse. In addition to his many other talents, Morse had an eye for landscape architecture and fashioned the grounds surrounding his house (which he designed in conjunction with Andrew Jackson Davis) in a manner that calls to mind many of Downing's aesthetic prescriptives, including the dominant placement of the house, plantings that frame and accentuate the picturesque views, and cozy woodland spaces within the landscape. Proximate to the house is a flower garden planted by a later owner, which is being expanded to include a vegetable garden indicative of the Morse period in the late-nineteenth century. Lilacs, roses, and other shrubbery plantings fill out the floral display at present, although there are plans to commence a restoration project that would return the bedded-out annuals and formal lawns that once adorned the property.

LOCUST GROVE GARDEN OPEN: dawn–dusk, weather permitting. HOUSE OPEN: 10am–4pm daily, May–October; by appointment, November, December, March, and April. SPRINGSIDE OPEN: when the local preservation group is working in the garden, usually Saturday. ADMISSION: free.

FURTHER INFORMATION FROM: 370 South Road Poughkeepsie 12601-5234. (914) 454-4500

NEARBY SIGHTS OF INTEREST: Washington's Headquarters, Clinton House

A central walk and lilac hedge connect several contrasting gardens.

Hyde Park: Vanderbilt Estate Italian Gardens

LOCATION: ROUTE 9, TEN MILES NORTH OF POUGHKEEPSIE

GARDEN OPEN: 9am–dusk daily. Admission: free. **HOUSE OPEN:** 9am–4pm daily. **ADMISSION:** $8 adults.

FURTHER INFORMATION FROM: P.O. Box 239, Hyde Park 12538-0239. (914) 229-6432 www.highlands.com/Vanderbilt

NEARBY SIGHTS OF INTEREST: Franklin D. Roosevelt Home, Eleanor Roosevelt Historic Site

"Barefoot Kate" considers a dip in the reflecting pool.

When Frederick Vanderbilt (grandson of Cornelius) purchased this estate on the hills overlooking the Hudson River, the grounds and gardens had already seen several designers come and go—including Belgian landscape architect André Parmentier, who fashioned the naturalistic entrance in the eighteenth century. The formal gardens, located in a woodland grove some distance from the house, however, retain the imprint of Vanderbilt, who held a horticulture degree from Yale University. Vanderbilt hired James Greenleaf of New York City and Thomas Meehan and Sons of Philadelphia to design the underlying structure of the gardens, but he himself was active in their continual evolution until his death in 1938. Today the gardens are experiencing a lengthy, oftentimes slow, restoration; although there is still much to be seen here. A tour begins in the annual gardens, which are bedded out in Italianate flourishes. The upper garden follows a geometric scheme of large ovals penetrated by curvilinear paths, while the lower garden exhibits a mélange of intricate shapes—crescents, hearts, and the like—all bubbling forth with white petunias, yellow marigolds, blue salvia, and other bold annuals. An esplanade of cherry trees leads to the walled perennial garden. Two long borders containing peonies, irises, and other old-fashioned varieties complement the handsome architecture of the wall. At the far end the space opens up into a reflecting pool planted with water lilies and overlooked by a bronze statue of a girl, nicknamed "barefoot Kate." Several freestanding columns were intended to provide architectural formality; however, in their contemporary and softened revival, they provide support for climbing Concord grape and bittersweet, which, combined with the hosta bed below the rim of the pool, imparts an informal sensuality more resonant of American tastes than Italian tradition. The path continues beyond this area, along a trellis, and into the rose garden, which has yet to be restored.

22 New Paltz: Mohonk Mountain House Gardens

LOCATION: MOUNTAIN REST ROAD, TWELVE MILES WEST OF POUGHKEEPSIE

In the nineteenth century, some of the world's greatest artists traveled to the mountains of the Hudson River Valley to imbibe the sublime landscape. Today, the imagery of Frederick E. Church, Thomas Cole, and many of the Hudson River school painters can still be found on the Shawangunk glacial ridge at the foothills of the Catskill Mountains. Here, the Mohonk Mountain House, a 129-year-old hunting lodge, offers a truly rustic experience of the Hudson valley. The enormous house, now operating as a hotel and spa, measures one-eighth of a mile long, in scale with the monumental vistas of the mountains and nearby glacial lake. The landscape is carefully sculpted by drives and punctuated by an intriguing juxtaposition of trees in the picturesque style of Andrew Jackson Downing, whose writings were being circulated at the time of the Mountain House construction. Some 35 acres of turf lawns and 150 garden structures create an inimitable experience that can literally consume an entire day of walking and observing. Not surprisingly, bird watching is a major activity at Mohonk. Near the house there are several formal gardens, the pinnacle of which is the Show Garden, a three-and-a-half-acre rectangular display garden of annuals and perennials which changes every year. There are 78 different flower beds planted thematically in solid masses of colors. An herb garden containing plants used in industry and medicine extends the botanical education. In recent years, the horticultural focus at Mohonk has been on introducing organic pest management practices into the landscape. Partly, this is just responsible horticulture. But there is also a focus on creating a rich floral and faunal environment—something pesticides don't encourage—evidenced by an emergent bluebird population on the property. A complex of greenhouses supplies the interior spaces daily with fresh-cut flowers, bringing the garden inside, which in turn bring people out.

GARDEN OPEN: dawn–dusk daily. ADMISSION: free.

FURTHER INFORMATION FROM: 100 Mountain Road, New Paltz 12561. (914) 255-1000

NEARBY SIGHTS OF INTEREST: Delaware and Hudson Canal Museum, Franklin D. Roosevelt Home

ABOVE: *Catskill architecture enmeshed with tapestries of color*

23 Millbrook: Innisfree Garden

LOCATION: TYRREL ROAD, OFF ROUTE 44, FIVE MILES EAST OF
THE TACONIC PARKWAY

GARDEN OPEN: 10am–4pm
Wednesday–Friday;
11am–5pm Saturday and
Sunday. **ADMISSION:** $3.

FURTHER INFORMATION FROM:
RR 2 Box 38A, Millbrook
12545. (914) 677-8000

NEARBY SIGHTS OF INTEREST:
Trevor Zoo, Eleanor Roosevelt
National Historic Site

While the du Ponts, the Vanderbilts, and other American barons were reworking the garden traditions of Europe on their palatial estates, Walter and Marion Beck were interpreting Chinese garden design in their rural Dutchess County valley. Innisfree was inspired by the scroll paintings of eighth-century artist and garden designer Wang Wei, which Beck unearthed in a London library in the 1930s. An artist, Beck switched milieus when he married Marion, a wealthy heiress to a Minnesota iron fortune. Central to Beck's interpretation of Chinese gardens was the idea of enclosed space—or "cupped" space. In his garden he experimented with framing features—typically unusual rock formations—with the surrounding landscape. However, unlike the ubiquitous nineteenth-century idea of a framed vista, Beck worked with three-dimensional, sculptural space that could be viewed from many different angles and perspectives. After Beck's death in 1954, Lester Collins, Chair of the Landscape Architecture department at Harvard University, took over management of the garden with an eye to opening it to the public. In order to effect this transition, Collins expanded Beck's vision beyond individual scenes or nodes to encompass the entire landscape, which is, in fact, one large cup. The lake that dominates the center forms the bottom of the cup, and the verdant meadows and woodlands that climb up the gentle slopes of the adjoining hills comprise the sides. A single path takes you through the garden, past many of Beck's constructions, as well as those fashioned by Collins. There is the striking trio of lichen-covered rocks—the Dragon, the Turtle, and the Owl—that sit poised in a frozen ballet of horizontal (yin) and vertical (yang) thrusts. The artful placement of a stone border and pine trees captures the scene as if in mid-dance. Throughout Innisfree these living images are presented beautifully, requiring extensive time and attention to catch them all.

*An oxbow "cup" cradles
the landscape.*

The experience is organized as one long stroll around the lake that passes by each individual work. The walk is magical, imparting a peacefulness reminiscent of Yeats's own description of Lake Isle Innisfree: "There midnight's all a glimmer, and noon a purple glow."

24 Millbrook: Institute of Ecosystem Studies

LOCATION: ROUTE 44 TO ROUTE 44A, FIFTEEN MILES EAST OF POUGHKEEPSIE

For gardeners in New York and New England, deer have replaced ground hogs as the number one offender. Each year, a booming—and therefore hungry—deer population ravenous for such delectables as arborvitae attacks homes across the suburban and rural stretches of the region. At the Institute of Ecosystem Studies the problem has become so profound that scientists have developed an entire test garden for deer-resistant plant species. The Institute was founded in 1983 by the New York Botanical Garden, but broke off to become its own entity in 1993. Although oriented to scientific research, the Institute has a strong public education mission and a wonderful selection of gardens. The 1817 brick manor that houses the visitor's center was originally the Herman Gifford residence and sat above a sunken garden. This area has been transformed into display gardens of perennials and several specialty gardens. The three perennial beds are divided into shade-loving, sun-loving, and hardy, low-maintenance perennials. A butterfly garden is planted with high-nectar flowers, such as coreopsis, hollyhock, and coneflower, arranged around a birdbath, which provides necessary water. Nearby, a hummingbird garden is designed with plants that exhibit a long, tubular flower, such as petunias and delphiniums, arranged around quince and rose of Sharon. A raised octagon of annuals resides in the center of the garden, giving a strong and colorful body to the layout. An arbor hosts all five varieties of clematis and connects the display gardens to the deer demonstration garden. Much to the horror of suburban homeowners, the garden is left open for deer browsing, and each year the Institute publishes a report of which plants are more resistant to deer than others. So far, volatile oils in such woody shrubs as barberry and compact juniper have proven distasteful to Bambi and her cohorts. Surrounding the Institute are informal, oblong beds containing several notable collections. The Howard Taylor Lilac Collection presents over sixty varieties of French lilacs that form a frame against which a display of the twelve divisions of daffodils are set. Hostas frame the Gifford house, while at the end of the perennial garden sits a rose garden that has been divided into chemically treated and organically grown roses, in order to assess the viability of a postmodern rose that can be grown without fertilizers and still remain beautiful. The Institute's gardens give way to the Mary Cary Flagler Arboretum, a 2,000-acre preserve of winding trails.

GARDEN OPEN: 9am–6pm Monday–Saturday; 1pm–6pm Sunday, May–September; 9am–4pm Monday–Saturday; 1pm–4pm Sunday, October–April. ADMISSION: free.

FURTHER INFORMATION FROM: Box AB, Millbrook 12545-0129. (914) 677-5343

NEARBY SIGHTS OF INTEREST: Eleanor Roosevelt National Historic Site, Trevor Zoo

A water-conserving landscape teaches as it beautifies.

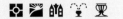

Amenia: Wethersfield

LOCATION: PUGSLEY HILL ROAD, OFF ROUTE 44, THIRTY MILES
NORTHEAST OF POUGHKEEPSIE

GARDEN OPEN: noon–5pm
Wednesday, Friday, and
Saturday, June–September.
ADMISSION: free.
Reservations required for
house tours.

FURTHER INFORMATION FROM:
RR#1, Box 440, Amenia
12501. (914) 373-8037

NEARBY SIGHTS OF INTEREST:
Gay-Hoyt House

Late-twentieth-century estates are rarely viewed by the public
for the simple fact that most of them are still residential.
Financier Chauncey Stillman's home of Wethersfield, in the
rolling valleys of Dutchess County, presents a splendid example of postwar neo-classical landscape design. Beginning in
1947, Stillman hired landscape architect Evelyn Poehler to
design a series of formal garden rooms that would eventually
cover ten acres around his house. In most areas the landscape
serves as a dramatic backdrop to Stillman's collection of statuary and architectural artifacts. But in others the clipped hedges,
layers of flowering deciduous shrubs, and picturesque vistas
exist of and for themselves. The garden rooms are laid out
either along a strict east-west or north-south axis. Nearest the
house is the keyhole-shaped Inner Garden, ringed by a perennial bed containing hosta, phlox, lady's mantle, and peonies.
Two marble putti stand watch at the iron gates, while at the far
end, a quiet pool situated beneath a grape arbor provides
Rondo, a redstone figure by sculptor John Flannagan, with
reflective silence. Trickery and enchantment were themes of
seventeenth-century Italian gardens, and they make an appearance throughout Wethersfield in playful statues, such as the
pan pipers gracing the arborvitae arch, and in unusual plant
formations, such as the tunnel of beech and intricate knot garden. A generous allée of arborvitae—190 feet long—ends in an
ellipse that encloses a still, granite pool and *Naiad* by Swedish
sculptor Carl Miles. A woodland walk beautifully frames a
belvedere perched at the edge of the gardens. From here there
are excellent views of the far-off Catskills (to the northwest)
and the Berkshires (to the northeast). The six-columned temple
was designed by Stillman himself. The edge of the woodland,
which gives way to rolling, open farmland was planted with
hawthorn, lilac, and other northeastern woodland ornamentals
by Poehler in order to provide a transition from the formal
landscape to the natural one. Stillman's Georgian house contains paintings by Mary Cassatt and John Singer Sargent and a
notable collection of antique furniture. The carriage house,
which is only open by appointment, contains antique carriages
from the nineteenth century.

26 Annandale-on-Hudson: Montgomery Place

LOCATION: ROUTE 9, TWENTY-FIVE MILES NORTH OF POUGHKEEPSIE

GARDEN OPEN: daily, year-round.

FURTHER INFORMATION FROM: P.O. Box 32, Annandale-on-Hudson 13504. (914) 758-5461

NEARBY SIGHTS OF INTEREST: Old Rhinebeck Aerodome, Mills Mansion

The landscape tradition goes back to 1804 at Montgomery Place when Janet Livingston Montgomery first resculpted the west meadow, which looks out over the Hudson River. Thirty years later, Mrs. Montgomery's descendants began in earnest one of the most celebrated landscape architecture projects of its time. The meadows were planted as great rolling lawns, vistas were framed and enhanced by specimen trees, and a romantic forest was thinned and managed to provide a place of respite and enjoyment. The architect Andrew Jackson Davis was hired to expand the mansion, while Andrew Jackson Downing came on board to oversee the design of the landscape. The original bones of this design still exist in several places, most evidently in the juxtaposition between the large-scale vistas and the romantically enclosed woods. Downing was also hired to complete some gardenesque features around the mansion, but what exists today reflects later generations' floral tastes. Beneath the vista, on the underside of the balustraded retaining wall, exists a spring- and fall-blooming flower border planted by Violetta White Delafield, matron of Montgomery Place in the 1920s. Working from a handwritten plan found in Mrs. Delafield's papers, gardeners have executed a modern re-creation. The garden follows a narrow, semicrescent movement that slightly tapers at each end and is fashioned in distinct layers of massed perennials. Although spectacular in the spring, the garden also includes chrysanthemums and other fall-blooming plants. Down a drive

The garden path cuts through a historic landscape.

alongside the great meadow, a path leads into the romantic woodland. Here Mrs. Delafield planted a naturalistic garden over a wooded ravine. In the 1920s the garden contained an abundance of flowers, however, today the terraces crafted from fieldstone and the bucolic stream provide the context for a display of ferns and other shade-tolerant plants owing to the encroachment of the forest. An axial path leads from here to an elliptical pool, planted with a single flowering dogwood. Across a country lane, a greenhouse is adorned with several garden plots. Two of these are designed with formal gardens: a rose garden and an herb garden, and each follows a rectilinear pattern around a central axis. Other plots, probably intended to host formal gardens as well, are planted with border gardens. The architecture of these spaces is large and open (although they are overplanted in a lush style) and reminds one of the taste for the European formalism and the Beaux-Arts style that influenced gardening in the early years of the twentieth century. They contrast vividly with the rest of the landscape, which is quintessentially American romantic. Taken together, moving from one experience to the next can be marvelously exciting.

GARDEN OPEN: 11am–5pm Tuesday–Sunday, April– October; 11am–4pm weekends, November and December. ADMISSION: $3 adults, $2 seniors, $1 children.

FURTHER INFORMATION FROM: 1 Clermont Avenue Germantown 12526. (518) 537-4240

NEARBY SIGHTS OF INTEREST: Olana

27 Germantown: Clermont

LOCATION: ROUTE 9G, BETWEEN THE KINGSTON-RHINECLIFF BRIDGE AND OLANA, FORTY MILES SOUTH OF ALBANY

The Livingston clan owned large amounts of property in pre-Federal New York, at one time owning most of this portion of the Hudson River valley. As landed gentry, they established their base here, south of the little hamlet of Germantown, and named it Clermont for the clear views of the Catskill Mountains. Three gardens crafted by the hand of Alice Delafield Clarkson Livingston in the 1920s and 1930s grace the estate. The South Spring Garden was planted in 1909 based upon Mrs. Livingston's observation of European gardens, particularly in Britain and Italy, gleaned from a two-year honeymoon in Europe. Although today the garden is a shady spot of herbaceous shrubs and groundcover, the underlying structure can still be seen in the winding staircase (derived from Italian gardens) and the retaining walls (borrowed, perhaps, from Britain). This juxtaposition of styles is carried further in the Walled Garden, dating to 1930. Statuary and wrought iron gates express Italian sentiments, whereas masses of flowering perennials reflect a study of twentieth-century English garden writers William Robinson and Gertrude Jekyll. Some iris, tulips, and phlox remain; however, several magnolia trees planted in the 1940s have doused the garden in shade, making it more hospitable for maidenhair

An ancient feeling pervades Clermont.

fern and other shade-loving plants. A path leads from here into a woodland, where graceful stalks of astilbe wash into streams of daffodils and tulips to create a Wilderness Garden. Barberry, quince, and smoke trees complete the romantic understory. A wooden footbridge passes over a stream, flanked on the left by a pond of water lilies, on its way to a cutting garden that once supplied the manor house with fresh roses. Heirloom varieties are in abundance, including the damask Madame Hardy and the deep purple Bourbon Louise Odier. There are several rustic structures in this area, including the cottage that the reclusive Mrs. Livingston lived in during the last years of her life, when she became more consumed with gardening than much else in the world, as well as an allée of pine framed by tulip trees. Although located in a corridor of historic homes, Clermont seems a little neglected by time. But many aficionados consider it the best of the lot for just this reason. The gardens are all somewhat of a secret, blooming by and seemingly for themselves in the silent woods above the Hudson.

28 Elizabethtown: Elizabethtown Colonial Garden

LOCATION: ROUTE 9, EXIT 31 OFF THE NEW YORK THRUWAY, THIRTY MILES SOUTHWEST OF BURLINGTON, VERMONT

Alden Hopkins, a landscape architect at Colonial Williamsburg, designed this exquisite garden in the 1950s, in cooperation with Lake Placid landscape architect Frank Politi and horticulturists from Cornell University. Like its brethren in Williamsburg, it is less a faithful re-creation of history than a set piece that evokes the spirit of that history. A white colonial fence modeled on one at Monticello and lined with hedges encloses the garden. Arranged around a center green are rectangular, brick beds of old-fashioned flowers that are arranged to provide

GARDEN OPEN: 9am–5pm Monday–Saturday; 1pm–5pm Sunday. ADMISSION: $3.50 adults, $2.50 seniors, $1.50 children.

FURTHER INFORMATION FROM: Court Street, Elizabethtown 12932. (518) 873-6466

NEARBY SIGHTS OF INTEREST: John Brown House, Adirondack Park, Lake Champlain bloom throughout the summer. After spring and early summer bulbs, daylilies take over before giving in to tiger lilies. Hopkins originally called for a southern mixture of plants, but his choices couldn't compete with the climate. Along one side is a wooden gazebo that provides a shady place to take in the tranquil, lilting atmosphere. An herb garden, complete with sundial and water trough for birds, was appended to the garden in recent years to include a display of historic herbs used in medicine and cuisine. The garden is situated behind the Adirondack County History Museum within a lovely landscape of birch, hemlock, hawthorn, viburnum, and quince, which infuses a bit of coastal charm into the Adirondack setting.

GARDEN OPEN: always.

ADMISSION: free.

FURTHER INFORMATION FROM:
Cornell Plantations, Ithaca
14850-2799. (607) 255-3020
www.plantations.cornell.edu

NEARBY SIGHTS OF INTEREST:
Owasco Teyetasta/Iroquois
Museum

29 Ithaca: Cornell Plantations

LOCATION: CORNELL UNIVERSITY CAMPUS

Few lovelier landscapes adorn a college than at Cornell University, which is situated amid a series of interconnected arboreta and gardens established in 1935. Cornell Plantations, as this green ring is called, include many significant tree collections, including dogwoods, azaleas, pin oaks, and rhododendrons. The Dean's Garden of woody plants includes such rarities as Persian parrotia, Japanese stewartia, and cinnamon clethra. There are also several botanical gardens, such as a rock garden, an orchid garden, and the macabre Poisonous Plants Garden, located behind the veterinary science building (which includes plants poisonous to pets and livestock, as well as to humans). The Mundy Wildflower Garden occupies a former landfill on campus and features flowering plants native to the Cuyuga Lake basin, including mayapple and wild columbine. An international crop garden displays the nine major crops that "feed the world" and, to be fair, the weeds that plague farmers. A nationally famous peony garden graces the landscape near Emerson Field. The collection contains a number of stunning, exotic varieties. Alongside the common bulbous flowers are more daisy-like and rose-like confections. The peonies are planted individually as specimens among grasses and flowering sedum. River birch, ash, and cherry trees serve to heighten the contrast, filter the light, and enhance the color of the flowers. Although commenced in 1935, the plantations are a work in progress and new gardens—many of which are memorials to alumni—continue to be added all the time. Many of the gardens are teaching gardens and provide plenty of scientific information about species, habitat, and taxonomy.

30 Canandaigua: Sonnenberg Gardens

LOCATION: OFF ROUTE 332, TWENTY-ONE MILES SOUTHEAST OF ROCHESTER

The little lake town of Canandaigua in western New York is known for its strong, intelligent women. Susan B. Anthony argued for women's suffrage in the Ontario County Courthouse in 1873 when she was brought up on charges of illegally voting in the 1872 election. (She lost her case, but its repercussions galvanized support for the cause elsewhere.) Mary Clark Thompson made her impact in other ways—through philanthropic giving and patronage of the arts. Some of the arts that Thompson generously supported were garden design, architecture, and ornamentation, each brought to perfect cultivation at her summer estate at Sonnenberg, which means "sunny hill" in German. The luxurious Victorian landscape and gardens were designed and implemented between 1902 and 1919 by Boston landscape architect Ernest Bowditch, a protégé and competitor of Frederick Law Olmsted. Thompson eventually hired the principal in charge of the monumental project, John Handrahan, away from Bowditch to reside permanently at Sonnenberg, and ensure its completion. Today's gardens are the result of an extensive restoration process begun in the 1960s, with augmentations by Syracuse University Professor Emeritus of landscape architecture Noredo Rotunno. Thompson's tastes are a throwback to the mid-nineteenth-century estates of aristocratic France, where each carefully sculpted room responds to a specific aesthetic theme or time period, of which the Italian Garden is the most visually representative. Designed by Bowditch in 1906, the garden consists of a brilliant display of annuals arranged in *fleur-de-lis* patterns within a sunken carpet of lawn. Two strong, transverse axial paths bisect the garden and provide excellent views of its stylish composition. Small, conical yews, spaced evenly along these paths reinforce the sense of rigid symmetry. The rectangular space is anchored at its farthest end by a semicircular pool adorned with a fountain depicting Hercules slaying the Hydra. A stately wooden pergola with white, clematis-covered columns and a brick walkway surround the Italian garden and provide a sensual transition between areas in the landscape. Other formal gardens include a re-creation of the original rose garden, an intimate pansy garden, a moonlight garden consisting of light-colored night-blooming flowers, and a Japanese garden designed by K. Wadamori that is typical of the period's interest in the Orient. To accommodate her massive project, Thompson commissioned the architecture firm of Lord and Burnham to design a glasshouse adjacent to the mansion, but this was subsequently moved to its present location near the parking lot. An exhibition of tropical exotics, including an excellent collection of orchids, are on display here, as well as a profusion of annuals

GARDEN OPEN: 9:30am– 5:30pm daily, mid May–mid October. Seasonal events October–December.
ADMISSION: $7.50 adults, $6.50 seniors, $3.00 children.

FURTHER INFORMATION FROM: 151 Charlotte Street, Canandaigua 14424. (716) 394-4922 www.sonnenberg.org

NEARBY SIGHTS OF INTEREST: Women's Hall of Fame, Curtiss Museum

Aged statuary reflects resilience amid decay in the Italian Garden.

propagated for the property. Besides the formal gardens there are a series of naturalistic rock gardens on the premises designed by Handrahan. Regionally quarried limestone and a small rivulet transform this area into a shaded paradise punctuated by grottos and subterranean nooks. Thompson's mansion, designed by Boston architect Francis Allen, is a superb example of the Queen Anne style. A perpetual cosmopolite—an apocryphal story holds that she held tickets on the Titanic but fortuitously prolonged a trip to Europe—Thompson surrounded herself with antique Old World furnishings. Unfortunately, all the original pieces are gone; what remains today is a generous re-creation of the magnificence that once pervaded this Gilded Age summerhouse.

GARDEN OPEN: 10:00am–4:30pm Tuesday–Saturday; 1pm–4:30pm Sunday. Closed Thanksgiving, Christmas, and New Year's Day. Open on Mondays in May. **ADMISSION:** $6.50 adults, $5.00 seniors and students, $2.50 children.

FURTHER INFORMATION FROM: 900 East Avenue, Rochester 14607-2298. (716) 271-3361

NEARBY SIGHTS OF INTEREST: Strong Museum, Susan B. Anthony House

31 Rochester: George Eastman House Gardens

LOCATION: EAST AVENUE, BETWEEN GOODMAN STREET AND CULVER ROAD

According to popular history, George Eastman came to photography accidentally when a friend suggested he take a camera on a trip to Central America. Although the trip never panned out, Eastman became interested in photography and eventually produced modern film and developing processes. The rest of his life was a lot less accidental. In 1905 Eastman hired architect J. Foster Warner to build his mansion and landscape architect Alling S. DeForest to design the estate as both an elegant urban landscape and a working farm. During his lifetime, Eastman constructed several formal gardens around the house, including the Terrace Garden that contained a profusion of perennials framed by boxwood parterres and pathways of brick to echo the architectural accents of the house. In the center of this garden was an oval pool set within a lovely sunken lawn. Much of the garden was destroyed and replanted during the 1930s and 1940s, but it has recently been restored to DeForest's specifications. As such the original Venetian pergola that lines the outside edge of the terrace contains a bare covering of the original Chinese wisteria—from the original root stock but cut back. Most of the original landscape was altered when the estate was owned and managed by the University of Rochester, from Eastman's death in 1932 until 1947. Today the house contains a museum of photography, which has dedicated itself to restoring as much of the original design as possible. In some cases, faithful reproductions are impossible, such as in the Library Garden. Intended as an adaptation of DeForest's cutting garden, it is actually a rooftop garden atop a subterranean structure. An axis lined with arborvitae cuts through the space, giving it a pleasant

formality. Other garden features include a naturalistic lawn of native shrubs, such as viburnum, spirea, and winterberry; some remnants of original wisteria and borders of annuals and perennials in the West Garden; and hemlock and elm punctuating the graceful Front Lawn. Work is underway to restore the wooden tubs of bay trees and boxwoods that once enlivened the entry.

A pergola, pool, and plenty of perennials at the restored Terrace Garden.

32 Mumford: Genesee Country Village and Museum

LOCATION: GEORGE STREET OFF ROUTE 36, TWENTY MILES SOUTHWEST OF ROCHESTER

Unlike the museum villages of New England, this settlement depicts nineteenth-century life. However, because this area of New York wasn't heavily settled until that time, many of the gardens are decidedly "frontier" in nature. There are typical colonial dye and herb gardens, including a shaker herb garden containing medicinal plants. The MacKay Homestead presents a strange little gem—a "parlor garden," which would have adorned the aristocratic residence of this Scottish immigrant around 1814. Also unique is the Foster-Tuft garden, a kitchen garden containing solely berries used in jams and jellies, including gooseberries and currants. Surrounding the transplanted Livingston-Backus city mansion (circa 1838) is an early Victorian garden, arranged around a formal boxwood parterre with flowering wisteria and pear trees, illustrating the inroads of European classicism among the upper classes. This trend is further explicated in the picturesque garden adorning the Octagon House (1870). Here, rigid European styles have been softened and further expressed. The tradition comes from England but here begins to receive American treatment in a manner that is reminiscent of the mid-nineteenth-century development of rural aesthetics. Agricultural lands surround much of this model village, including orchards, pumpkins, and a field of hops located (where else?) behind the brewery. A nature center and trail system are located in the woodlands and wildflower fields that border the museum.

GARDEN OPEN: 10am–5pm Tuesday–Sunday, May 10–October 13; 10am–4pm Thursday and Friday; 10am–5pm Saturday and Sunday, November–April. **ADMISSION:** $11.00 adults, $9.50 seniors and students, $6.50 children.

FURTHER INFORMATION FROM:
1410 Flint Hill Road
Mumford 14511-0310.
(716) 538-6822
www.history.rochester.edu/gcmuseum

NEARBY SIGHTS OF INTEREST:
Holland Land Office Museum

GARDEN OPEN: 9am–4pm daily. Closes at 5pm on weekends and 6pm on Wednesday. **ADMISSION:** free.

FURTHER INFORMATION FROM:
2655 South Park Avenue
Buffalo 14218-1526.
(716) 696-3555

NEARBY SIGHTS OF INTEREST:
South Park, Our Lady of
Victory Basilica, Fort Erie

33 Buffalo: Buffalo and Erie County Botanical Garden

LOCATION: SOUTH PARK ROAD, ON THE SOUTH SIDE OF BUFFALO

The magnificent Lord and Burnham glasshouse at the edge of Buffalo's South Park is an iconographic reminder of the industrial age splendor of this city by the lake. South Park was one of several parks Frederick Law Olmsted designed for Buffalo, where he envisioned a "green ring" similar to the Emerald Necklace in Boston. The conservatory was built in the waning years of the nineteenth century to house a growing and increasingly popular collection of tropical exotics at the nearby Albright Conservatory (now gone). John F. Cowell, a professor of botany at the State University of New York–Buffalo, was chosen as the institution's first director in 1894, and he left his indelible mark on the wildly diverse collections. The botanical garden, like so many other civic jewels across the country, fell into disrepair in the 1970s, but was resurrected in the early 1980s, receiving an extensive makeover of the entire structure and a many new plantings. Like its sister glasshouse at the New York Botanical Garden, the conservatory is built around a central annex, which towers 67 feet in the air, and two perfectly balanced, transverse wings anchored by two smaller domed rooms, at 36 feet. As at the New York Botanical Garden (*page 79*), this garden greets visitors with a vertiginous palm house containing varieties gathered from the Americas, Pacific Islands, and the Mediterranean and planted in tight islands so that their canopies droop and hang over the pathways. A corridor to the right contains an extensive display of ferns, hydrophytes (aquatics), and cycads (rare, fernlike plants found mainly in Australia). For the grand reopening in 1985, a tremendous rabbit's foot fern, a gift from Longwood Gardens, was placed above the fishpond. A waterfall at the end of this area contributes a structural element to a

A world of plants in a magnificent structure

changing plant display that often involves orchids from the Orchid and Anthurium Room. Other displays include a spine-tingling cactus garden, annuals useful in home gardening, and a learning garden containing plants that are used in everyday life to make textiles, chemicals, and medicines—all arranged in a single loop. Like the domed house that culminates the fern display at the other end of the garden, the show house contains a changing exhibit of floriculture.

34 Ringwood: Skylands

LOCATION: MORRIS ROAD, OFF ROUTE 17N, THIRTY MILES
NORTHWEST OF NEW YORK CITY

GARDEN OPEN: 8am–8pm
daily. ADMISSION: free.

FURTHER INFORMATION FROM:
Box 302, Ringwood 07456.
(973) 962-1553
www.njskylandsgarden.org

NEARBY SIGHTS OF INTEREST:
The Hermitage, Ringwood
Manor House

Skylands began as the private residence of Clarence McKenzie
Lewis, a trustee of the New York Botanical Garden, who hired
architect John Russell Pope to design his Tudor-style manor
house here in 1922. Over the years, Lewis implemented a horticulturally satisfying landscape with the assistance of several
prominent landscape architects. Although he lived in the twentieth century, Lewis's tastes were emphatically Victorian and
resulted in a wonderfully varied selection of formal gardens. A
handsome annual garden is bedded-out in typical Victorian
fashion, in large, colorful flourishes anchored and defined by
subtle architectural features: a wellhead, benches, and statuary.
A perennial border garden follows Lewis's original design, with
pillar roses and buddleia alternating through the early summer.
Several floral landscape features complement these formal
designs in the same old-fashioned vein—most notably a collection of lilacs and a crabapple walk. Lewis's penchant for the
dictates of Victorian fashion makes a grand appearance in the
azalea garden, arranged around a reflecting pool, and in a
peony garden. Although rhododendrons and several specimen
trees dot the area, including a Japanese maple and mountain
silverbell, which afford wonderful contrast in color and form to
the floral arrangements, the focus here is on azaleas in and
of themselves. A more contemporary feel is conveyed by the
rock garden, which features dwarf conifers, although the inclusion of several exotics, such as a particularly strange variety of
sedum (*Sedum gypsicolum*) and the mystical monkshood
(*Aconitum anthora*) indigenous to the Pyrenees mountains, tell
of the garden's roots.

*The Manor, illuminated
for the holidays*

GARDEN OPEN: dawn–dusk
daily, May–June.
ADMISSION: free.

FURTHER INFORMATION FROM:
474 Upper Mountain Avenue,
Upper Montclair 07043.
(973) 783-5974

NEARBY SIGHTS OF INTEREST:
Lambert Castle, Newark
Museum

ABOVE: *A rainbow
crescent of iris in full
summer splendor*

35 Upper Montclair: Presby Memorial Iris Garden

LOCATION: WATCHUNG AVENUE (EXIT **151** OFF THE GARDEN STATE PARKWAY)
TO UPPER MOUNTAIN AVENUE, TWENTY MILES WEST OF NEW YORK CITY

The venerable iris, a staple of traditional perennial gardens, is
the main attraction here. In fact, it is the only attraction. As a
result, the garden is only open in the spring and for a few weeks
in the fall, when a handful of late bloomers make a show. Frank
Presby (1857-1924) was a founder of the American Iris Society,
and befitting his stature as a demigod of iris cultivation, the garden dedicated to his memory features a stunning variety of
irises, which seem to come in all sorts of strange and wonderful
shapes and colors. Bearded irises, of course, garner much attention. Their alien forms swirl in the landscape. But the *Floren-
tina*, the oldest iris, which dates from the 1500s, and the
Honorabile, a variety that nineteenth-century pioneers carried
west also appear like much-anticipated divas. John C. Wister,
Harvard University landscape architect, designed the gardens
in 1927. His singular gesture makes a definitive arc across a
slightly concave field. It is graceful as well as quietly intriguing.
And the bands of color have elicited more than a few remarks
on the garden's similarity to a rainbow.

36 Morristown: Frelinghuysen Arboretum

LOCATION: EXIT 36 (HEADING SOUTH) OR EXIT 36A (HEADING NORTH) OFF INTERSTATE 287, ON WHIPPANY RD, THIRTY MILES WEST OF NEW YORK CITY

GARDEN OPEN: 8am–dusk daily. ADMISSION: free.

FURTHER INFORMATION FROM:
53 East Hanover Avenue
Morristown 07962-1295.
(973) 326-7600

NEARBY SIGHTS OF INTEREST:
Morris Museum, Fort Nonsense

The Frelinghuysen family purchased the Whippany Farm in 1891 to construct their Colonial Revival summer residence, complete with Palladian accents and Ionic columns. The landscape was designed in the English romantic style with a graceful lawn that descends through a carefully wooded slope of calculated vistas. Collections of cherry trees, silverbells, dogwoods, and other specimens fill in the lower areas. Near the house lie a few remnants of the original gardens, including a Victorian knot garden with gazebo and a rose garden. The park commission that now administers the site as a public arboretum has augmented these areas with a series of educational demonstration gardens, such as the Mary Linder Clark Perennial Garden, which showcases different plants and plant combinations and includes tips on how to grow certain varieties, as well as a mixed border garden that illustrates the use of cool colors. In addition to these, there are other gardens aimed at a specific visitor or idea, such as a garden designed for people with special needs (plants are situated in raised beds for easy wheelchair access) and a garden devoted entirely to the color blue (larkspur, Delft blue hyacinth, great blue lobelia, and others). Situated in the midst of a Braille nature trail is the Pikaart Garden, designed specifically to appeal to the blind, with unusually textured plants such as goatsbeard and ferns. The educational tour proceeds through a shade garden, fern garden, and rock garden before its conclusion. A public park as much as a garden, the Arboretum hosts summer concerts in the evening.

Patterned plantings guide the educational gardens.

GARDEN OPEN: 10am–4pm Monday–Friday; 10am–5pm Saturday; noon–5pm Sunday. Closed on weekends and major holidays December–February. **ADMISSION:** $1 donation.

FURTHER INFORMATION FROM: 11 Layton Road, Far Hills 07931. (908) 234-2677

NEARBY SIGHTS OF INTEREST: Cooper Mill, Drake House

37 Far Hills: Leonard Buck Garden

LOCATION: FAR HILLS ROAD OFF ROUTE 202, SEVENTEEN MILES NORTHWEST OF NEW BRUNSWICK

Leonard Buck had rocks in his head, literally. A wealthy mining engineer, Buck translated his love of geology into an impressive 33-acre rock garden. The setting Buck chose was a picturesque glacial valley called Moggy Hollow in western New Jersey, where the retreat of the Wisconsin glacier some 30,000 years ago left behind a stunning geological landscape. Buck augmented this scene by arranging boulders and rocks into naturalistic displays that are almost sculptural in their presentation: frieze-like ledges, statuesque outcroppings, and dioramas of conglomerations. Swiss-born landscape architect Zenon Schreiber prepared a planting plan for each display that responds to specific soil and light conditions, both of which vary subtly as each display creates its own microclimate. Using primarily shrubbery and flowers, Schreiber wove a tapestry of color around Buck's rock arrangements, animating the still-life garden. Many delicate plants, such as primrose and pheasant's eye *(Adonis amurensis)*, deepen the canvas, while off-season woody plants, like winterberry and red maple, provide an architectural element that contrasts with the rock in winter months. In 1986 the Leonard Buck Garden received a collection of hardy ferns from a benefactor, which were subsequently planted in the damp, acidic area near Moggy Brook. The collection includes the gigantic, gawking ostrich fern (*Matteuccia struthiopteris*) and the giant shield fern (*Dryopteris goldiana*), as well as other uncommon varieties. Near the parking lot, contemporary gardeners have created a garden of heathers, truly the most impressionistic of flowers. The collection focuses on *Calluna* and *Erica* genera, and hybrids that are acclimated to zones 5, 4, and even 3.

Unique geology provides a stunning backdrop for Leonard Buck's collection of plants.

38 Somerville: Duke Gardens

LOCATION: ROUTE 206, 16 MILES NORTH OF PRINCETON

Doris Duke spent fifty years perfecting her acre of gardens, and perfection is an appropriate word for these conservatories. Tobacco tycoon James B. Duke originally built the central glasshouse in 1908, designed by Lord and Burnham; yet not until 1958 did his daughter, Doris, begin designing the exquisite plant collection. Eleven interconnected rooms contain the gardens, each devoted to a specific gardening style or region. The most stunningly formal garden is a French parterre situated within three barrel vaults of deep green lattice, called trelliage. "Majesty," a marble statue, holds court at the far end of the space. Traditions of the Mughal emperors inform the Indo-Persian garden. A 70-foot channel that drops through successive stages forms the centerpiece for an arrangement of shades and screens (commonly employed to deflect the sun) and desert plants. Elsewhere, Duke designed a Chinese garden, a Japanese garden, a Mediterranean Italian garden, a colonial garden, and an English garden that features an excellent collection of succulents. She also planted an Edwardian garden, where stag horn ferns, orchids, and palms replicate the findings of intrepid botanists—a collection that might have graced the greenhouse of an English gentlemen in the early part of this century. Typical greenhouse displays of arid, semitropical, and jungle plant communities round out the displays, but the heart of the gardens resides in the delicately manufactured spaces derived from a careful study of gardening traditions.

GARDEN OPEN: by reservation only, October–June. Garden tours: noon–4pm daily, October–June. ADMISSION: $5.00 adults, $2.50 seniors and children.

FURTHER INFORMATION FROM: P.O. Box 818, Somerville 08876-0818. (908) 722-3700

NEARBY SIGHTS OF INTEREST: Old Dutch Parsonage, Hopewell Museum

Doris Duke's tastes were exquisite.

39 Millstone: Rudolph van der Goot Rose Garden

LOCATION: EXIT 12 OFF INTERSTATE 287, SOUTH ON WESTON CANAL RD, TEN MILES WEST OF NEW BRUNSWICK

Rudolph van der Goot, a local horticulturist, designed three rose gardens over a seven-year period on the site of a former working farm that had been converted into a municipal park. When he began, Goot had inherited the bones of the Front Garden—an Italianate geometry that provides the underlying structure. A central fountain is underplanted with miniature roses, while the four proximate beds all contain modern hybrid teas. Brick-edged beds, flagstone paths, and clipped hedges give the space its architectural cast, while Goot's sensitive plant demarcations travel through the range of colors to impart a delicate feeling. The adjacent Central Garden remains true to Goot's original

GARDEN OPEN: dawn–dusk daily. ADMISSION: free.

FURTHER INFORMATION FROM: 11 Layton Road, Far Hills 07931. (908) 234-2677

NEARBY SIGHTS OF INTEREST: East Jersey Olde Towne

Radial symmetry defines the limits of Adolf van der Goot's rose collection.

design. A central axis of polyantha roses lined by brick walkways form the spine of a crucifix-shaped bed. The transverse axis is formed by two semicircular areas of radial beds containing a mixture of floribundas and hybrid teas arranged in flows of alternating texture and form. A wooden trellis wends its way around the entire garden, wearing a cloak of climbers. At the base are many fragrant heritage varieties, including damask, bourbon, and musk. In the final garden Goot mounted a tribute to traditional Dutch rose gardens; the area is compressed by narrowing the space between the beds, which has the effect of pushing the visitor over the roses so as to view them from above. Outside the rose gardens, the park's gardeners have designed a vibrant, four-acre perennial garden around a rustic gazebo. The flower combination relies heavily on daffodils and peonies, with accents of lilacs, irises, and ornamental grasses. Nearby lies a Fragrance and Sensory Garden, designed specifically for the blind and disabled, which makes use of strongly fragrant flowers, such as lavender and autumn clematis, and highly textured plants, such as lamb's ear and sedum.

GARDEN OPEN: 8am–8pm daily, summer; 8am–4pm daily, winter. **ADMISSION:** free

FURTHER INFORMATION FROM:
352 Red Hill Road
Middletown 07748.
(732) 671-6050

NEARBY SIGHTS OF INTEREST:
Longstreet Farm, Sandy Hook

40 Middletown: Deep Cut Gardens

LOCATION: EXIT 114 OFF THE GARDEN STATE PARKWAY, ON RED HILL ROAD, TWENTY MILES SOUTHEAST OF NEW BRUNSWICK

These gardens are named for the vertiginous rivulet that traces its way through the property; however, one might get the impression that "deep cut" implies something more sinister, something more in keeping with their original owner, mafioso Vito Genovese. Genovese owned the property from 1935 to 1947 and constructed a series of elaborate gardens on the grounds. They fell into disrepair after he sold them, and today only a single pergola set on a stone terrace in the back of the property still exists. A county park agency took over the property in 1977 and converted Genovese's landscape into an informal woodland park, dotted by several notable garden collections. In the Rockery, a juxtaposition of dark boulders, weeping hemlocks, and dwarf conifers is particularly striking. A recently planted native garden includes several species of rare ferns and trillium, arranged beneath a shady woodland. A koi pond with water lilies lies nearby a bog and provides a strong contrast of landscape types. Several on-site greenhouses contain orchids, succulents, and displays of common houseplants. The spirit of Genovese lies behind the current construction of formal perennial gardens, which will be planted in parterres on axis with the pergola. In the spring an azalea and rhododendron walk attracts many locals, but Deep Cut still remains pleasantly beyond the radar screen of most garden aficionados.

41 Swainton: Leaming's Run Gardens

LOCATION: EXIT 13 ON THE GARDEN STATE PARKWAY, THIRTEEN MILES
NORTH OF CAPE MAY

GARDEN OPEN: 9:30am–
5:00pm daily, May 15–
October 20. **ADMISSION:**
$4.50 adults, $1.00 children.

FURTHER INFORMATION FROM:
1845 Route 9 North, Swainton
08210. (609) 465-5871

NEARBY SIGHTS OF INTEREST:
Cape May lighthouse,
Wetlands Institute

Unlike most places constructed by eccentrics, Jack Aprill's constitutes one of the most intriguing and beautiful gardens in New Jersey. Located in the southern half of the state, almost at Cape May, Leaming's Run (named after an early settler in the area) is the culmination of Aprill's 40-year love affair with annuals. The gardens stretch over thirty acres of wetlands, woodlands, and cleared meadows—all of which bear the mark of the gardener's hand. Color combinations reign supreme and each year the garden is frosted with a rich mixture of annuals, designed in bold swaths of color. For instance, a yellow garden contains some 60 varieties of yellow-blooming or yellow-foliage flowers and shrubs. A blue garden is more subdued, with grasses and varieties of spruce complementing the mix of flowers. Cape May County lies within the "holly belt" of the East Coast, yet the area is classed as zone 7—semitropical. To emphasize this strange conjunction, Aprill juxtaposes the winter ornamentals with stands of bamboo, vibrant floral displays within deep forests, and wetlands. Careful editing of the woodlands creates shade gardens, while a wetland has been planted with rare cinnamon ferns. Although Leaming's Run emphatically rejects formalism—what Aprill calls the "square, European style"—the garden bears the unmistakable stamp of Aprill's vernacular meditations. In a grassy meadow, a serpent of red flowers—sometimes impatiens, sometimes celosia—approaches and encircles a summerhouse in a vibrant, dramatic sweep. The iconoclasm of the garden has a stultifying effect on the hummingbirds that flock here in August crazy for cardinal flower and scarlet cypress. (Aprill speaks out passionately and clearly against sugar feeders, which ferment in the heat and kill the birds.) Unlike fussy perennial gardens, the eclectic and varied collections at Leaming's Run remain relevant all summer long, particularly in early September, when blooming white clematis makes its appearance. Elsewhere on the property lies an old vegetable farm, settler's cabin, and chicken coops containing a wild display of some fine poultry—all part of Aprill's emphatic individualism.

*A riot of color in the
pine barrens of southern
New Jersey*

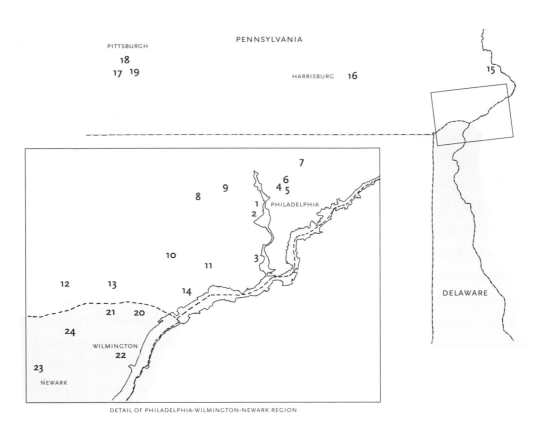

PENNSYLVANIA

PITTSBURGH
18
17 19

HARRISBURG 16

15

PHILADELPHIA

7

6
4 5

8   9

1
2

3

10

11

14

12   13

21   20

24

WILMINGTON
22

23

NEWARK

DELAWARE

DETAIL OF PHILADELPHIA-WILMINGTON-NEWARK REGION

MID-ATLANTIC REGION:

Pennsylvania and Delaware

The presence of Longwood Gardens (*pages 131–33*) makes this region especially notable. It is common to hear Pennsylvania and Delaware garden proprietors describe their gardens with the prefatory disclaimer, "well, we're not like Longwood." The technical showmanship of the fountains that Pierre du Pont began constructing on his property in 1925 have been matched over the years with a horticultural vigor that supersedes most gardens in America. But Longwood presents a specific kind of experience, and the region is home to plenty of other gardens that are important to visit. Cousin Henry du Pont's garden at Winterthur is one such place. There are probably no two such wildly contrasting gardens of similar caliber within such a short distance of each other anywhere else in the country. While Longwood is spectacle, splash, and showmanship—vibrant displays that dazzle the eyes—Winterthur reflects a quieter, more profound understanding of plants and devotion to the deeper levels of design. One leaves Longwood exhausted; one leaves Winterthur inspired. Each garden presents something for every garden enthusiast, and sometimes it's easy to think that the garden world can be divided into two camps according to which of these one prefers.

The spiritual energy propagated by these great twentieth-century gardens is felt most strongly in the western suburbs of Philadelphia, where both Longwood and Winterthur have influenced younger, yet equally inspirational idylls. Chanticleer (*pages 126–27*) is one upstart with veracious pretensions. The Henry Foundation (*page 128*) and

OPPOSITE: *Spring is heralded by newborn crocuses at Winterthur.*

Roberto Burle Marx's astounding Cascade Garden in the Conservatory at Longwood Gardens

Meadowbrook Farm (*page 125*) are iconoclastic places that, if they haven't risen to the status of their southerly neighbors, are treasured by their own select audience. In contrast the Hershey Gardens (*pages 137–38*) present Victorian visions of the garden in the hubristic dreams of Milton Hershey—but do so in such a consistent manner that they seem to belong to the same spirit. Other gardens seem oblivious to the competitive context of the region. Within Philadelphia proper, Shofu-So (*page 119*), the Japanese house and garden, is one of the best contemplative gardens in the East, while the Morris Arboretum (*page 122*) stands alone—an eclectic Victorian pleasure ground as wondrously delightful today as it must have been in the nineteenth century.

Although garden history in Pennsylvania and Delaware is centered upon the early twentieth century, several gardens, such as E. I. du Pont's at the Hagley Museum (*pages 140–41*) and the estates of North Philadelphia, date back to earlier eras. In this vein Bartram's Garden (*pages 120–21*), in particular, is a must-see for anyone visiting Philadelphia. Here the exuberance of the du Ponts finds its precursor in the fascinating characters of Bartram and his son Willie, the country's first botanists who set out for the frontiers in search of new and wonderful plants in the eighteenth century. Today its silence on the banks of the Schuykill River, in an impoverished part of Philadelphia, serves as a filter, or lens, to perceive the voluminous history and presence of gardening in this region.

Philadelphia: Shofu-So

LOCATION: BEHIND THE HORTICULTURAL CENTER, FAIRMONT PARK

The Japanese house, as Philadelphians informally call Shofu-So, was designed by Junzo Yoshimura in 1953 in the Shoin-zukuri style (the "desk style") employed in the houses of government officials, priests, and scholars. The structure was exhibited at the Museum of Modern Art in 1954 before being brought to Philadelphia as a gift to the city. The house sits within a pond garden designed by Sano Tansai in the style of a seventeenth-century garden that approximates a Japanese landscape vista, in miniature. In reverie, the small pond evolves into a large lake, framed by a mountain range of evergreens. In reality, the garden consists of a selection of dwarf conifers and Japanese flowers that recede in false perspective toward an increasingly lush, and larger, backdrop. A narrow path of stones leads around the edge of the pond toward a small bridge that connects to a rock island. But the garden is not meant for strolling. It is meant for passive contemplation from afar. To heighten this experience the house is raised a few feet above the view, a traditional feature of Japanese gardens. To the occidental visitor, the effect may be too subtle, but for one versed in these things the slight elevation contributes a fuller perspective of the scene.

The garden contains a wide selection of traditional Japanese plantings, including bamboo, cypress (of which the house is constructed), cryptomeria, and several vibrantly blooming dogwoods (*Cornus florida*). Although 250 rocks were imported from Japan, hard forms are at a minimum. Instead, the garden has a decidedly lush, soft, and inviting character. Architectural features such as the bridge, a small stone pagoda, and a statue of Jizo, a Buddhist deity, train the eye to certain spaces, although the main joy is achieved by casting a glance across the entire scene and experiencing the plays of depth and perspective.

HOUSE AND GARDEN OPEN:
10am–4pm Tuesday–Sunday, May–August; 10am–4pm Saturday and Sunday, September–October. Closed November–May.
ADMISSION: $2.50 adults, $2.00 seniors and children.

FURTHER INFORMATION FROM:
Box 2224, Philadelphia 19103. (215) 878-5097
www.libertynet.org/~jhg

NEARBY SIGHTS OF INTEREST:
Belmont Mansion, Horticultural Center, Philadelphia Zoo

ABOVE: *A sense of enclosure, a sense of landscape*

GARDENS OPEN: 8am–6pm daily. Admission: free. **GREEN-HOUSES OPEN:** 9am–3pm daily. **ADMISSION:** donation requested.

FURTHER INFORMATION FROM:
P.O. Box 21601, Philadelphia 19131. (215) 685-0096

NEARBY SIGHTS OF INTEREST:
Belmont Mansion, Shofu-So, Philadelphia Zoo

2 Philadelphia: Philadelphia Horticultural Center

LOCATION: HORTICULTURAL DRIVE AND MONTGOMERY AVENUE, FAIRMOUNT PARK

The Philadelphia Horticultural Center serves as the potting shed for the entire city. Amid the grungy tools and utilitarian greenhouses, however, are a lovely hothouse and several acres of botanical gardens that are engagingly designed, if underused by city residents. Canary Island palms predominate the Tropical House, located as an appendage off the propagation greenhouses. The brick-and-stone terrace encompasses several stream-like water features, around which are established banana plants, coconut plants, and other palms. Although hotter than Hades in July and August, the Tropical House is popular for weddings in the fall and winter and is often closed in preparation for this on weekend afternoons. The grounds surrounding the greenhouses slope down toward a wilderness-choked creek containing a plethora of excellent trees, including redwoods and dramatic weeping hemlocks. Extending west from the entrance to the hothouse lies a long reflecting pool surrounded by a terrace. The walk continues further to a butterfly garden set about a sundial created by Alexander Calder. Statues of German literati Goethe and Schiller look on. Winding around the back of the building are a series of demonstration gardens, including an herb garden, a garden designed for people with disabilities, a butterfly garden, a night garden consisting of plants with white foliage, and a grass garden. Picnic groves throughout attest to the garden's park status; however, on most days, even in the heat of summer, the place is empty. Nooks containing statuary of Verdi and other European luminaries offer bucolic spots for a peaceful hour—only a mile from busy downtown.

GARDEN OPEN: dawn–dusk daily. **HOUSE TOURS:** 12 noon–4pm Wednesday–Sunday. **ADMISSION:** $3.

FURTHER INFORMATION FROM:
54th Street and Lindbergh Boulevard, Philadelphia 19143. (215) 729-5281

NEARBY SIGHTS OF INTEREST:
University of Pennsylvania

3 Philadelphia: John Bartram Gardens

LOCATION: 54TH STREET AND LINDBERGH AVENUE, ON THE SOUTH SIDE OF PHILADELPHIA

According to myth, Quaker farmer John Bartram was inspired by the sight of a single daisy in his field to put down the hoe and to take up the magnifying glass, thus becoming the first botanist in the American colonies. Regardless of the truth of this story, Bartram typified the independent intellectual spirit of the day—his deist philosophy proved his ouster from the Quaker meeting—and through extensive travels compiled a stunning documentation of the exotic flora of the New World. Many of the plants that Bartram discovered were brought back with him to his 128-acre farm along the banks of the Schuykill River, just south of Philadelphia, where he assembled his botanical curiosities in a magnificent garden. Today, many specimens from the original collection still exist. The landscape is arranged in a rustic manner, showing less of an interest in design as a whole than in its individual components. There are a number of flower gardens and herb gardens near the 1728 stone house; however, Bartram's greatest fascination was with trees and shrubs, with which he littered the slope beyond. There are some marvelous specimens, including the Franklin tree (*Franklinia altamaha*), which Bartram discovered near the Altamaha River in Florida in 1765 but which has been extinct in the wild since 1803. Supposedly, all *Franklinias* growing today are descended from this tree, which Bartram named in honor of his friend Benjamin Franklin. Bartram's son, William, accompanied his father on most of his travels and became his "little botanist." In 1773 Willie set off alone, however, on a journey that was as much about self-discovery as plant science. Gifted with an ability to depict and describe the word, his notes and drawings of this trip were published in a book titled *Travels*, today considered a classic of travel writing and early American botany. While the elder Bartram was concerned with documenting the scientific details of nature—he also published a catalogue of some 220 new species he'd discovered—William had a more romantic bent, describing the effect of these details on his inner life. The indissoluble connection between these two modes of thinking is abundantly clear within the garden today—an oasis in postindustrial Philadelphia, where one can still contemplate the sublimities of nature.

Bartram's flower garden adorns the house.

Immediately behind the house lie the flower gardens, differentiated according to whether Bartram was growing species for trading with other collectors or cultivating exotics he had received for his own use. The area is very much an adjunct to the house: the large oak and yellowwood trees (the latter allegedly a gift from French botanist and explorer André Michaux and dating to the 1780s) cradle the dark stone structure, while a brick terrace and wild beds create an unorganized, organic feel. Beyond this spot, a path descends into an area of shrubs, shaded by larger canopy trees. Most of the specimens are carefully labeled with names and dates of when (approximately) Bartram first acquired them. Of particular note is an ancient gingko tree thought to be among the first three of these species imported from China in the eighteenth century. Halfway down the slope is a newly restored fish pond, which Bartram planted with aquatics that caught his fancy. The trail continues down to the edge of the Schuykill River that runs along the east side of the property. A wetland is currently being constructed here, and a riverboat runs from the small dock, taking passengers up the heavily exurban waterway.

4

Philadelphia: Morris Arboretum

LOCATION: NORTHWESTERN AVENUE, CHESTNUT HILL

GARDEN OPEN: 10am–4pm daily; open until 5pm on weekends, April–October. **ADMISSION:** $4 adults, $3 seniors, $2 students.

FURTHER INFORMATION FROM: 100 Northwestern Avenue Philadelphia 19118. (215) 247-5777 www.upenn.edu/morris

NEARBY SIGHTS OF INTEREST: Woodmere Art Museum, historic Chestnut Hill

A Venusian temple and adoring swans

Siblings John and Lydia Morris were eccentrics. Wealthy Philadelphia Quakers who traveled throughout aristocratic Europe, the pair developed a taste for the various passions of the Victorian age while keeping an extremely open mind to new and inventive American ideas. In 1887, when they purchased a 92-acre hilltop in the suburb of Chestnut Hill on which to build their summer home, the Morrises set about designing the estate (called Compton) in an amalgam of styles. Today, the Morris Arboretum, which is owned and managed by the University of Pennsylvania as a public garden and research center, stands as a most vivid example of the Victorian eclectic in American landscape. Picturesque rolling landscape, formal gardens, representative and abstract sculpture, and built forms taken liberally from the panoply of historic architecture all present a wildly varied and exciting spectacle. Within a short space the visitor is treated to a visual festival of garden styles and landscape forms.

A single path makes one grand loop through the garden so the landscape reads as a series of consecutive rooms. The first, discovered as the path dips below a rise, is a romantic rose and herb garden. Neatly proportioned lines and a central fountain demarcate the arrangement of the roses while an uninterrupted border of flowering dogwoods provides an attractive frame to excellent views of the rest of the arboretum. The path continues downhill through an array of exotic trees, many of which date to the nineteenth century. The Morrises originally began installing sculpture in the landscape in the early part of the twentieth century, and the tradition is carried out today with noticeable gusto. Many of the University's holdings are on display at any one time, although the playful bronze statues of John and Lydia as well as the steel x marking the location of the now-destroyed Compton manor are permanent. Other eclectic ornaments include the classically inspired seven arches and Mercury Temple, fountains illustrating the Italian Renaissance and English Victorian aesthetic, and even a pioneer's rustic log cabin. Of particular note is the newly restored H. Hamilton Fernery, built to showcase tropical ferns in the late nineteenth century. The structure sits below grade in order to achieve the right balance of humidity and temperature, much like a wine cellar, and yet its 350 panels of glass provide ample light for the dozens of species of exotic ferns. As a major urban educational center, the Morris Arboretum mounts numerous exhibitions throughout the year, often several at one time. Recent educational displays have included an exhibit of plants commonly used to heal in cultures around the world and a riparian streambed restoration demonstration project.

Philadelphia: Awbury Arboretum

LOCATION: CHEW AVENUE AND WASHINGTON LANE, GERMANTOWN

During the nineteenth century, Philadelphia's rapidly growing upper classes colonized Germantown, a bucolic burb located in the wooded hills on the north side of the city. Many of these millionaires were also Quakers, who, in constructing their large estates, chose to temper Victorian ostentation with a touch of Pennsylvanian humility. Henry Cope was one of these. Cope purchased fifty-five acres in 1852, and for the next seventy years, Awbury (named for the English village from which his family had emigrated) was home to a widely extended family of Copes. The landscape was designed by William Saunders, first landscape architect of the U.S. Capitol grounds in Washington, D.C., in the romantic English style. Rolling lawns wind around copses of trees that are artfully placed to frame distant vistas and heighten the dramatic impression of scale. Miraculously, in the midst of the city that has grown up around it, there are no modern intrusions visible, giving one the sense of total dislocation with the outside world. Although the Cope house is now privately owned, the Arboretum does possess the garden, which is designed as a kind of secret garden, accessed through a stone wall and planted with beds of perennials in the Victorian style. The original structure on the property, a farmhouse dating to 1797, still stands, although most of the historic structures are in private hands.

GARDEN OPEN: dawn–dusk daily; self-guided tour.
ADMISSION: free.

FURTHER INFORMATION FROM:
1 Awbury Road, Philadelphia 19138. (215) 849-2855

NEARBY SIGHTS OF INTEREST:
Cliveden, Maxwell Mansion

ABOVE: *The eighteenth-century farmhouse still stands on the site.*

LOCATION: GERMANTOWN AVENUE AND WALNUT LANE, IN GERMANTOWN

GARDEN OPEN VIA GUIDED WALKING TOURS: 1pm–4pm Tuesday, Thursday, and Saturday, April–December 15, or by appointment.
ADMISSION: $5 adults, $4 seniors and students, $10 families.

FURTHER INFORMATION FROM:
6026 Germantown Avenue
Philadelphia 19144
(215) 848-1690

NEARBY SIGHTS OF INTEREST:
Cliveden, Awbury Arboretum

ABOVE: *An ancient rose garden lends romance to a Philadelphia estate.*

The famous rose garden at Wyck has changed little in the past 150 years. Originally planted in the 1820s by the Haineses (descendants of the Quaker family that lived on-site since the seventeenth century), this intimate formal garden—composed of a quadrangle of boxwood-parterres and enclosed on one end by a wisteria arbor and the other by a romantic garden shelter—retains a rare, old-world charm. The roses are all old varieties, which are typically far more fragrant and wild in appearance. Age has brought the bushes into a stately, yet free-flowing character that demands pause. The small and solitary garden has an integral connection with the handsome house on-site, extending the lines of architecture into the landscape. Perhaps it is the graceful shady lawn, or the rural character of the orchard, but at Wyck one seems far away from downtown Philadelphia, only a short seven miles away. The affluent flocked to Germantown in the nineteenth century, building a number of notable mansions, such as the manor house now gracing the Morris Arboretum. Time, of course, has taken its toll on most of these, with the exception of intimate Wyck, which has been preserved, intact (and therefore requiring no extensive restoration) since the 1820s. The Haines family produced several horticulturists who made their impact on Philadelphia history, including Ruben Haines III, a founder of the Academy of Natural Science and Jane Bowne Haines, a founder of a school of horticulture for women and the designer of the rose garden.

7 Meadowbrook: Meadowbrook Farm

LOCATION: WASHINGTON LANE AND WELSH ROAD (ROUTE 63),
SEVEN MILES NORTH OF PHILADELPHIA

Philadelphia flower designer J. Liddon Pennock, a mainstay at
the local flower show for many years, created floral arrangements for the Nixon White House. Since then he's been quietly
ensconced at his home north of Philadelphia creating a magnificently detailed garden for his own edification. Each small
room at Meadowbrook Farm has been placed on strict axis so
that one might experience the entire garden as a visual progression through a canal of successive spaces. From the Eagle
Garden—a round room containing a large bronze eagle that is
given classical treatment with vibrant annuals—visitors may
peer down a passageway to the begonia-lined fountain in the
Round Garden. Each detail has been calculated by a discerning,
visual mind. The surrounding space is intimate but with plenty
of room. Beyond these first rooms, the eye continues onward
to a rectangular pool and a summerhouse. On perfect transverse axis (one need never move in order to experience almost
the entire garden) lies a small dipping pool surrounded by
miniature plantings—a dollhouse effect. Around a corner lies
the Lyre Garden, named for the statuesque bard that adorns
the center of the space and the lyre-embedded fence that runs
around the edge. Here again annuals provide a manicured,
classical touch to the architectural and sculptural focus.

GARDEN OPEN: 10am–5pm to
groups of fifteen or more,
Monday–Sunday.

FURTHER INFORMATION FROM:
1633 Washington Lane
Meadowbrook 19046-2917.
(215) 887-5900

NEARBY SIGHTS OF INTEREST:
Glencairn Museum, Briar
Bush Nature Center

*A precise arrangement
of conifers and begonias
define this formal garden
and its vista.*

GARDEN OPEN: 10:00am–
3:30pm Wednesday–Saturday,
April–October. **ADMISSION:** $5
adults, $3 children.

FURTHER INFORMATION FROM:
786 Church Road, Wayne
19087. (610) 687-4163

NEARBY SIGHTS OF INTEREST:
Finley House

8 Wayne: Chanticleer

LOCATION: OFF BROOKS ROAD, FIFTEEN MILES WEST OF PHILADELPHIA

Christopher Woods describes his gardens at Chanticleer as a
traditional English garden on hormones. The characterization
is typical of Woods, a witty British expatriate. But it is also
appropriately applied to Chanticleer, one of the most exuberant
gardens in this region. Adolph Rosengarten Jr., who had inherited the estate from his father, donated Chanticleer to the public
in 1993. At that time the landscape, though containing lovely
rolling lawns, a stream, and many significant trees, included little in the way of formal gardens. Then Woods came along, and
everything changed. The garden design follows no predeter-
mined scheme and in fact seems to snub tradition in a playful
manner. The entry court presents itself as a lush Mediterranean
terrace: tropical fronds and delicate hothouse flowers adorn a
brimming urn that spills a gentle trickle of water into a fountain. But on closer inspection, the comparison falls short.
Everything is tweaked; the lushness goes beyond anything that
would be found in a typical Mediterranean garden. The overlarge banana plant leaves create a jungle atmosphere, whereas
a wild variety of annuals, vibrant in color and texture, swirl
around the architectural feature to create less the idea of the
garden as a space than the idea of the garden as a three-
dimensional painting. The main focus at Chanticleer is on
extremely diverse and unusual plant combinations that, in the
words of their creator, "are simply beautiful." Taking advantage
of a worldwide network of plant hunters, the gardens include
many species that simply are not found elsewhere, such as the
potted *Amorphophallus rivieri*, a compact tuberous perennial
with strangely spotted skin garnering it the moniker "snake
plant" in its native Indonesia. But for all this horticultural

ABOVE: *Effusive plantings*
transform a knot garden.

bravado, Chanticleer emphatically eschews pure scientism. The main focus is on beauty in all its various forms. None of the plants—with the one exception of the snake plant—are labeled, due to Woods's inability to find a labeling system that wouldn't disrupt the eye. Behind the Rosengarten house, designed by Philadelphia architect C. Louis Borie, lie a series of formal terraces. Although a large rectangle of turf ringed with a masonry balustrade and focused on a spotless swimming pool impart a stolid, pristine structure to the space, Woods has leavened the mix with several florid displays: a vaguely knotlike herb garden swirls together lavender, dusty miller, and ornamental onion in a dizzying pattern that is underlaid by orange portulaca. Pots that bake in the sun on the railing contain a rare succulent sent by a friend from South Africa. Espaliered apricots along the garden wall and handmade chairs beneath a white cherry tree lend the serious air of a pleasure garden, while two yew hedges beside the house trimmed to mimic buttresses play a little joke, expressing a central dictum of Chanticleer that "gardens should always have a sense of humor."

Perhaps because Woods believes that horticulture is not a radical art, humor is largely achieved by employing iconoclastic spins to traditional norms. A border garden that reaches down toward the Summer Perennial Garden exemplifies this point. The space seems to scream for a Jekyllian hand—delightfully impressionistic mixtures that lead the eye toward the flower garden. To some extent this is achieved through the use of black-eyed Susans and other vertical plants that serve to shield the wall behind them. But smack in the middle of this display is a topiary evergreen cut into a severely pyramidal shape, a shocking treatment that may bother purists while delighting those of lighter disposition. Elsewhere, this heresy becomes more subtle and inevitably more intriguing. An Asian woodland employs Eastern species, such as Japanese iris and stewartia trees, in the nascent, eclectic American manner—a winding path provides specifically controlled vistas. A wooden arbor built into a stone retaining wall looks down over Woods's most recent creation, a series of stepped pools surrounded by a swirling and ever-changing pastiche of perennials and aquatics. The imperfect relationship of the garden's scale—it forever seems too far away—makes it difficult to comprehend the tremendous diversity of plant material, a trick, one supposes, calculated to draw the visitor down into the garden proper, via one of several grass paths, to investigate more closely. It is an invitation difficult to turn down. The most architectural of the gardens is currently under construction. Two streams of wheat punctuated with columnar trees and stone columns weave down a slight hillside to achieve what Woods says will be "a mad, pagan, Italianate" effect. Although it sounds strange, one has faith it will blend in with the rest of the engaging landscape.

9 ## Gladwyne: Henry Foundation for Botanical Research

LOCATION: STONY LANE, THIRTEEN MILES WEST OF PHILADELPHIA

GARDEN OPEN: 10am–4pm Monday–Friday.
ADMISSION: free.

FURTHER INFORMATION FROM:
801 Stony Lane, Gladwyne
19035-0007. (610) 525-2037

NEARBY SIGHTS OF INTEREST:
Plymouth Meeting Hall,
Finley House

Mrs. Henry's old stone manse presides over the gardens.

Mary Gibson Henry traveled the globe with a spade and a keen eye on the lookout for unusual plants. Beginning in 1926, she sent back most of her loot (predominently seeds) to her estate in the western suburbs of Philadelphia, which now comprises an energetic garden of earthly delights. The garden rolls across a magnificent natural landscape of boulders and rock outcroppings, culminating in a rock garden at the summit. Displays are arranged according to geographical region, including plants from lush British Columbia and semi-arid Texas. The geological strata provide a setting for New Mexican hespaloe and arid varieties from the Yucatan. Magualias, an atypical selection in this region, are abundant throughout the garden and culminate a champion *Magualia ashei* of impressive stature. Each garden area is self-contained but linked to the rest of the landscape by vistas that allow the visitor to see other nodes, outcroppings, and nooks. Magnolia and rhododendron, pierced with unusual collections of Styrax, silverbell, and *Lilium,* cover the grounds in an inviting tapestry. Mrs. Henry was legend among horticulturists and plants people in her time, winning many awards from the prestigious Pennsylvania Horticultural Society as well as an award from the Royal Geography Society of Scotland. The collections continue to grow because the garden is a working garden, and its caretakers are continually searching out new additions.

10 ## Media: Tyler Arboretum

LOCATION: OFF ROUTE 352, ADJACENT TO RIDLEY CREEK STATE PARK, TWENTY-FIVE MILES WEST OF PHILADELPHIA

GARDEN OPEN: 8am–dusk daily. **ADMISSION:** $3 adults, $1 children.

FURTHER INFORMATION FROM:
515 Painter Road, Media
19063-4424. (610) 566-5431

NEARBY SIGHTS OF INTEREST:
Ridley Creek State Park, Caleb Pusey House

William Penn, the founder of Pennsylvania and designer of Philadelphia, extended his reach far beyond the boundaries of that city, leasing and selling lands throughout the rolling hillside of what today we call the metropolitan area. One such property was sold to the Minshall family in 1691. In 1825, descendants of those first settlers, Jacob and Marshall Painter, began cultivating an extensive arboretum of exotic tree specimens. Today some of that collection exists as the pristine and beautiful Tyler Arboretum, a 650-acre preserve in the ever-developing woodlands of Delaware County. Like the other major gardens in the area, the Arboretum has always been engaged in a lively dialogue with horticulturists, receiving seeds and plants from the various du Ponts and providing like in return. A walk commemorating the Painter brothers passes by the major tree specimens including a giant sequoia, which greets visitors as they enter the compound, false cypress, cedar of Lebanon, and the curiously hollow Yulan magnolia. There are also several groves that feature classic nineteenth-century varieties, such as magnolia, lilac, cherry, and crabapple. A handful of pretty flower gardens calculated to attracted butter-flies and birds are neatly knitted into the overall presentation

11 Swarthmore: Scott Arboretum

LOCATION: ROUTE 320 AND COLLEGE AVENUE, JUST OFF ROUTE 476,
TEN MILES SOUTHWEST OF PHILADELPHIA

Scott Arboretum is located near some pretty tough competi-tion; yet, it is the students at Swarthmore College who enjoy one of the most significant arboreta and gardens anywhere. The entire campus of this liberal arts college (student popula-tion 1,300) is considered a garden, in some manner. Notable specimen trees dot the landscape as do several tree gardens, such as a bewitching metasequoia allée, a pinetum, and the Frorer Holly Collection, which contains over 200 specimens of holly and provides a particularly vibrant place in winter. Although designed and cared for as a public garden, the Scott Arboretum is integrated into the fabric of Swarthmore life. Each year, graduating seniors wear a rose from the Dean Bond Rose Garden—an extraordinary collection of 200 varieties— and participate in the service held in an outdoor amphitheater stitched through with a thin grove of tulip trees, which actually grow between the curvilin-ear seats. On the eastern edge of campus, a drainage ditch was converted into a biostream. A meandering streambed helps reduce the amount of runoff that empties into nearby Crum Creek, while also feeding a healthy ecosystem of bluestar, goldenrod, and switchgrass. Recent additions to the arboretum include the Nason Garden, devoted to test plants, which include broad-leafed paulownia and *Rudbeckia*. The real joy at Scott is simply walking around cam-pus, where one assumes random plantings of daylilies and viburnums, containers brimming with annuals and grasses, as well as the occasional hidden copse or courtyard, would release the undergraduate mind from its harried contemplation of the conjuga-tions of Goethe or the perambulations of Thoreau— not to mention other, far less esoteric concerns.

GARDEN OPEN: dawn–dusk daily. Arboretum office open: 8:30am–4:30pm Monday–Friday. ADMISSION: free.

FURTHER INFORMATION FROM: 500 College Avenue Swarthmore 19081-1397. (610) 328-8025

NEARBY SIGHTS OF INTEREST: Tyler Arboretum, Bartram's Garden

The Dean Bond Rose Garden in full bloom

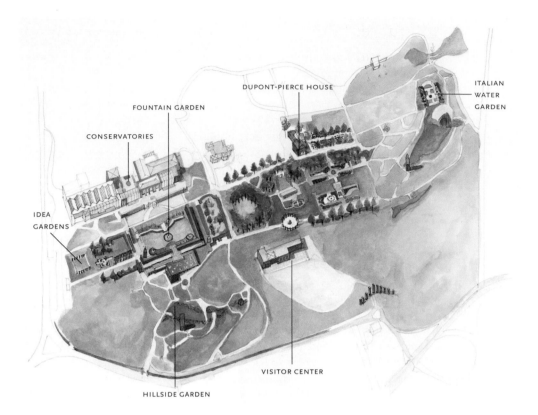

CONSERVATORIES

FOUNTAIN GARDEN

DUPONT-PIERCE HOUSE

ITALIAN
WATER
GARDEN

IDEA
GARDENS

VISITOR CENTER

HILLSIDE GARDEN

*Christmas time in the
Orangerie sees poinsettias,
orange trees, and other
artful combinations.*

12 Kennett Square: Longwood Gardens

LOCATION: ROUTE 1, TWELVE MILES NORTH OF WILMINGTON, DELAWARE

For many people the tacit, though sometimes overt, du Pont horticultural competition finds its culmination in Longwood Gardens, the former estate of Pierre du Pont, a chairman of the Dupont chemical company and General Motors Corporation and cousin to Alfred (of Nemours) and Henry (of Winterthur). Du Pont purchased the land from the Pierce family, which had been in residence since 1700. The landscape surrounding the 1730 manor house was designed as a pleasure ground and arboretum, including croquet lawns, summerhouses, and a wonderful collection of trees—an excellent assortment of natives, such as wild tulip trees, as well as others from afield, such as Kentucky coffee trees imported from western Pennsylvania and gingkos acquired through trade. Although owned privately, the Pierces maintained the property as a public arboretum; in part this character (combined with the natural beauty of the place) is what enticed Pierre du Pont to purchase it in 1906. In his hands, the gardens would remain dedicated to public enjoyment while undergoing a radiant transformation.

The two most defining characteristics of Longwood are its eclecticism and its rigorous horticultural focus—both of which are due to the vision and persona of du Pont, who personally oversaw the design, development, and maintenance of the property until his death in 1954. The prize of Longwood are the conservatories, a string of greenhouses some quarter-mile in length, in which a staff of master gardeners prepare exuberant displays that change through the seasons. The major display rooms are the Orangerie, East Conservatory, and Exhibition Hall. Set within a handsome architectural context of bronze arched windows and Corinthian columns, plantings arranged in a highly wrought and meticulous aesthetic comprise floral exhibits of a grandeur and magnificence unequaled on American soil. Although the displays change from season to season and year to year (an exception being an exuberant chrysanthemum festival held every November), the underlying character of each room imparts a certain amount of constancy to the displays. The Orangerie, owing to its rectilinear layout, focuses on the geometric interplay of form and color, with large masses of delphiniums or rows of fuchsias playing against lines of evergreen, for instance. The East Conservatory, by contrast, is arranged in a flowing manner, with a looping path winding around several pools. Here the displays tend more toward the naturalistic, with vertical elements (such as trees) giving the idea of a landscape rather than a canvas. The Exhibition Hall, a moody and more serious space, has the most "interior" feeling of all the rooms, a sensation heightened by the thin film of water that lines the balustraded center court

GARDENS OPEN: 9am–6pm daily, April–October; until dark Tuesday, Thursday, and Saturday, summer; 9am–5pm daily, November–March. CONSERVATORIES OPEN: 10am–5pm daily. ADMISSION: $12 adults, $6 youth (ages 16-20), $2 children (ages 6-15).

FURTHER INFORMATION FROM: Route 1, P.O. Box 501 Kennett Square 19348-0501 (610) 388-1000 www.longwoodgardens.org

NEARBY SIGHTS OF INTEREST: Winterthur, Nemours, Brandywine River Museum and Conservancy

TOP: *Du Pont drew inspiration from his European travels in designing the Italian Water Garden.*

BOTTOM: *The Cascade Garden was designed by Roberto Burle Marx.*

and casts a cavernous feeling. Beyond these central areas, the
conservatories contain many other displays, most of which are
permanent. The Cascade Garden, at the westernmost corner of
the facility, was designed by Brazilian landscape architect
Roberto Burle Marx in 1992 and reveals his artful understanding of the verticality of tropical plants. In the fern passage witness fly catchers, venerable stag-horns, and the spiderlike, rare
colysis. Other collections include a lily pond, a palm house,
Mediterranean garden, desert garden, bonsai and espaliered
fruit gardens, and a superior collection of orchids.

Although the conservatories alone can occupy several visits to Longwood, the grounds contain dozens of important garden areas worth visiting. Throughout its history, a major
attraction at Longwood has been the acrobatic water displays,
the result of continuous experimentation and technical tinker-
ing, and which today are culminated in the grand Fountain
Garden, constructed in 1931 and located just south of the conservatories. A total of 380 jets, 675,000 gallons of water, and an
18-pump circulation system feed a series of pools in magically
timed sequences. Inspired by the water gardens of Europe, particularly Versailles, and an exhibit of water-jet technology discovered at the 1893 World's Columbian Exposition in Chicago,
du Pont created this garden to entertain his friends and the
public. Although considered theatrical eye-candy by garden
purists, the fountains are still a technical wonder; and at night
the illuminated effect is stunning. Throughout his life and
work in the garden, du Pont was interested in technology, and
the electrical control system for the Fountain Garden was the
most advanced of its day. Today, that futurism has brought a
computer system on board, which coordinates the water dance
to music, echoing to dazzling precision the cadence and

rhythm of a contemporary soundtrack. This Disney-like effect is couched within a beautiful setting. A rectangular allée of Norway maples—an unusual selection for such use—outlines the garden, beyond which du Pont planted a dense deciduous woodland (importing full-grown trees to the amazement of locals) to give the blue-and-white spectacle of splash a strongly contrasting background of deep green.

The Italian Water Garden, located in the less heavily visited eastern corner of Longwood, was a precursor to the grandiose Fountain Garden. Inspired by a visit to Villa Gamberaia near Florence, the garden is a more-refined, gentle feature than its counterpart. Constructed in 1925, the pools are made of limestone, with Italianate ornamentation. A grove of lindens encloses the space on two sides.

A major change in focus since du Pont's time has been a concentration on education at Longwood, which now runs one of the best-known gardening schools in the country. A direct manifestation of this is in the idea gardens that occupy the western precinct of the grounds. Individual gardens devoted to perennials, annuals, vegetables, plants of unusual texture, and ornamental grasses are just some of what can be found here. Each plant is well labeled with not only genus and species but also a brief line about its use in the landscape. As well, short broadsides describe each garden's focus and address pertinent issues, such as staking, blooming periods, and plant sources. The entire area is patrolled by a small army of cats, which the garden intentionally breeds as a sustainable and natural solution to pests and hungry rodents. Although the gardens appear to be free from such maladies, most of the time the cats can been seen lounging around the herb garden, where the catnip is located.

Connected to these gardens geographically and conceptually is the most homely garden at Longwood, but also one of the most beautiful: the Hillside Garden. Here a steep slope is covered with an impressionistic combination of creeping junipers, mosses, and flowers. A delicate staircase weaves through the scene, controlling the experience in a thoughtful way and giving views to a pond and the Chimes Tower nearby.

Longwood is perhaps one of the most decadent gardens in America. It is a plant-lovers dream, with horticultural expertise applied in great fanfare throughout the conservatories and grounds. But the upper reaches of the garden, where portions of the original arboretum still exist, also provide something of interest to the aficionado of pleasure grounds. Architecturally, too, the garden is ablaze with elaborately staged constructions, all calculated to strong effect. The aesthetic is inspired by the fanciful gardens of the European aristocracy; however, in execution, Longwood is more than anything else an American statement—both a forerunner of modern amusement parks and a celebration of American ingenuity and individuality.

TOP: *The Eastern Conservatory displays tend toward a story-book effect.*

BOTTOM: *The Pierce-du Pont house*

GARDENS OPEN: dawn–dusk daily. **ADMISSION:** free.
MUSEUM OPEN: 9:30am–4:30pm daily. **ADMISSION:** $5 adults, $2.50 students, seniors, children.

FURTHER INFORMATION FROM: Route 1, P.O. Box 141, Chadds Ford 19317. (610) 388-2700 www.brandywinemuseum.org

NEARBY SIGHTS OF INTEREST: Longwood Gardens, Nemours

Native plants and a naturalistic setting

13 Chadds Ford: Brandywine Museum and Conservancy

LOCATION: ROUTE 1, TWENTY-FIVE MILES SOUTHWEST OF PHILADELPHIA

Nestled into the forested banks of the pristine Brandywine River, these naturalistic gardens are wonderful examples of the many different uses and characters of native plants. Besides housing a significant collection of American art, including landscapes by Edward Moran and Thomas Doughty and an extensive collection of Wyeth family paintings, the Brandywine complex also contains the conservancy, an environmental preservation and education organization. Native plants are the focus of this ecosensitive garden, which includes a beautiful array of black-eyed Susans, bluebells, various species of phlox, native azaleas, and wild ginger. Although aesthetically pleasing, this garden is meant to be educational. The lessons start in the parking lot, where a sewer basin has been designed as a wetland. Not only does this smack of ecosensitivity, it makes great engineering sense. The profusion of plantlife helps capture water and retain it, preventing erosion elsewhere. It is what we call today an excellent example of sustainable design. Such examples are in abundance here without knocking us about the head with self-righteous admonishments. Even wildflower plantings along the riverbank serve an important purpose (besides their aesthetics). The river provides downstream Wilmington, Delaware, with much of its drinking water. Here again the use of plant mass prevents erosion, which in turn prevents silting and degradation of the river. Some of spirit of the museum spills into the garden at places. Sculptures by Clayton Bright and Gordon Parks adorn the setting and serve as visual focal points for the displays. In the spring the woodland garden becomes interpenetrated by superb displays of wildflowers, while in the fall sumac and viburnums come alive.

14 Upland: Crozer Arboretum

LOCATION: MEDICAL CENTER BOULEVARD, OFF INTERSTATE 95,
FIFTEEN MILES SOUTHWEST OF PHILADELPHIA

The Victorian houses within the confines of this garden testify
to its earlier incarnation as a campus of the Crozer Seminary,
where Martin Luther King Jr. received his divinity education.
Today the arboretum is joined to the large Crozer Medical
Facility, although it is a separate entity and open to the public.
The 12 acres of parkland are devoted to mature trees, which are
labeled, and trails. The collections include an ornamental grass
garden, a holly collection, and a small Japanese-style garden, as
well as many azaleas and rhododendrons. Natural springs that
bubble through the earth in the area contribute to the profusion
of bogs, which have been transformed into naturalistic garden
areas and planted with indigenous varieties. The Leona Gold
Garden forms the epicenter of the arboretum. This naturalistic
woodland garden of understory plantings, rock outcrops, and
carefully arranged groups of coniferous and deciduous plantings were actually transported from the Gold property in Delaware to this spot along Chester Creek. Patients and staff of the
medical center, who come here to recuperate and relieve stress,
actively use the garden. Greenhouses on-site provide cut flowers
for the rooms of nonambulatory patients, while within the garden there is an abundance of cozy nooks placed in opportune
spots that provide meditative and therapeutic experiences.

GARDEN OPEN: 7:00am–
3:30pm daily.
ADMISSION: free.

FURTHER INFORMATION FROM:
1 Medical Center Boulevard
Upland 19018. (610) 447-2281

NEARBY SIGHTS OF INTEREST:
Caleb Pusey House, Morton
Homestead

ABOVE: *Crozer offers
hospital patients a place
to reflect and recuperate.*

GARDEN OPEN: 8:30am–dusk daily. Visitor's center open: 9am–5pm Monday–Saturday; noon–5pm Sunday.
ADMISSION: free.

FURTHER INFORMATION FROM: P.O. Box 685, New Hope 18938-0685. (215) 862-2924

NEARBY SIGHTS OF INTEREST: Carousel World Museum, Washington Crossing Park

15 New Hope: Bowman's Hill Wildflower Preserve

LOCATION: RIVER ROAD (ROUTE 32), TWO MILES SOUTH OF NEW HOPE

The Delaware River cuts a path through some of the most romantic landscape in the country: shady streams, winding roads, and cozy towns with bucolic names, such as New Hope. Bowman's Hill Wildflower Preserve, opened in 1934, is a naturalistic garden of woodlands, streams, and meadows where some 1,000 species of vascular plants (i.e., flowers) native to the region are on display. The selections are arranged in beds along trails that weave through the site, often individual plants or bunches that highlight botanical interest rather than large drifts of color that bespeak a concern for design. But color is profuse here, with plenty of azaleas and marigolds. Of particular note is Pidcock Creek, where a famously intoxicating selection of bluebells and trilliums bloom in late April. For the most part, the garden has been created by editing the existing woods and weaving in a diverse understory of flowers, shrubs, and smaller trees. But there are also several specialized habitats—such as a limestone barren, a hemlock grove (which creates its own microclimate), and a small bog, which have been created to illustrate some of the various ecological conditions found in this region. A newly acquired parcel of land has recently been transformed into a meadow, displaying native wildgrasses. Bowman's Hill Tower sits on a vertiginous rise (some 400 feet above the lower portions of the garden) and provides an athletic walk and a chance to spy down on the rest of the landscape. Bowman's Hill is a haven for plant lovers eager to delve into the more subtle study of native species. The garden's annual Mother's Day plant sale and continuous educational programs are popular events that aim to educate the public about the botanical abundance of the area.

Pidcock Creek cuts through a naturalistic garden.

16 Hershey: Hershey Gardens

LOCATION: HOTEL ROAD, OPPOSITE HERSHEY HOTEL, FIFTEEN MILES
EAST OF HARRISBURG

Hershey is most emphatically the town of chocolate tycoon
Milton Hershey, who not only established his business here
but hired Philadelphia landscape architect Ogelsby Paul to
design the town from the ground up, imprinting almost everything with his client's enthusiasm. In 1936, Hershey hired horticulturist Harry Erdman to create a public rose garden for the
citizens of the town. It quickly became a consuming passion for
the candy baron and by 1955 included 42,000 roses of 1,200
different varieties. The original layout is formal and geometric
in nature, but spread across three-and-a-half acres, it creates an
exuberant scene. The beds are laid out in linear fashion, extending from a formal pond and fountain surrounded by a fence of
climbers toward a lovely gazebo that mimics the hotel. In the
1970s, twenty-five years after the death of Hershey, the gardens
were expanded to include several theme gardens. A tulip and
chrysanthemum garden, designed in semi-radial fashion, lies
on axis with the rose garden and gives brilliant bloom throughout the summer and deep into the fall. There are also two
vibrant bedded annual gardens, one designed as a gigantic fan
with successive bands of color. Beyond the rose garden, the
majority of the gardens are set into a wooded landscape that
includes Japanese maples, hollies, and a large selection of evergreens, many of which are planted amidst stone formations to
create a rock garden. The Japanese Garden, one of the jewels
contains a naturalistic pond enclosed by redwoods and giant

GARDEN OPEN: 9am–6pm
daily, mid April–October 31;
open until 8pm Friday and
Saturday, Memorial Day–
Labor Day. ADMISSION: $5.00
adults, $4.25 seniors, $2.50
children.

FURTHER INFORMATION FROM:
170 West Hersheypark Drive
Hershey 17033. (717) 534-3492

NEARBY SIGHTS OF INTEREST:
Hershey Museum

ABOVE: *An old rose garden
is the epicenter of an entire
array of gardens.*

137

sequoias. In 1942 Mrs. Hershey's rose garden of old European varieties was relocated from the mansion to a small corner of this ever-growing area. Butterfly gardens have been a mainstay at Hershey for years, and in 1998 the garden opened a new Butterfly House, a dome structure of mesh supported by steel arches that were used in a 1930 greenhouse on the premises. Nectar-rich plants are used to retain a stock of rare butterflies, while the dense mesh provides filtered shade and shelter crucial to the development of the eggs and larvae. Beginning in the 1930s with Hershey's ostentatious display of roses, the gardens have always focused on amusing visitors from far and wide. While the Hershey amusement park and chocolate museum both extend that focus to modern incarnations, the gardens today seem quaint, like a botanical Coney Island.

17 Pittsburgh: Phipps Conservatory

LOCATION: SCHENLEY PARK, EAST OF DOWNTOWN PITTSBURGH

GARDEN OPEN: 9am–5pm Tuesday–Sunday. **ADMISSION:** $5.00 adults, $3.50 seniors and students, $2.00 children.

FURTHER INFORMATION FROM: 1 Schenley Park, Pittsburgh 15213-3830. (412) 622-6914 www.phipps.conservatory.org

NEARBY SIGHTS OF INTEREST: Carnegie Museum of Natural History, Carnegie Museum of Art

A Grecian presence in the palm house

It was Henry Phipps's idea to merge a couple of fledgling Pittsburgh iron interests in 1864 into what eventually became the Carnegie Steel Company. Like his partners, the enterprising Phipps profited greatly, a boon that he equaled with philanthropic giving, of which the conservatory that bears his name remains the greatest testament. The structure was designed by Victorian glasshouse savants Lord and Burnham in 1893 and immediately stocked with exotic tropicals from the recent World's Columbian Exposition in Chicago. The vaulted glass Palm Room forms the central annex, adorned with a Romanesque stone entrance designed by Henry Hobson Richardson (removed in 1967), from which three transverse wings radiate. Today, thirteen garden rooms that cover just under an acre contain a rich assortment of plants, including palms (some possibly dating back to 1893), orchids, ferns, desert flora, and tropical fruits and spices. A combination of eye-dazzling displays has been the garden's specialty since its inception. In a frequent summer performance, the flower collections of the Stove Room play host to a bevy of butterflies. Outside the confines of the conservatory lay a Japanese courtyard garden, an aquatic garden featuring water lilies, five terraces of perennials, and a children's garden. In 1993, at 100 years old, the conservatory experienced a rebirth as the city of Pittsburgh, in financial straits, relinquished management to a private foundation, which has since infused the venerable institution with new life. Educational and artistic programming fills the seasons, and the collections and displays receive the care and attention befitting such an important garden.

18 Pittsburgh: Pittsburgh Civic Garden

LOCATION: MELLON PARK

GARDEN OPEN: dawn–dusk
daily. ADMISSION: free.

FURTHER INFORMATION FROM:
1059 Shady Avenue
Pittsburgh 15232.
(412) 441-4442

NEARBY SIGHTS OF INTEREST:
Frick Art Museum

Richard Beatty Mellon and his wife, Jenny King, built their opulent mansion on this rise in 1911. Mrs. Mellon immediately set about designing terrace gardens that descended down the knoll to the outlying park grounds. The architectural firm of Alden and Harlow designed an elaborate system of retaining walls, balustrades, and ornamenture that gave the landscape a European formalism and attracted national attention in its day. The manor was raised in 1940. After the Mellon family donated the property to the city for a park, the gardens fell into disrepair. Today, a group of volunteers maintains a perennial garden and herb garden on-site. Little of the original garden exists, save a knot garden of lavender, which makes the barest reference to the spirit of Mrs. Mellon, and remnants of the fine architectural details that haunt the landscape like specters. Beneath a tangle of vines and undergrowth are some magnificent specimens of terra cotta and ironwork, accessible only to the adventurous. The local gardeners are active, and the garden serves as an adjunct of the park, hosting an abundance of visitors (and their dogs) throughout the summer. The surrounding landscape is handsomely planted with mature trees, shrubs, and graceful lawns.

19 Pittsburgh: Rodef Shalom Biblical Botanical Garden

LOCATION: FIFTH AVENUE AND DEVONSHIRE STREET, IN OAKLAND

GARDEN OPEN: 10am–2pm
Sunday–Thursday; noon–1pm
Saturday, year-round; 7pm–
9pm Wednesday, June–
August. ADMISSION: free.

FURTHER INFORMATION FROM:
4905 5th Avenue, Pittsburgh
15213. (412) 621-6566
trfn.pgh.pa.us/orgs/rodef

NEARBY SIGHTS OF INTEREST:
Carnegie-Mellon University,
Frick Art Museum

For the faithful, the landscape of the Middle East conjures up images of Eden. The juxtaposition of different topographies and climate, and the wild floral beauty thus created, are like none other in the world. At Temple Rodef Shalom, a spirited congregation has re-created a bit of the Jordan River valley in the heart of Pittsburgh. The one-third-acre garden adjacent to the 1907 landmark temple designed by architect Henry Hornbostel contains temperate and tropical plants from Israel that have Biblical significance—such as figs, pomegranates, cypress, and tamarask—and which are planted in a warm, flowing manner. Accompanying each plant is the verse that describes it. A small stream, designed to symbolize the Jordan River, trickles over a waterfall and cuts through the garden, forming pools filled with water lilies and lotuses and that symbolize Lake Kineret and the Dead Sea. Several architectural features, such as a footbridge and benches, complete the scene. Each summer, the temple creates a special exhibit and sponsors a series of lectures and tours of the garden that focus on a certain aspect of horticulture in ancient Israel. Some examples have included the ancient art of dyeing and the role of beer in Jewish tradition. For the faithful, Rodef Shalom holds special religious significance, evoking the visual texture of Biblical experience. But in addition to its role as a sanctuary for spiritual reflection, the garden also provides people of all faiths an excellent educational experience of the ancient world, from which all of western civilization sprang.

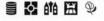

MUSEUM OPEN: 9:30am–4:30pm daily. **ADMISSION:** $9.75 adults, $7.50 students and seniors, $3.50 children.

FURTHER INFORMATION FROM: P.O. Box 3630, Wilmington 19807-0630. (302) 658-2400

NEARBY SIGHTS OF INTEREST: Nemours, Brandywine Museum and Conservancy

20 Wilmington: E. I. du Pont Garden, Hagley Museum

LOCATION: THREE MILES WEST OF THE INTERSECTION OF ROUTES 141 AND 202, SEVEN MILES NORTH OF DOWNTOWN WILMINGTON

The du Pont legacy in Delaware begins at Hagley, a Quaker farm purchased by French immigrant Éleuthère Irénée du Pont and converted into a gunpowder mill. Although he'd trained as a chemist and worked as a printer and publisher, when he immigrated to the United States in 1799 with his brother and father, E. I. put down his occupation as *botaniste*. The moniker speaks to the ancient tradition of the family, a tradition that E. I. transported to the banks of the Brandywine River and bequeathed to his descendants. They, of course, propagated it in such diverse ways throughout the region (Longwood, Winterthur, Nemours). This original du Pont built a gunpowder mill along the Brandywine, and although a large portion of the business was destroyed in successive explosions through the nineteenth century (culminating in one very serious blast in 1890), much of the estate still remains, including the family mansion and outbuildings, a series of canals and the small stone powder mills that they powered, and a re-creation of E. I. du Pont's formal French garden. The garden occupies a gentle slope just in front of the mansion and is laid out in a strict, rectilinear fashion. Like the baroque gardens of eighteenth-century France—most notably Le Notre's designs for Versailles—the garden adheres to a strict geometry. Enclosing the space on two facing sides are single rows of espaliered apple trees—one row trained in the shape of upright forks bearing two tines, the other woven into a crisscrossing pattern. In the interior of the garden, a one-foot-tall parterre of espaliered apple trees—trained from a handful of massive plants, creates a living banister around the beds. The beds are mostly planted with well-tended vegetables, such as squash, cauliflower, and broccoli, and flowers like dahlias and larkspur. While the plants themselves are often impressive—the result of good gardeners—the relationship between the size of the beds and their arrangement is so perfectly calculated as to give this simple vegetable garden classical beauty.

E. I. du Pont's daughter, Louise Crowninshield, was also an avid gardener. She helped found the National Trust for Historic Preservation and was a major figure in the Colonial Revival movement in the late nineteenth century. With the assistance of her husband, Frank Crowninshield, she built a classical garden behind the house. To create an ancient ambience, it is said that Mr. Crowninshield would walk through the garden during construction and pull out bricks from the porticos and arches to create the sense of Roman ruins. Today the gardens have yet to be restored, which would no doubt please Mr. Crowninshield, and can only be viewed from the bus that brings visitors onto the site from the welcome center. Museum admission includes a tour of the house and the grounds, where docents demonstrate how the gunpowder mills operated.

An apple banister encloses E. I. du Pont's vegetable and flower garden.

21 # Wilmington: Nemours

LOCATION: TWO MILES WEST OF THE INTERSECTION OF ROUTES 141
AND 202, SEVEN MILES NORTH OF DOWNTOWN WILMINGTON

GARDEN OPEN: 9am–3pm
Monday–Saturday; 11am–
3pm Sunday, May–November.
ADMISSION: $10 for two-hour
tour of house and gardens.

FURTHER INFORMATION FROM:
Rockland Road, Wilmington
19803. (302) 651-6912

NEARBY SIGHTS OF INTEREST:
Hagley Museum, Wilmington
Museum of Art

Of all the cousins, Alfred I. du Pont made the most decidedly historic statement. Pierre may have been spiritually influenced by Versailles and Henry may have been expressing the botanical roots of the family, but Alfred created a real French baroque garden, replete with prancing putti and Grecian urns, which he named Nemours, after the family's ancestral home in France. Unfortunately, in the past five years, a lack of care and maintenance has taken its toll on the planted landscape at Nemours; however, the bones of its design remain intact and merit a visit.

Two impressive iron gates grace the forecourt of the mansion: the first, rescued from Henry VIII's Wimbledon estate, and the other, an eighteenth-century French commemorative gate to Catherine the Great, containing some magnificently detailed iron roses. To the west of the house is a series of formal garden rooms focused on a sweeping knot garden created in English boxwood. Farther along, the Southern Garden contains a grand lawn surrounded by a parterre border partially filled with herbaceous plants presided over by an enormous tulip poplar. The main gardens slope away from the forecourt along a grand axis and present a stunning perspective. The first room consists of lawn terraces graced with stone urns planted with petunias and emitting a slight stream of water into shallow pools. An unusual and visually stimulating combination of mature pin oaks, horsechestnuts, and Japanese cryptomeria form an allée along the sides and frame the view back toward the mansion. This vista ends in a rectangular reflecting pool edged in marble and adorned by neoclassical sculptures of the four seasons by Henri Crenier in white Carrera marble. Sloping upward, the next room is the Maze Garden, formed by hedges of hemlock and Helleri holly, and which is really more of a large knot garden than an actual maze. An impressive grand colonnade transects the axis. Constructed of Indiana limestone, the structure serves as a memorial to Pierre Samuel du Pont de Nemours and his son E. I. du Pont, the first du Pont immigrants to America. The next room, a sunken garden, is revealed by one of the greatest gestures of surprise in any American formal garden, rolling out behind the colonnade like a great carpet—an entirely new landscape. A dramatic series of fountains, a large pool, and several grottos give the space a subterranean feel. A strangely naturalistic pond forms the end of this space. Beyond, a great lawn slopes up to the misnamed Venus Temple, where the huntress Diana, sculpted in bronze by Jean Houdon, surveys the scene.

Walking the grounds at Nemours can be inspiring, as well as depressing. The plant material has been so poorly managed over the past ten years that most of the force of the formal French design has been dissolved. What were intended to be rigid lines of meticulously pruned boxwood exist today as undulating, half-destroyed hedges. Many of the wonderful trees are in need of a skilled arborist. Limbs litter the site. Algae clogs the reflecting pool and the naturalistic pond. Goose excrement litters the ground. And the flower and ivy beds, which are supposed to give depth and a sense of spirit to the hedges of the Maze Garden and Southern Garden, are little more than patches of dirt with the occasional sad-looking perennial. According to the foundation that administers the property, this pitiful situation is due to a recent outsourcing of gardening responsibilities—however the landscape bears the scars of years of mismanagement. Nonetheless, the underlying structure, in terms of built elements, plant arrangement, and landscape form, remains intact and offers an excellent view of Alfred du Pont's original design intention: to re-create a French country estate on American soil.

22 Wilmington: Rockwood Museum

GARDEN OPEN: dawn–dusk daily. Admission: free.

HOUSE TOURS: on the half hour, 11am–4pm Tuesday–Saturday, March–December.

ADMISSION: $5 adults, $4 seniors, $2 students.

FURTHER INFORMATION FROM:
610 Shipley Road
Wilmington 19809.
(302) 761-4340
info@rockwood.org

NEARBY SIGHTS OF INTEREST:
Delaware Art Museum,
Kalmar Nyckel Foundry

Joseph Shipley was the great-grandson of William Shipley, a founder of Wilmington. So it seems fitting that when this English millionaire decided to build a summer residence, he would choose aristocratic Wilmington. Rockwood was designed and built between 1851 and 1857 by architect George Williams in the style of a typical English country estate. The landscape carries this motif to its fullest expression, mimicking many of the aesthetics of the gardenesque movement that were beginning to make their way to this country (eventually informing the ideas of the great American parks builders) in the mid-nineteenth century. Near the house, Shipley constructed a walled garden that contained fruits and vegetables. Today the wall encloses a formal parterre garden planted by a descendant in the early twentieth century. In the 1800s, Shipley could watch his merchant ships sailing up the Delaware River from the lovely terrace behind the house. However today, a young forest obstructs the majestic view. Outside this area, the landscape rolls into a single pleasure ground. Trees are used in a highly romantic way, like strokes of paint on a canvas. The spikes of conifers are thrust against the bellowing canopy of maple and oak to create a vivid contrast—a far cry from today's ubiquitous arborvitae screen. The effect is also carried into autumn, when deciduous plantings bring forth a calculated polychromatic symphony. Elsewhere, there are more standard expression of the Victorian love of specimen trees, especially in the giant weeping beech that was grafted onto a European beech and planted by Shipley in 1856 (notice the swelling at its base). A ha-ha wall—a drop-off constructed to keep farm animals away from the main house—creates an attractive border to the property by cutting an unobtrusive, curving line along its edge. In 1974 the house was converted into a period museum containing an extensive collection of furniture belonging at one time to Shipley and his heirs.

ABOVE: *The picturesque lawn and romantic enclosures at Rockwood*

23 Newark: University of Delaware Botanic Gardens

LOCATION: SOUTH COLLEGE AVENUE, OFF ROUTE 896, THIRTEEN MILES WEST OF WILMINGTON

GARDEN OPEN: dawn–dusk daily. ADMISSION: free.

FURTHER INFORMATION FROM: Department of Plant and Soil Sciences, Newark 19717-1303. (302) 831-2531

NEARBY SIGHTS OF INTEREST: Upper Bay Museum, Mount Harmon Plantation public gardens of Wilmington

The University of Delaware boasts an outstanding botanical studies department, in part because of the school's proximity to some of the finest gardens in the world. So it comes as no surprise that the university itself contains an impressive botanical garden. The garden is first and foremost a place for study, and the main attractions here are plant specimens. Immediately adjacent to the department's utilitarian greenhouse is a lovely meadow garden of wildflowers punctuated by native shrubs. A collection of white wood asters (*Aster divaricata*) beneath the Canadian hemlock at the edge of the meadow are excellent in late summer, when their white daisy foliage blossoms in stark contrast to black stems. Across the way from the greenhouse lies the herbaceous garden, a 7,000-square-foot lot filled with a profusion of geraniums, goldenrods, and more asters. Unfortunately, the labeling is not great, but there are always students and teachers around ready to identify material. The Emily B. Clark Garden, situated about a mound in front of Townsend Hall, is a collection of many exotic species—such as the sweet pepper bush (*Clethra alnifolia*), a summer-blooming shrub with great fragrance—and several kinds of groundcover. More contemporary emphases are reflected in the extensive native plants collection and a wildflower garden which was designed by university master gardeners, who must periodically design a garden to retain their certification. The university also boasts a parklike campus, the major feature of which is a central mall containing 100-year-old elms.

Demonstration gardens highlight Delaware natives.

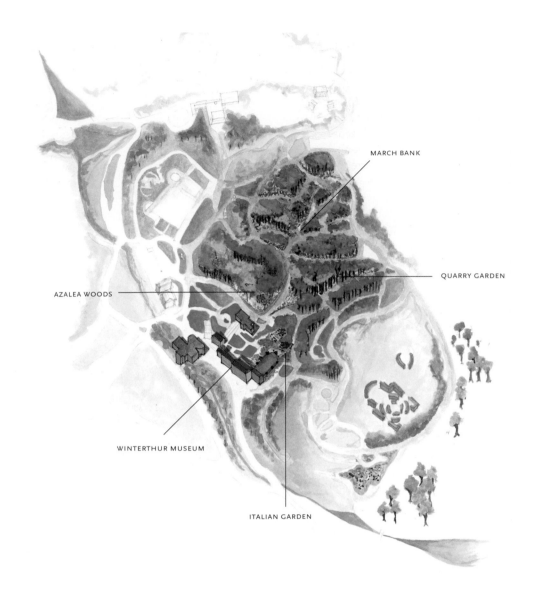

MARCH BANK

QUARRY GARDEN

AZALEA WOODS

WINTERTHUR MUSEUM

ITALIAN GARDEN

24 Winterthur: Winterthur Museum

LOCATION: ROUTE 52, NINE MILES NORTHWEST OF WILMINGTON

"Green is one of the prettiest colors," wrote gentleman gardener Henry F. du Pont, who is largely responsible for the world-famous Winterthur Museum and gardens. But in order to gauge what this normally nonbelletristic figure might have meant, it is imperative to make a pilgrimage to Winterthur, where the beauty of green is fully expressed.

Winterthur, in sharp contrast to its sister gardens, Longwood in Kennett Square and Nemours in Wilmington, is a naturalistic garden, composed primarily of sixty acres of meticulously edited and managed woodlands that have been carefully planted with a rich understory and groundcover of flowering plants. Lush collections of azaleas, peonies, hostas, grandifloras, and narcissi attract thousands of visitors each year; however, there is much more to Winterthur than simply color—though there's plenty of that. The true accomplishment is the intricate, sometimes minute, manipulation of nature to create something perhaps superior. Its beauty is not always readily observable, but rather Winterthur is a garden that must be absorbed over long periods of time.

The tradition of absorbing Winterthur stems from Henry Francis du Pont (1880–1969), who walked these grounds almost every day of his life, quietly observing the progression of plants and the varying conditions of places, which he noted in a small pocket notebook. Henry, of course, was one scion of the wealthy French family that populated these hills beginning in the early nineteenth century, and that in turn, increased its wealth in America in various industrial pursuits, such as gunpowder and, later, chemicals. Du Ponts first settled the property that comprises Winterthur in 1839 when Evelina du Pont and her husband, Jacques Antoine Biderman, purchased the land and named it after Biderman's ancestral home in Switzerland. Evelina and her husband were absentee owners and entrusted the development of the property to her brothers Alfred and Henry du Pont (grandfather of Henry Francis). Although they carried forth in dairy farming per their parents' wishes, Henry, in particular, was more interested in landscape and gardens than cows, and when he finally purchased the property after his sister's death in 1867, he set about planting several small gardens around the property. After his death in 1889, Winterthur passed to his son, Col. Henry Algernon, a man of politics who served in the U. S. Senate. While Henry Algernon was a gentleman farmer who enjoyed gardening and showed a penchant for conifers, in particular, it wasn't until his son, Henry Francis, began to manage the estate in the early years of the twentieth century, that Winterthur as we know it today began to take shape.

GARDEN OPEN: 9am–dusk Monday–Saturday; noon–dusk Sunday. MUSEUM OPEN: 9am–5pm Monday–Saturday; noon–5pm Sunday. Closed Thanksgiving, Christmas, and New Years Day.
ADMISSION: $8 adults, $6 seniors and students, $4 children.

FURTHER INFORMATION FROM: Winterthur 19735. (302) 888-4600

NEARBY SIGHTS OF INTEREST: Longwood Gardens, Nemours, Delaware Art Museum

ABOVE: *The Winterthur Museum galleries are neatly woven into the landscape.*

OPPOSITE: *A spare use of architecture enlivens the peony garden.*

As a young man, Henry du Pont attended Harvard University, where he studied botany under Asa Gray and spent his afternoons in the newly opened Arnold Arboretum, at the same time that Charles Sprague Sargent was assembling his world-class collection of exotic trees. Accompanying Henry on his forays into the Arboretum was the landscape architect Marian Coffin, who for a time, was the only female student of landscape architecture at MIT. Together they admired the Frederick Law Olmsted-designed landscape and exotic trees of the Arnold Arboretum and developed a friendship that would last a lifetime. In 1902, after the death of his mother, Henry returned to Winterthur to help his father, who was becoming increasingly involved in politics, with the estate, and he set himself to gardening.

The star attraction at Winterthur is the eight-acre Azalea Woods. Tucked beneath a canopy of tulip poplars, white oaks, and American beech trees, du Pont planted a dappled tapestry of Kurume azaleas that bloom in a variety of colors. Unlike most azalea gardens, in which this effusive plant is splayed across the open landscape like so much colorful jelly on toast, here the plants are situated within the cool grove of the woods. Without the bleaching effect of the sun, the colors are far more vivid and clear. To heighten the experience, du Pont planted different cultivars of the same variety together; the slight differences in shade and form give a single color added depth. The woods are also planted with a light smattering of dogwoods, the nimble trunks of which give stability to otherwise overflowing pastiche of color. Beneath the flowering azaleas, there is a groundcover of ferns and trilliums. The great show of azaleas takes place from early April to mid-June, a constant cycle of orchestrated color. However, after the blooms die the dogwoods and trilliums provide continued interest.

The parti of the Azalea Woods—the artful placement of hardy (as opposed to strictly native) plants within a carefully designed woodland—extends beyond its borders to the March Bank, an esker planted with naturalized daffodils, crocuses, and snowdrops. Although ensconced in the woodland, this ridge offers some excellent views, particularly of the Bristol Summerhouse, on the other side of the ravine just outside the edge of the woods. Curiously, gazing back from that spot, it is difficult to discern exactly where the March Bank is located in the dense woodland. Near the summerhouse is the seemingly hidden Quarry Garden, which is a reclamation of an actual stone quarry on the site. Cut through by several stone-lined rills, the garden is planted with English primroses, which an apocryphal story holds was inspired by correspondence with Gertrude Jekyll (although this part of Winterthur was the last garden to be built, in 1969, more than thirty years after her death). Smaller and more modest than the rest of the gardens, this quiet and sublime place nonetheless shows du Pont at the height of his powers.

Although he devoted his life to the gardens, du Pont made little provision for them in his estate, which was mostly concerned with turning the house and his extensive collection of Americana into a museum. As a result the Winterthur gardens devolved into mayhem for several years until the current garden director, Thomas Buchter, mounted an aggressive reclamation in 1987. After a decade the restoration is best seen close to the house, while outlying gardens continue to be reworked. The first areas to be restored were in the formal gardens located behind the house. Here du Pont enlisted the help of his friend Marian Coffin, whose tastes ran to the more formal and geometric. Italianate in inspiration, the gardens descend from the back of the house in a series of steps and terraces to a swimming pool that has since been converted into a reflecting pool. The handsome stone stairs were once lined with boxwood, however without proper management they became too unwieldy and had to be removed. Coffin's axial relationships provide an interesting counterbalance to the general tenor of the naturalistic gardens and remind us, in the hush of the woods, that there are other, radically different worlds than that of Henry du Pont's Winterthur.

TOP: *A Sargent cherry explodes in the spring.*

BOTTOM: *The March Bank in early spring*

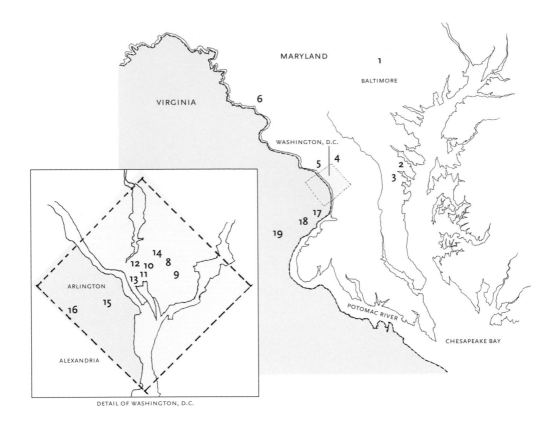

MARYLAND

BALTIMORE

1

VIRGINIA

6

WASHINGTON, D.C.

5 | 4

2

3

17

18

19

POTOMAC RIVER

CHESAPEAKE BAY

ARLINGTON

14
12 10 8
13 11 9
15
16

ALEXANDRIA

DETAIL OF WASHINGTON, D.C.

CAPITAL REGION:

Washington, D.C., Maryland, and Northern Virginia

As with most other aspects of life in Washington, D.C., the presence of the federal government has had a visible effect on gardens. Most of the owners of the great gardens in the region were associated with government, either as a founder (George Washington of Mount Vernon) or as a civil servant (Mildred and Robert Woods Bliss of Dumbarton Oaks). In the District of Columbia proper, the federal government has bequeathed to America several wonderful gardens. The National Arboretum (*pages 160–61*) is an often-overlooked treasure due to its location on the periphery of the tourist precincts. Yet the grounds are magnificently designed and contain many important collections, such as the world-famous bonsai museum. The U.S. Botanic Garden (*page 159*) is unfortunately undergoing an extensive renovation at the same time that the new National Garden is being planted, but the adjacent Bartholdi Gardens are still a magical place to rest while strolling along the Mall.

The federal influence wanes, at least in terms of aesthetics, when we step into Georgetown and then into Dumbarton Oaks (*pages 164–67*). Here Beatrix Farrand found her greatest patron in Mildred Bliss, and together the duo converted a steep hillside into a series of distinct formal gardens, each with its own character and seemingly eternal beauty. Although Dumbarton Oaks dominates Georgetown, there are two pocket gardens that are delightful when stumbled upon. Tudor Place (*page 168*), a historic landscape around the corner from Dumbarton Oaks, exudes the same sort of intimacy but in an informal manner. The Old Stone Garden (*page 169*) is a lovely re-creation of an

OPPOSITE: *The hunt scene at Ladew Topiary Gardens*

The historic flower
knot at Tudor Place,
Washington, D.C.

eighteenth-century town garden, set off from the main road. Landscape architects Wolfgang Oehme and James van Sweden, who make Washington their home, have had a profound affect on gardening in America in the past ten years, and there are several places here to observe the gestation of their practice. Most noticeably are the gardens of the Federal Reserve (*page 163*), where classic themes of the "new American garden" can be discerned, such as layering, use of lush grasses, and borrowed vistas.

The tenor of life, and garden life in particular, changes outside of the city, especially when heading south. Although located only ten miles from the capital, George Washington's Mount Vernon (*pages 174–75*) and George Mason's Gunston Hall (*pages 175–76*) are southern landscapes that reflect the inimitable characters of these men. Washington's estate presents a palpable incarnation of his belief that gardening made one a better citizen by knitting us to the land. Gunston Hall seems to indicate the exact opposite. Here the reclusive and politically frustrated Mason took solace in solitary gardening after the death of his wife. These statements of individuality are echoed north of Washington, in Monkton, where Harvey Smith Ladew created his amazing topiary gardens (*page 153*), or in Bethesda, at the bucolic estate of William McCrillis (*page 157*).

But contemporary history continues to move on, and at Winkler Botanical Preserve (*page 170*) just outside the city, one can see the next wave in gardens—those that attempt to mitigate the harmful effects of development as our society continues to consume rural land.

Monkton: Ladew Topiary Gardens

LOCATION: JARRETTSVILLE PIKE, AT THE INTERSECTION OF ROUTES 146 AND 152, TWENTY MILES NORTH OF BALTIMORE

GARDEN OPEN: 10am–4pm Tuesday–Friday; 12noon–5pm Saturday and Sunday, mid April–October and second weekend in December; open until 8pm on Thursdays, Memorial Day–Labor Day. **ADMISSION:** $6 adults, $5 seniors, $1 children.

FURTHER INFORMATION FROM: 3535 Jarrettsville Pike Monkton 21111. (301) 557-9570

NEARBY SIGHTS OF INTEREST: Boordy Vineyards, Havre de Grace Decoy Museum

As a young man newly home from serving in World War I, Harvey Smith Ladew made a laudable declaration. He decided to reverse life's pattern and spend the first part gallivanting about from enjoyment to enjoyment, and then resume work after fifty. Of course, as Ladew remained independently wealthy all his life, the second half of the bargain was of less importance. When he wasn't jetting off to Britain to participate in fox hunts, Ladew spent his time on his luxurious estate in Maryland creating one of the most outlandish and impressive topiary gardens in the world. Luckily, the garden never fell into disarray (the death knell for topiary) and remains just as perfect today as it was 40 years ago. The iconographic Hunt Scene greets visitors as they come up the front drive to the house. Here Ladew trained yew hedge onto metal frames in a kinetic mimesis of a fox chase: a rider vaults a fence while before him several hounds give chase. Surrounding these fanciful forms are several areas of beautiful flower and woodland gardens. The romantic Victorian Garden includes azaleas and rhododendrons, spring bulbs, and bedded-out annuals. In the Berry Garden, immediately behind the house, viburnums, pyracanthas, and dogwoods provide winter food for a display of birds. Topiary takes over again off the north wing of the house, where a formal lawn garden is edged by tall yews that are trimmed into "garlands." A curious blend of obelisks and French hens sitting on nests alternate down a series of terraces that continue down a gently graded slope to an oval swimming pool nestled into the lawn; the entire garden is surrounded by an undulating wave of hedge supporting twelve graceful swans. Ladew loses himself in the topiary Sculpture Garden, where an eclectic assemblage of figures—magnificent lyrebirds with fan-like tails, a model of Winston Churchill's top hat, and the victory sign—are jumbled together in freak-show fashion, creating a sense of having truly stepped through the looking glass. A woodland that runs alongside these lawn gardens contains several theme gardens, including the White Garden, containing lilacs, dogwoods, and hundreds of white bulbs. Besides a presiding Anglophilia, there is little to connect the twenty-some garden rooms of Ladew Topiary Gardens except for the personality and whim of Ladew himself, who conceived and tended them with exuberance until his death in 1976.

Lyrebirds and other topiary are combined with statuary in the Sculpture Garden.

GARDEN OPEN: 10am–4pm
Monday–Saturday; 12noon–
4pm, Sunday. ADMISSION: $4.

FURTHER INFORMATION FROM:
186 Prince George Street
Annapolis 21401.
(410) 263-5553

NEARBY SIGHTS OF INTEREST:
U.S. Naval Academy,
Maritime Museum

2 Annapolis: William Paca Garden

LOCATION: PRINCE GEORGE STREET, DOWNTOWN ANNAPOLIS

It is hard to believe that historic Annapolis contains only one historic garden, that of William Paca, who in the 1770s, planted an impressive English pleasure garden behind his brick Georgian manor house. It was a fitting accoutrement for such an impressive man—Paca was a signer of the Declaration of Independence and governor of Maryland. Although the original garden has been lost to history, a faithful reproduction was created in the 1970s by landscape architect Lawrence Brigham, who worked from a historical portrait of Paca in his garden and a watercolor of the landscape painted in the mid-1800s. Much of the plant material was chosen from lists prepared by William Ferris, a local plantsman and a neighbor of Paca's in the eighteenth century who kept copious records of his own purchases. The architectural elements of the garden are faithful reproductions of those portrayed in the paintings. They include a two-story summerhouse and a Chinese Chippendale bridge—both vestiges of Paca's English aristocratic tastes. The brick wall surrounding the property is original and contains curious slits along its length in an effort to increase the healthful circulation of air through the garden. Nearest to the house, lining a lawn terrace, are two parterres of roses and perennials, overstuffed with selections from Ferris. A kitchen garden extends beyond these, including herbs, vegetables, fruit trees, and medicinal plants, such as lungwort and comfrey, a cure for psoriasis. The far reaches of the garden devolve into more romantic, wilderness areas, with a small spring-fed pond, a bathhouse, and many native plants. Two arbors with Chinese paneling were rebuilt here based on decaying originals at the Charles Carroll House nearby. Within the rich historical fabric of Annapolis, the Paca house provides a pleasant refuge for local garden history.

3 Edgewater: London Town

LOCATION: OFF ROUTE 2, TEN MILES SOUTHWEST OF ANNAPOLIS

London Town is in the process of becoming a living museum, like Colonial Williamsburg, Sturbridge Village, and Strawberry Banke. Several old structures exist on-site, including the 1760s William Brown House, which was also a public house for a time. But while the excavations take place (which should take several years) and reconstruction and preservation of the buildings occur (which should take even longer), there are eight acres of woodlands and cultivated gardens on display. The site overlooks the South River, an inlet of the Chesapeake Bay. Wood-chipped paths lead through naturalistic woodland colorfully planted with peonies and azaleas. There are notable collections of hollies and magnolias, as well as daylilies, stitched into the forest, while a wooded dell contains a wildflower garden. Behind the Brown house is the Richard Hill Garden, an herb garden of eighteenth-century medicinal plants reconstructed according to the letters of Hill, an early resident of the area (c. 1730) and a physician, who corresponded frequently with the Royal Society in London. The garden sponsors a plant sale on the last Saturday of April and the third Saturday of September.

GARDEN OPEN: 10am–4pm Monday–Saturday; noon–4pm Sunday. **ADMISSION:** $6

FURTHER INFORMATION FROM:
839 Londontown Road
Edgewater 21037.
(410) 222-1919

NEARBY SIGHTS OF INTEREST:
U.S. Naval Academy,
historic Annapolis

ABOVE: *A hill of azaleas beautifies a recreation of colonial London.*

4 # Wheaton: Brookside Gardens

LOCATION: GLENALLAN AVENUE AND RANDOLPH ROAD, TEN MILES
NORTHWEST OF WASHINGTON

GARDEN OPEN: dawn–dusk
daily, except Christmas Day.
ADMISSION: free.

FURTHER INFORMATION FROM:
1800 Glenallan Avenue
Wheaton 20902
(301) 949-0571

NEARBY SIGHTS OF INTEREST:
Clara Barton National
Historic Site, Washington
Mormon Temple

Brookside Gardens is a uniquely American place. Here is a
pleasure garden oriented not toward aristocratic tastes but to
public education. Designed by German garden designer
Hans Hanses in 1969 and situated within a small regional
park, the gardens are divided into formal and informal areas of
horticultural displays geared less toward botanical diversity
than engaging ongoing design combinations. The three formal
gardens are arranged on a common axial path; they follow no
particular scheme but are intended simply to display a smattering of ideas for the benefit of the everyday gardener. In the
spring, crocuses and other bulbs spawn impressionistic swaths
of color, but in other places, there are more geometric arrangements surrounded by clipped yew hedges. These culminate
in the Round Garden, an intimate setting of purple-leafed plum
trees and blooming groundcover. Specialty and theme gardens
surround these areas and include a collection of tea roses, a
garden of fragrant herbs, and a seven-acre woodland of azaleas
and rhododendrons. An arboretum fans out over fifty acres
beyond the azalea woods and encompasses a collection of
viburnums, a winter garden of paperbark maple and holly, and
early-blooming flowers. The Gude Garden, commemorating a
local nurseryman, is a Japanese garden in the grand landscape
tradition of sculpted topography, ponds, and dotted groves. In
the spirit of education that pervades Brookside, there is a horticultural library on the grounds where the librarians answer
common gardening questions. There are also several display
gardens here of continually revolving plant combinations.

*An open air tea house
sits above one of the
ponds at Brookside.*

Bethesda: McCrillis Gardens

5

LOCATION: NEAR THE JUNCTION OF INTERSTATE 270 AND THE BELTWAY, TEN MILES NORTHWEST OF WASHINGTON

When he wasn't serving in the department of the interior under Presidents Franklin D. Roosevelt, Harry S. Truman, and Dwight D. Eisenhower, William McCrillis was planting azaleas on his five-acre homesite in Bethesda. Hundreds of azaleas, planted in a shady, woodland setting comprise these gardens. For years the gardens, which are managed by nearby Brookside Gardens, have been experimenting with varieties and cultivars to create a longer blooming season. In 1981 the importation of over 300 Satsuki azaleas extended it as far as June—quite an accomplishment in this tricky climate. In fitting accompaniment, the forested backdrop for this springtime symphony of color consists of many Asiatics, such as stewartias, dawn redwood, and umbrella pine. Because the McCrillis Gardens collection are primarily monospecies, the best time to visit is between March and June when the azaleas are in full bloom. During this period, owing to the scope of the collection, each weekend displays an entirely different character of the gardens. McCrillis's house has been converted into an art gallery that regularly hosts new exhibitions of work by local artists.

GARDEN OPEN: 10am–dusk daily. Gallery hours vary.
ADMISSION: free.

FURTHER INFORMATION FROM:
6910 Greentree Road
Bethesda 20817
(301) 365-5728

NEARBY SIGHTS OF INTEREST:
Clara Barton National Historic Site, Washington Mormon Temple

ABOVE: *Springtime tulips adorn the galleries at McCrillis Gardens.*

GARDEN OPEN: 9:30am–
5:30pm Monday–Saturday;
11:30am–5:30pm Sunday.
ADMISSION: free.

FURTHER INFORMATION FROM:
6800 Lilypons Road
Buckeystown 21717.
(301) 874-5133

NEARBY SIGHTS OF INTEREST:
Harper's Ferry, Antietam,
Crystal Grottos Caverns

ABOVE: *Virginia waterlilies
spread across an informal
pond.*

6 Buckeystown: Lilypons
Water Gardens

LOCATION: OFF ROUTE 85, TEN MILES SOUTH OF FREDERICK

Usually nurseries are interesting to only the most enthusiastic
gardener, but Lilypons is the exception. Here the focus is on
aquatic plants, the presentation so artful, so utterly different
from most nurseries that it bears notice. A total of 500 ponds
and pools, many of which are cement lined and formal, are
spread out over 300 acres. A rich fabric of color schemes illustrates not only the diversity of aquatics but their use in garden
compositions. Each garden represents a typical home landscape within which a water garden is featured—including natural, irregularly formed ponds, formal pools, waterfall ponds,
and an octagonal pool. Water lilies and lotus predominate;
however such accessory plants as water iris and pickerel rush
are also used. Iconoclasm pervades Lilypons, which was named
after the opera singer; and each year, in June, an opera festival
takes place on the grounds.

7 # Washington: U. S. Botanic Garden

LOCATION: INDEPENDENCE AVENUE, BETWEEN 1ST AND 2ND STREETS,
JUST OFF THE NATIONAL MALL

The U.S. Botanic Garden was a dream of George Washington's, Thomas Jefferson's, and James Madison's, gentleman farmers all. Legislation authorizing the garden dates back to the early nineteenth century; however in typical Washington, D.C., fashion, today's conservatory was constructed as late as 1933. Traditionally the conservatory houses a collection of palms, orchids, cacti, and other exotics. Each year four major flower shows take place. In 1997 it was closed for extensive restorations, and will reopen in 2000, in conjunction with the National Garden unveiling nearby. In the meantime, across another street, is Bartholdi Park, a collection of seasonal gardens. Situated on an oddly shaped triangular block, the garden is cut into a complex pentagram by a network of paths. In the center is a fountain designed by Frédéric Auguste Bartholdi, architect of the Statue of Liberty, originally created for the 1876 centennial celebration in Philadelphia and purchased by Congress for the Mall. Around the fountain is a formal parterre garden, lined by clipped boxwood and columnar Japanese holly, both of which extend out in the garden to add definition to the pathway system. Fanning out around the fountain garden are annuals and perennials in stylized, formal patterns.

BARTHOLDI GARDENS OPEN: dawn–dusk daily. **ADMISSION:** free. **U.S. BOTANIC GARDEN:** closed for repairs until fall 2000.

FURTHER INFORMATION FROM: 245 First Street, SW Washington, DC 20024. (202) 255-8333

NEARBY SIGHTS OF INTEREST: U.S. Capitol, National Gallery of Art

A small urban garden wraps around the Bartholdi Fountain.

8

Washington: National Arboretum

GARDEN OPEN: 8am–5pm
daily, except Christmas Day.
**NATIONAL BONSAI AND PEN-
JING MUSEUM OPEN:**
10:00am–3:30pm daily,
except Christmas Day.
ADMISSION: free.

FURTHER INFORMATION FROM:
3501 New York Avenue, NE
Washington, DC 20002.
(202) 245-2726

NEARBY SIGHTS OF INTEREST:
U.S. Capitol, The Mall

LOCATION: OFF BLADENSBURG ROAD, IN NORTHEAST
QUADRANT OF WASHINGTON

The National Arboretum was established in 1927 on a patch of
forest along the Anacostia River in what was then the far
reaches of Washington's suburbs. Of course since that time, the
city has grown up around it, so that now this is truly an idyllic
patch in the middle of the concrete jungle. The arboretum occupies 444 acres of rolling woodland. A paved, one-way road takes
visitors around the site to where the different designed gardens
are located, while footpaths traverse the wooded interior. A
quick drive through the park, slowing down enough to get a
glimpse of the collections, can take an hour. Thoroughly perus-
ing just a handful of gardens can take all day. Two of the most
intriguing gardens are located near the visitors' center. The
National Bonsai and Penjing Museum was a gift from the people of Japan to the people of the United States in 1976 to honor
the latter's bicentennial celebration, and represent one of the
most significant collections of that centuries-old art in this
country. A mossy path leads through a dark, silent grove of
Japanese crytomeria, a tall conifer that has a haunting aspect
and gives the place an ancient atmosphere. A plaza joins three
open-air galleries devoted to Japanese bonsai, North American
bonsai, and Chinese penjing (the Chinese version of the art of
miniature trees). To the expert, there are great differences
between each of these traditions, reflecting differences in climate and geography, as well as the cultural evolutions of the art.
(The North American version, as to be expected, is less evolved
than both Asiatic forms.) An area of different formal gardens
lies across the road from the bonsai museum. It includes a mul-
ticolored sunken knot garden, a heritage rose garden planted
with a variety of perennials, and ten herb gardens representing
different uses or histories of herbs: such as culinary herbs and
fragrant herbs, traditional oriental herbs and eastern American
Indian herbs, early American herbs, herbs employed in modern
medicine, herbs used in industry, and a garden of the herbs
described by the Greek physician Dioscorides. Each garden is
labeled and well-laid out; and the conjunction of sight, smells,
and intellectual edification is engrossing.

At the other end of the arboretum, along the outer loop, is
historic Azalea Hill, the first collection in the garden. Over
70,000 plants of several thousand species line the road,
lumped in mounds that seem to tumble or undulate down the
slope when in bloom in early spring. Because azaleas do so well
in dappled shade, the garden is laid out beneath a verdant
canopy of ash, hickory, and elm—the official tree of the District
of Columbia—and are woven into a thin woodland of magnolias, whose blooms provide a delicate white contrast to the dra-

The former columns of the U.S. Capitol now adorn a meadow at the National Arboretum.

matic oranges, reds, and pinks of the azaleas. Passing by a field located in the center of the arboretum affords a glimpse of the original Capitol Columns, an arrangement of sandstone Corinthian columns that originally supported the east portico of the U.S. Capitol building. When they were replaced with marble ones in the 1950s, landscape architect Russell Page designed this visually delightful sculptural arrangement. The stone copse is inviting and spotlights several passive water features. However, the greatest effect is from the edges of the prairie meadow, where the handsome architectural aspect of the columns anchors the view and gives the entire landscape visual strength. Other notable features located farther along the road include a garden of native piedmont woodland containing a room of ferns and eastern prairie plants designed by Wolfgang Oehme and James van Sweden—known internationally for their native gardens. Across the road is the arboretum's Asian collection. With the exception of a pagoda-looking structure, this is not a formal Japanese garden but rather a display of plants typically found in Asian climates.

Farther along is a most impressive conifer garden—the Gotelli Dwarf Conifer Garden, donated by New Jersey nurseryman William Gotelli in 1962. Over 1,500 specimens of naturally dwarfed trees occupy a bend in the road. Although laid out rather unimaginatively, the natural variety of color, texture, and unusual architecture of the plants provide more than enough interest for the uninitiated. The theme is circus sideshow: some are fantastically thin and tall, sticking into the air like totem poles; others bulbous with scalloped leaves like an undersea arthropod; while still others, like the frightening Pendula spruce, creep across the ground as if hungry and seeking food. It is truly an otherworldly place, retrieved perhaps from outer space or some literary fiction.

The National Arboretum is a national treasure, often overlooked by visitors overburdened with museums and monuments located within walking distance of the Mall. For garden connoisseurs this is a good thing, as the gardens are hardly ever crowded.

GARDEN OPEN: 7am–4pm
daily. ADMISSION: free.

FURTHER INFORMATION FROM:
1900 Anacostia Drive, SE
Washington, DC 20020.
(202) 426-6905

NEARBY SIGHTS OF INTEREST:
U.S. Capitol, The Mall

9 ## Washington: Kenilworth Aquatic Gardens

LOCATION: OFF KENILWORTH ROAD IN THE SOUTHEAST QUADRANT
OF WASHINGTON

These unusual gardens were started in the 1880s as a hobby but quickly became an obsession, and later a business, for Civil War veteran Walter B. Shaw and his daughter, Helen Fowler. In the late nineteenth century, these two went to great lengths to obtain exotic water lilies, lotuses, and other blooming aquatic plants from as far afield as South America and Asia. In the 1930s, when an Army Corps of Engineers dredging scheme threatened the gardens, the National Park Service stepped in and rescued them for posterity. Today, the gardens contain over three dozen ponds separated by grassy dikes and situated within earshot of several busy highways and the lazy Anacostia River. During the summer, muddy paths, heavy humid air, and a plethora of buzzing, chirping, croaking wildlife strengthen the lowland experience. The ponds contain primarily lotuses and water lilies—exotic, otherworldly botanical forms that are perhaps the most mysterious and luxurious garden material, if only because they coyly stand out of reach. Beginning in May, a canvas of colors—pinks, whites, reds, and yellows—compete for attention. Predominantly the collection contains hardy plants that bloom in June and July, although there are smaller ponds of tropical lilies that are planted in submerged pots and propagated in a greenhouse during the winter. These bloom later, in August. Many of the lilies are day bloomers and some, night bloomers. So morning time is optimal for viewing this kinetic changeover. Behind the visitors center is a display pool of exotic tropicals. Another pool contains ancient lotuses grown from seed that were discovered in an ancient lakebed in Pulantien, China, in 1951. Estimates put their age at 960 years.

ABOVE: *A tropical lily pond, woven into the Anacostia riverscape.*

10 Washington: Federal Reserve Gardens

LOCATION: 20TH AND C STREETS, OFF VIRGINIA AVENUE, IN THE NORTHWEST QUADRANT OF WASHINGTON

GARDEN OPEN: dawn–dusk daily. **ADMISSION:** free.

FURTHER INFORMATION FROM: 20th and C Street NW, Washington 20551. (202) 452-3000

NEARBY SIGHTS OF INTEREST: White House, Vietnam Memorial, The Mall

A severe winter in 1977 decimated the gardens at the Federal Reserve, an indistinctive concrete box located on a triangular corner in such a way to create an accidental public park. David Lilly, then a member of the board of governors of the Federal Reserve, set about to repair the gardens and retained garden designers James van Sweden and Wolfgang Oehme, whose work was relatively unknown at that time. In this first major commission Oehme and van Sweden demonstrated the bold plant palette that would come to typify their work. A formal fountain plaza ties the building to its urban corner. Lush native grasses frame an undulating lawn to provide a green forecourt to the fountain that is neither ostentatious nor humble. This motif is carried to the front of the building, where it is extended and transformed into fanciful mounds of green to frame the facade and a rectangular lawn for sculpture. Informal garden rooms are created in the nether spaces: between these larger architectural forms and within a small and contained space, Oehme and van Sweden accomplish the seemingly impossible task of creating large, formal landscapes and intimate nodes. "Borrowed views" of picturesque Washington, such as a vista that focuses on the Washington Monument a couple of blocks to the south, are used to arrange certain plantings and pathways: the eye is constantly drawn forward and outward. The garden is actually located atop an underground garage, which left the designers only fifty centimeters of topsoil for the flowers and shrubs and one-meter mounds for trees. Even with these constraints, Oehme and van Sweden planted large swaths of luxurious perennials and grasses—the bold romantic style that has since become known as their "New American Garden."

The Federal Reserve Gardens was Oehme and van Sweden's first major commission.

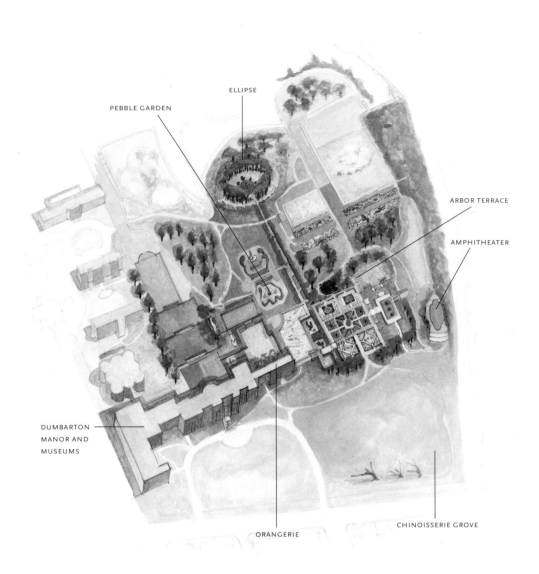

PEBBLE GARDEN

ELLIPSE

ARBOR TERRACE

AMPHITHEATER

DUMBARTON
MANOR AND
MUSEUMS

ORANGERIE

CHINOISSERIE GROVE

11   Washington: Dumbarton Oaks

LOCATION: 32ND AND R STREETS, GEORGETOWN

Dumbarton Oaks was carved from the wilderness by Ninnian Beall, a Scottish planter who surveyed and purchased the land in 1703, and bequeathed to it the name "Rock of Dumbarton" after a geological formation on the Scottish coast. A cast of Virginia notables all put their mark on the property over the next 200 years—the Beverleys, vice president John C. Calhoun (under Andrew Jackson), and a shrewd merchant—of which the Georgian manor that exists on site today is the most notable example. In the 1920s, diplomat Robert Woods Bliss and his wife, Mildred, purchased the fifty-acre estate, located within a crow's mile of the White House. The Blisses were extremely cosmopolitan and spent most of their professional lives in Europe and South America, where they acquired a taste for fine art, particularly Byzantine and Pre-Columbian—which Mr. Bliss continually advocated should be gauged on its artistic merits, not anthropological ones—rare books, and historic gardens. While the first three interests involved extensive collecting and shipping back to the United States of some of the world's finest rarities, the process of collecting gardens was more internal and, hence, more imaginative.

The gardens at Dumbarton Oaks are the result of a ten-year collaboration—often conducted by letter—between Mildred Bliss and her close friend and ally, landscape architect Beatrix Farrand. Although the gardens bear the unmistakable imprint of Bliss and her taste for the gardens of Europe, they are also considered some of Farrand's greatest work. A tour begins in the Orangerie, a roofed, open-air garden room appended to the east wing of the house. A single fig tree, dating to the Civil War, is the sole source of the entire foliage here—notice the large trunk at the western edge of the room. Beyond this semi-enclosure, formal garden rooms encompass the house in a system of terraces that step down the slope toward the outlying woods. In architectural design, form, and detail the rooms closest to the house were intended to be a direct extension of the interior living spaces, places where the family could eat, talk, and swim in the large pool. Proceeding away from the house and down from the first tier, however, they become progressively informal, until finally opening up into landscape grounds and naturalistic woodlands.

The several formal rooms near the house offer a diversity of experiences, from the effusive Rose Garden, planted with some 1,000 roses and ringed by a stone balustrade inscribed with the family motto, *Quod Serveris Metes* (As you sow, so shall you reap), to the delicate and sparse Fountain Terrace, containing two water-spurting putti designed by Farrand and surrounded by ivy-covered stone walls and beds of perennials.

GARDEN OPEN: 2pm–6pm daily, April–October, except holidays. ADMISSION: $3 adults, $2 seniors and children.

FURTHER INFORMATION FROM: 1703 32nd Street, NW Washington, DC 20007 (202) 339-6401

NEARBY SIGHTS OF INTEREST: Tudor Place, Woodrow Wilson House

OPPOSITE: *The Fountain Terrace bordering the formal gardens*

The most secluded spot in the garden is nearby, in the Arbor Terrace, where a wisteria-draped reproduction of an arbor designed by the Renaissance architect Jacques Androuet du Cerceau and a trickling fountain offer respite from the heat. From here there are excellent views—once framed by the trees, but now a little obscured—of the rest of the garden below.

One of the great achievements of Dumbarton Oaks is the design of the transitions from one room to the next. Each part of the garden is radically different from every other, in both theme and atmosphere; but through the careful manipulation of the entrances and exits to each room, there is never a sense of shock. Rather, gentle surprise and expectation infiltrate one's mind while moving through the landscape. A great example of this occurs in moving between the diminutive amphitheater, which sits above Lover's Lane Pool, and the kitchen gardens. The path, called Melisande's Allée, passes through narcissus and silver maples as it proceeds downslope in a graceful arc. However, its entire sweep is never fully visible, thereby creating a sense of wonder and continually infusing the mind with wonder.

A major attraction at Dumbarton Oaks is the Ellipse, constructed with rare and unusual linden trees. As with the rest of the garden, the magic here relies on the acute sense of proportion and the employment of magisterial, and surprising, materials. A pool once sat in the center of this area, although Mrs. Bliss had it removed, along with many other water features onsite, in the 1960s when the property was being transformed into a more public institution. Another transformation made at this time occurred with the tennis courts, which were removed and converted into the Pebble Garden, an ornate tile-and-stone landscape sculpture in the form of a sheaf of wheat (the family motto again) designed by Ruth Havey, a landscape architect in

TOP: *A quiet colonnade on the middle terrace*

BOTTOM: *The seasonal cutting garden*

Farrand's office. On the north end of the house, the four terraces descending down a hill mark one of Farrand's first and
most auspicious designs here. By progressively narrowing each
terrace, she created a sense of false perspective, as if the space
were actually longer than it is. The design also serves to mitigate the precipitous character of the slope.

Elsewhere on the property are many other wonders large
and small, formal and informal, as paths lead around toward
the front of the house or back into the reaches of Forsythia Hill.
A favorite place of seclusion is located along the path heading
up behind the amphitheater and toward the front gate. At a
bend in the row, a small copse with two seats emerges. The
seats and accompanying swing, which has been partially dismantled, are indicative of the French chinoisserie style. To
complement their oriental aesthetic, the surrounding area is
planted in bamboo, and a brilliant split-leaf Japanese maple
hangs over the scene.

Throughout their lives here, the Blisses always considered
Dumbarton Oaks a kind of intellectual and artistic center in
the grand Mediterranean tradition dating back to the courts of
the Medici. In this spirit, delegates from nations around the
world met here in 1944 for a series of conferences that resulted
in the creation of the United Nations. In 1940, the Blisses
donated their art and rare book collections, and the mansion
and grounds of Dumbarton Oaks, to Harvard University.
Today, the facility operates as a private research institution,
although much of the artwork is on rotating display in two
small museums—the Byzantine collection is located in the
main house, while the Pre-Columbian is located in a building
designed by Philip Johnson in 1963.

TOP: *The restful hornbeam
Ellipse designed by Beatrix
Ferrand*

BOTTOM: *The Bliss mansion,
rebuilt in 1920 from an 1801
manor house*

GARDEN OPEN: 10am–4pm
Monday–Saturday.

ADMISSION: $2 donation.

**DOCENT-LED HOUSE AND GAR-
DEN TOURS (AVAILABLE BY
APPOINTMENT):** 10am–3pm
Tuesday–Saturday.

ADMISSION: $6.

FURTHER INFORMATION FROM:
1605 32nd Street, NW
Washington, DC 20007.
(202) 965-0400
www.tudorplace.org

NEARBY SIGHTS OF INTEREST:
Dumbarton Oaks, Old Stone
Garden

ABOVE: *Broccoli-like
undulations of boxwood
are a southern touch.*

12 Washington: Tudor Place

LOCATION: 31ST, 32ND, Q AND R STREETS, GEORGETOWN

Cozy Tudor Place is tucked into the neighborhood of Georgetown like a hidden gem. All eight acres of garden are peppered
by nooks, crannies, copses, shaded arbors, and the most meticulously and tastefully arranged nodes, which transport the visitor
far away from the fashionable shops of Wisconsin Avenue and
the bustle of downtown Washington. The estate originally
belonged to Thomas Peter and his wife Martha Custis, grand-
daughter of Martha Washington. Dr. William Thornton, the
first architect of the U.S. Capitol, designed the neoclassical
structure, which was built in 1816. The gardens were designed
on the instructions of Martha Custis Peter, an astute but somewhat obtuse gardener, whose personal imprint is evident
throughout. First evidence of this is spied in the English boxwood trimmed into undulating mounds in the drive. The
pungent fragrance and protean shape of this shrub make
appearances throughout the landscape. The garden is finely
planted with a variety of leafy herbaceous plants and specimen
trees and contains a few jaw-dropping mature oaks that cover
large tracts of the garden with their canopy. Formal garden
rooms set within a naturalistic woodland context occupy the
north end of the property, while open lawns and flower borders
comprise the southern half. Peter's tastes tended toward the old
English. The Flower Knot, a boxwood matrix filled with old

roses, adorned the property from earliest times, although the present garden is a 1923 re-creation. A wooded dell occupies the western edge of the property. Here the path dips down into a shady glen of native woodland plants such as the slope of plantain lilies, all situated beneath a mature canopy. The garden can be viewed from the stone-and-wrought-iron semicircular seat on the trail above. With the guarded exception of this space, there are no grand vistas here, rather, the emphasis is on quiet observation of nature within small enclosures that often seem to have been discovered for the first time. The effect can be transformative, especially in the romantic copse beside the brick-lined lily pond. Two chairs are set here for contemplative souls. The spirit of the place transfixes even the bronze of young Bacchus (cast from the original located in the U.S. Capitol).

13 Washington: Old Stone Garden

LOCATION: M STREET BETWEEN 30TH AND 31ST STREETS, GEORGETOWN

The Old Stone Garden is located, appropriately enough, next to the Old Stone House, a prehistoric structure dating back to 1765, when Washington was little more than an alluvial swamp. The National Park Service created the garden in the 1950s as a model for historic gardens. Apple, crabapple, Virginia cedar, and huge, multistemmed crepe myrtles enclose a small, three-tiered garden that is reminiscent of small, English city gardens. The scale is intimate without being precious, owing to a formality that increases as the garden is experienced successively. After passing through a white picket fence the first room is a shaded brick terrace lined with hostas, plum trees, and *Magnolia grandifloras*—deep, luxuriant foliage that blends nicely with the venerable architecture of the house. The second terrace becomes more formal, with a central grass path lined by full-season perennial borders containing a festive combination of larkspur, thistle, bearded iris, and tree peonies. The third garden leaves behind color and mood for pure geometry: a boxwood parterre framing a grass lawn in a single, lazy arc. A small bird garden planted with coneflowers and acanthus infuses a breath of life around the fringe.

GARDEN AND HOUSE OPEN: 10am–4pm Wednesday– Sunday. GARDEN OPEN: 9am–2pm Monday and Tuesday. ADMISSION: free.

FURTHER INFORMATION FROM: 3051 M Street, NW Washington, DC 20008 (202) 426-6851

NEARBY SIGHTS OF INTEREST: Washington Harbor, Kennedy Center

14 Washington: National Cathedral Gardens

GARDEN OPEN: daily.

ADMISSION: free.

FURTHER INFORMATION FROM:
All Hallows Guild
Massachusetts and
Wisconsin Avenues, NW
Washington, DC 20016-5098.
(202) 244-0568

NEARBY SIGHTS OF INTEREST:
U.S. Naval Observatory,
National Zoo

LOCATION: MASSACHUSETTS AND WISCONSIN AVENUES, NORTH OF GEORGETOWN

Negotiating the political pitfalls and securing the funding to build a monument in Washington, D.C. takes a long time. Take the National Cathedral for instance. President Theodore Roosevelt laid the cornerstone in 1907, but it wasn't until 1990 that President George Bush dedicated the structure. In a curious twist on established norms, the grounds actually predate the cathedral, to when the Olmsted Brothers firm was hired at the turn of the century to "prepare the grounds." The cathedral close, today, is an aggregate of many different gardeners' influences, most predominantly Ms. Florence Bratendahl, who planted several gardens within the Olmsted landscape. Atlas cedars and fig trees, transplants from Israel, flank the entrance to the gardens, which is lined with historic boxwood taken from the estates of Thomas Jefferson and George Washington. Medieval religious sculptures, as well as such heathen images as a statuette of Pan located near the herb cottage, are interplanted with peonies, roses, and irises in subdued but inspirational combinations. Numerous architectural elements dot the landscape. A Norman courtyard lies along a curving cobblestone path, the entrance to which is marked by a twelfth century carriage arch. Set within the garden proper is the Shadow House, an octagonal garden structure designed by cathedral architect Philip Frohman. Three small herb gardens are planted nearby, with such medieval varieties as sage, fennel, and wormwood, culled from an essay by Abbot Strabo. Five acres of the original woodland designed by the Olmsted firm still exist at the base of the hill as public parkland.

Hortulus font surrounded by boxwood

15 Alexandria: Winkler Botanical Preserve

LOCATION: ROANOKE STREET OFF BEAUREGARD STREET, EXIT 4 OFF
INTERSTATE 395, FOUR MILES SOUTH OF WASHINGTON

There is little open space left in the suburbs of northern
Virginia, a region that everyday gives new meaning to the word
"sprawl." In response to the inexorable progression of the suburbs, the Winkler preserve was established in the 1980s. The
garden is a naturalistic botanical preserve that focuses on
species native to the Potomac River region. Woodland trails run
through 43 acres of reclaimed land that was once a dumping
ground and a pig farm. Those days are long past thanks to careful forest management and the planting of thousands of plants
annually. Most of the collection of Virginia bluebells, alder, vio-
lets, and larkspur were rescued from other sites in the area. In
the spring the wildflowers come alive beneath a tapestry of
mixed oaks and chestnuts. A highlight of the garden is a wetland meadow planted with goldenrod and coneflower. Hidden
within the vegetation are a series of check dams that carefully
regulate the water volume. As the surrounding areas have
become more developed, stormwater runoff into the Preserve
has increased. The meadow garden provides a smart (and beautiful) way to mitigate this consequence. The 25-foot waterfall
and abundant plantings also serve to improve water quality. The
peace and calm of the scene is always kept in perspective by the
hum of the highway nearby, an appropriate and critical component of this particular garden experience.

GARDENS OPEN: 7:30am–3pm
Monday–Friday.
ADMISSION: free.

FURTHER INFORMATION FROM:
5400 Roanoke Avenue
Alexandria 22311.
(703) 578-9109

NEARBY SIGHTS OF INTEREST:
Arlington National Cemetery

ABOVE: *Beautiful vistas
conceal the garden's
engineered purpose.*

Alexandria: Green Spring Gardens Park

GARDEN OPEN: dawn–dusk daily. **ADMISSION:** free.

FURTHER INFORMATION FROM: (703) 642-5173.

NEARBY SIGHTS OF INTEREST: Meadowlark Gardens Regional Park, Winkler Botanical Preserve

LOCATION: LITTLE RIVER TURNPIKE, NEAR ANNANDALE, EIGHT MILES SOUTH OF WASHINGTON

The last owners of this 1760 manor house in the far reaches of Alexandria were good friends with Beatrix Farrand and hired the garden designer to design the landscape around this home and their estate on Long Island in the middle of this century. Farrand sketched the bones of the design, but it has evolved considerably over the years under the guidance of the Fairfax County Park Authority, which now manages the property. Public demonstration gardens are now the modus operandi at Green Spring, including townhouse gardens that communicate ideas for planting a small, often shady area, and several border gardens. During the latter years of her career, Farrand conducted a close study of Gertrude Jekyll's work and began designing border gardens in that vein. A blue border garden of delphiniums, lobelia, and other azure combinations that lead down a slope from a gazebo gives us hints of this direction, whereas a mixed border of perennials in an interwoven pastiche works in an entirely different direction from Jekyll's signature clumping. Elsewhere, the gardens around the manor include a shade garden, a rock garden, an orchard of pears and apples (some of which are espaliered), and a native plant garden featuring common northern Virginia varieties, such as Virginia bluebells and trillium. A horticultural center was erected on-site in recent years, which provides the local community with a library and classes on gardening.

17 # Alexandria: River Farm

GARDEN OPEN: 8:30am– 5:00pm daily, except holidays. **ADMISSION:** free

FURTHER INFORMATION FROM: 7931 East Boulevard Drive Alexandria, VA 22308 (703) 768-5700. www.ahs.org

NEARBY SIGHTS OF INTEREST: Alexandria, Arlington National Cemetery

LOCATION: OFF MOUNT VERNON MEMORIAL PARKWAY, SEVEN MILES SOUTH OF WASHINGTON

By 1787 George Washington's acquisitional spree along the Potomac River extended to five different farms, totaling nearly 8,000 acres. River Farm, now separated by several subdivisions from Mount Vernon, was the farthest reach of the property. Although it passed to successive generations of Washington, by the twentieth century the property had fallen on hard times. In the 1970s, a desperate owner even courted the Soviet Union as a potential buyer (Moscow considered establishing an embassy here), which outraged many patriotic souls, including Enid Annenberg Haupt, patron of the New York Botanical Garden and board member of the American Horticultural Society. She

A rustic, natural perennial garden at George Washington's old farm

purchased the property in 1973 and donated it to the society, which now uses it as its administrative base and cultivates gardens on-site. In front of the 1757 brick house there are several collections of dogwoods, azaleas, and fruit trees, and a Front Yard Garden that showcases common American yard plants. Behind the house there are more formal gardens, many of which are sponsored by plant organizations, including a rose garden, a perennial border, and an herb garden laid out in a radial manner with peach trees anchoring each bed. A heavy wisteria arbor lines the far end of the property. A children's garden designed by different school groups in conjunction with professional landscape architects, horticulturists, and nurseries proves the most eye-catching from afar. The garish competes with the provocative in this visually eclectic space, with the most evocative contribution being the very simple, very beautiful Native Plant Butterfly Garden, featuring rue, hollyhocks, and milkweed. While the rest of River Farm, surprisingly, lacks extensive plant labeling, this area is fairly well interpreted and should prove educational for children. The vistas of the Potomac River are better at Washington's other, better-known property downstream. At the edge of the sloping lawn is a Wildlife Garden planted with coneflowers to attract butterflies and designed around a small pond tucked into a copse of trees like a grotto. The most attractive garden at River Farm is immediately behind the house in the Garden Calm, an enclosed room of shady plants presided over by a 200-year-old osage orange tree.

🗄 🍽 🔲 🌱
⚗ 🏛 🎋 🏆

GARDEN OPEN: 8am–5pm
daily, April–August; 9am–
5pm daily, March, September,
and October; 9am–4pm daily,
November–February.
ADMISSION: $8.

FURTHER INFORMATION FROM:
Mount Vernon Memorial
Parkway, Mount Vernon, VA
22121. (703) 780-2000

NEARBY SIGHTS OF INTEREST:
Old Town Alexandria,
Arlington National Cemetery

18 Mount Vernon: Mount Vernon Estate

LOCATION: MOUNT VERNON MEMORIAL PARKWAY (ROUTE 400),
TEN MILES SOUTH OF WASHINGTON

By the end of the Revolutionary War, George Washington was as close to an American saint as the country would ever produce. While his national popularity would eventually force him back into public life, his first thoughts after the end of the war were of farming his estate along the Potomac River. In imitation of his fellow Virginians, Washington first planted tobacco at Mount Vernon, which a cast of three hundred slaves cultivated. But the temperamental plant disliked the clay soil, and Washington found he couldn't compete with the more productive farms farther south in Virginia and the Carolinas. This economic fact caused him to investigate other, innovative agricultural options—wheat, flax, and hemp—and spurred his naturally inquisitive mind to seek out European writings on "new husbandry" farming by such writers as Arthur Young, Jethro Tull, and Monceau. As a young man Washington had worked as a land surveyor in Northern Virginia, and when he moved into Mount Vernon, he set about laying out the landscape in such a way as to accommodate his agricultural pursuits with other, less utilitarian uses. Formal lawns surround the house, offering vistas of the Potomac and a central Bowling Green, lined with enormous tulip poplars that frame the house from the approaching circular drive. Extending down the slope Washington experimented with seeds gathered from friends and planted an arboretum of locusts and crabapples that roll down toward the fields.

In addition to landscape architecture, Washington was an avid gardener. In the Lower Garden, or kitchen garden, located south of the Bowling Green, vegetables and fruit were planted in square beds cut through the middle by a single allée of natural boxwood. Downslope, this formal but unadorned geometry is continued, with the exception of a radial herb garden, and framed in brick. The sunken beds are still planted with vegetables and herbs, many of which were common in the eighteenth century and reflect the letters and diaries of Washington himself; however they are roped off to visitors. The gnarled and overgrown boxwood dates to Washington's time. In the upper half of the garden the beds are now planted with flowering perennials and annuals, including peonies and foxglove. A handsome brick wall lined with espaliered fruit trees forms the northern border, while a hedge and white fence progress to an octagonal summerhouse along the east. To the south a sunny view opens over fields and country lanes.

On the opposite side of the Bowling Green, the upper garden mirrors the lower garden in design, however the beds contain a dynamic display of well-labeled perennials that include

Restored colonial gardens at George Washington's former estate

coneflower and poppy set amidst carpets of lamb's ear, all flut-teringly alive with butterflies. Originally this too was a working garden, however Washington transformed it into a pleasure garden in 1785. The diversity of plants reflects Washington's own tastes, which were often encouraged by friends and col-leagues who sent him exotic seeds and cuttings. The last gar-den at Mount Vernon is the diminutive Botanical Garden, located just outside the walls of the Upper Garden. Although not much to look at, this is where Washington experimented with horticultural varieties. Today the garden is sown each year with a different plant to reflect its appearance 200 years ago.

19 Lorton, VA: Gunston Hall

LOCATION: MASON'S NECK

The force of George Mason's strong-willed personality was very much felt in the famous Philadelphia meeting hall in the sum-mer of 1787. In the end, however, this enigmatic Virginian refused to vote in favor of the U.S. Constitution because it did not include a bill of rights. Mason's ideas about individual human rights, and his language used to describe them in the Virginia Declaration of Rights, influenced both the Declaration of Independence and the Bill of Rights when they were finally drawn up in 1791. Mason's actions would have assured him expulsion from modern-day politics, and perhaps from the eighteenth-century's as well, if he hadn't opted for private life on his own accord. He was, first and foremost, a gentle-man farmer. Like his neighbor George Washington, Mason

GARDEN AND HOUSE OPEN: 9:30am–5:00pm daily, year-round, except Thanksgiving, Christmas, and New Year's Day. ADMISSION: $5 (includes video orientation and house tour).

FURTHER INFORMATION FROM: Gunston Hall Plantation Mason's Neck, VA 22079. (703) 550-9220

NEARBY SIGHTS OF INTEREST: Mount Vernon

175

believed that working the land elevated the spirit of man and contributed not only to his well-being but to the individual's liberty. Gunston Hall, Mason's home and wheat and tobacco plantation on the Potomac River, is the physical manifestation of these ideals. Built in 1775, the house contains many period furnishings, some of which belonged to Mason and his descendants, and some of which were later brought in to fill the historic structure. Of the original 5,500 acres of croplands, forest, and gardens that once surrounded the house, 500 remain, including many outbuildings and garden areas. The Georgian manor is approached through a stately allée of magnolias, shrouded from the wind by an outer row of arborvitae, planted by a subsequent owner. In form, it echoes Mason's original allée of cherry trees. Behind the house lie the formal gardens. The overgrown, aromatic boxwood allée that splits the area (and mirrors the allée in the front) was planted by Mason, however the surrounding beds were designed when the museum first opened in the 1950s, by Alden Hopkins, a landscape architect at Colonial Williamsburg. Hopkins' interpretation is widely regarded as beautiful but far more indicative of the Colonial Revival style than anything Mason would have planted. Victorian parterres filled with perennials, and cutting a striking geometry from the lawn, were probably not in Mason's rural, no-nonsense vocabulary. For a few years, debate centered around whether to preserve Alden's design (a shining example of Colonial Revival style) or to excavate the garden in an effort to reveal what Mason's original garden looked like. The decision was made to excavate. As a result the landscape is fairly unattractive, if highly interesting. More fascinating information about the garden is likely to come out of the archeological techniques being applied to the site presently.

A smaller, sunken garden—also designed by Hopkins—remains at the edge of the property. The woods beyond this and separating the house from the river were fenced off as a deer park in Mason's day. Around the side of the house there are several herb and vegetable gardens planted with authentic colonial varieties, although they are not labeled. The slave quarters—and Mason owned many slaves—were located near the kitchen garden. The foundation of one structure—a tiny, windowless building that would have housed two families—remains intact. Regardless of these facts, Mason's ideas, as articulated in the preamble of his Declaration of Rights, in which he asserted "That all men are by nature equally free and independent," remains his greater legacy.

The lower parterre garden looks out over Mason's "Deer Park."

Biographies

BOWDITCH, ERNEST (1850–1918) A protégé and competitor of Frederick Law Olmsted, who designed the private estates Sonnenberg and The Elms, as well as several notable public commissions in the Midwest.

BIGELOW, JACOB (1797–1887) Physician/botanist/ educational reformer who spearheaded the campaign for Mount Auburn cemetery in the 1830s and designed its parklike, romantic landscape and gothic structures that inspired landscape architects and garden designers for half a century.

DIOSCORIDES (1st century AD) Roman physician who wrote *De Materia Medica*, a treatise on the medicinal uses of herbs that continued to be used until modern times.

DAVIS, ALEXANDER JACKSON (1803–1892) Architect of country residences who collaborated with Andrew Jackson Downing on many commissions.

DOWNING, ANDREW JACKSON (1815–1852) After Jefferson, the father of landscape architecture whose *Treatise on Landscape Gardening and Rural Architecture* influenced American tastes for half a century.

FARRAND, BEATRIX JONES (1872–1959) American landscape gardener whose designs for Dumbarton Oaks and her home at Reef Point translated European traditions and trends, notably those of Gertrude Jekyll, into an American context.

HOPKINS, ALDEN (1905–1960) Landscape architect of Colonial Williamsburg and purveyor of Colonial Revival gardens in the 1940s and 1950s including those at Gunston Hall and Elizabethtown.

JEKYLL, GERTRUDE [pronounced JEE'kul] (1843–1932) Artist and garden designer famous for the English "cottage garden" style.

LEIGHTON, ANN *nee Isadore L.L. Smith* (1902–1985) Garden historian and author of a three-volume history of American gardens. Her design for the John Whipple House signalled the end of the Colonial Revival and the advent of garden restorations that are more faithful to the original.

LORD AND BURNHAM An Irvington, New York-based architecture firm that specialized in Victorian glasshouses, and built some of the most spectacular ones in the world.

OEHME, WOLFGANG AND JAMES VAN SWEDEN Washington, D.C.-based landscape architects whose "new American garden" style advocates (among other things) the bold use of plant materials organized in layers that evoke a sense of natural lushness. Van Sweden has also authored several books.

OLMSTED, FREDERICK LAW (1822–1903) Landscape architect who designed Central Park, Prospect Park, Boston's "Emerald Necklace," and many residential estates throughout New England and New York.

OLMSTED FIRM (known alternately as "the Olmsted brothers") Landscape architecture firm created by Frederick Law Olmsted. Commissions designed by the firm during Olmsted's lifetime are usually credited to him, while those executed after his death are credited to the firm.

OLMSTED, JOHN CHARLES (1852–1920) Stepson and nephew of Frederick Law Olmsted, he took over his uncle's landscape architecture firm when Olmsted senior died; John Charles managed Olmsted Brothers, with more than 3500 commissions, from 1898 until he died.

ROBINSON, WILLIAM (1838–1915) Irish gardener and writer whose *English Flower Garden* (1883) brought new focus to country gardens. Along with Gertrude Jekyll, he is credited with creating the English "cottage garden" style.

SARGENT, CHARLES SPRAGUE (1841–1927) Brother of painter John Singer Sargent and founder of the Arnold Arboretum. He advised many estate owners in the Northeast on issues of horticulture and influenced an entire generation of botanists, including Henry F. du Pont.

ARTHUR SHURCLIFF (1870–1957) Born Arthur Shurtleff; he changed his name in 1930. He was a co-founder of the landscape architecture program at Harvard University (the first in the country) and lead designer for Colonial Williamsburg. He was tremendously influential on the development of the Colonial Revival in New England.

WHITE, STANFORD (1853–1906) Architect who, along with partners Charles Follen McKim (1844–1909) and William Rutherford Mead (1846–1928), defined the Beaux-Arts style at the turn of the century. Their works include the original Pennsylvania Station and Madison Square Garden, as well as numerous country estates.

Index

Acknowledgments

I'd like to thank all my friends and family who spared their couches and enthusiasm for the cause: Gigs and Emily, Kerith and Scott, Christine and Lindsey, Mom and Dad, Barry and Marilyn. John Gallagher and Tom Buchter provided much guidance on gardens and garden history in Pennsylvania and Delaware. Thanks to Jan Cigliano, my editor, for all her help.

Of course, I could not have accomplished any of this work without the love and support of my wife, Lani, to whom this book is dedicated.

Photograph credits

Cover, ii, 118, 130–133: L. Albee/Longwood Gardens
iii, 129: Terry Wild Studio
viii, 89: Mick Hales
xi, 112, 114: Ellyn Meyers, courtesy Somerset County Park Commission
xii, 3: Jo Ann Botta
2, 18: R. Lynes
5: Acadia National Park, National Park Service
8 top, 9, 11, 43, 44: SPNEA
16: ©Jane Billings
17: John Evarts
18: R. Lynes
20: Shelburne Farms
22: Thomas Neill, Old Sturbridge Village
24 top: Robert Nash
26: John Kennard
27: Museum of Fine Arts, Boston
28–31: Courtesy Mount Auburn Cemetery
32: Longfellow House, National Park Service
34: Peter Del Tredici
37: Michelle Bosch
41: ©Fredrik D. Bodin
45: Hal Horwitz
46: Ken Druse
47: Thomas Neill, Old Sturbridge Village
48–51: courtesy Trustees for Reservations
53: Pat Valiasek
54: Paul Rocheleau; Chesterwood, National Trust for Historic Preservation
55: Lala Searle
56: Rick Sippel
57, 58: Preservation Society of Newport
76: Metropolitan Museum of Art
79: Jake Rajs
80 top, 81 bottom: Fred Charles
80 bottom, 81 top: Tori Butt
83: B. Pinover
86: Nassau County Museum of Art

88: Maggie Oster
90: Patti Courville, courtesy Longhouse Reserve
91: Jim Frank
92: Tiger Hill Studios
93: Charles Lyle
94: Caroline Burgess
95: Samuel F. B. Morse Historic Site
96: Lois E. Pan
97: Ruth Smiley
98: Lester Collins
99: E. M. Ashton
101: Historic Hudson Valley
103: PFK
108: Greater Buffalo Convention and Visitors Bureau
110: George M. Aronson
111: Molly Adams
115: Cape May County Department of Tourism
116: Winterthur Museum
119: Japanese Gardens
122: Nick Kelsh
128: ©1998 The Henry Foundation
134: Brandywine Museum and Conservancy
143: Nemours
144: C. Zullinger
145: Paul Dennison
146–149: Winterthur Museum
152, 168: Bill Lebovich, Tudor Place Foundation
154: Lucy Coggin
159: Sharon Phillips
160: James Adams
162: William L. Sigafoos
163: ©James A. van Sweden, 1992
164–167: Jan Cigliano
170: Joe Luebke
171: William H. Dunn
173: Mount Vernon Foundation